African Stars

Chicago Studies in Ethnomusicology
Edited by Philip V. Bohlman
and Bruno Nettl

Editorial Board
Margaret J. Kartomi
Hiromi Lorraine Sakata
Anthony Seeger
Kay Kaufman Shelemay
Bonnie C. Wade

Veit Erlmann

African Stars

Studies in Black

South African

Performance

The University of Chicago Press
Chicago and London

VEIT ERLMANN is a Heisenberg Fellow in the Department of Anthropology, Free University, Berlin. He was visiting professor at the University of Chicago 1990–91.

THE UNIVERSITY OF CHICAGO PRESS, CHICAGO 60637
THE UNIVERSITY OF CHICAGO PRESS, LTD., LONDON
© 1991 by The University of Chicago
All rights reserved. Published 1991
Printed in the United States of America
00 99 98 97 96 95 94 93 92 91   5 4 3 2 1

ISBN (cloth) 0-226-21722-1
ISBN (paper) 0-226-21724-8

Library of Congress Cataloging-in-Publication Data

Erlmann, Veit.
    African stars : studies in Black South African performance / Veit Erlmann.
        p.   cm. — (Chicago studies in ethnomusicology)
    Includes bibliographical references and index.
        1. Blacks—South Africa—Music—History and criticism.   2. Music—   South Africa—History and criticism.   I. Title.   II. Series.
    ML350.E77   1991
    780'.89'968—dc20   91-13927
                                                          CIP
                                                          MN

∞ The paper used in this publication meets the minimum requirements of the American National Standard for Information Sciences—Permanence of Paper for Printed Library Materials, ANSI Z39.48-1984.

You cannot deprive or take away a
person's land and at the same time expect
him to draw and sing about the landscape.
Mi Hlatshwayo

Contents

Illustrations

Musical Examples

A Note on Orthography and Translations

All song texts in chapters 3–6 have been translated from Zulu. English words in the original song appear in italics. No attempt was being made to standardize the different systems of Zulu orthography that have been in use in South Africa over the last seven decades or so. Most of the spelling on record labels, Tonic Sol-fa scores, and other documents prior to the 1960s differs from current practice and was left unaltered for the sake of documentary accuracy.

Preface

This book was written at a time when Paul Simon's Grammy Award–winning album *Graceland* was topping the world's pop charts and when South African music of all styles and descriptions enchanted audiences throughout the world. Songs by Miriam Makeba had of course been on the charts a long time before that, and a tune such as the indestructible "The Lion Sleeps Tonight" was in fact first recorded in Johannesburg as early as 1939. As an ethnomusicologist interested in popular African music I had long been familiar with these and other memorable compositions by Hugh Masekela and Miriam Makeba, and I had always admired the piano artistry of Abdullah Ibrahim. But it was only after reading Bloke Modisane's *Blame Me on History,* that marvelously evocative account of life in the South African townships in the 1950s, that I decided to gain some firsthand experience of the wealth of performance traditions and styles that I suspected was hidden underneath the international fame of the country's more successful and exiled musicians. What thus began in August 1981 by adjudicating an *isicathamiya* competition of Zulu migrant worker choirs in Durban, ended as a six-year-long exploration into a wide spectrum of black performance traditions ranging from nineteenth-century minstrel shows in Cape Town to Basotho migrants' dance culture. The findings of some of these research projects now form the essence of this book.

Most of the chapters in this book took more definitive shape in Johannesburg, at a time when South Africa was being thrust into one of the deepest crises in its history, and the apartheid regime was being shaken to its roots. Writing a book about South African music in a city where most of the country's corporate headquarters, including those of large media and record companies, are located implied a closeness to the arena of political conflict that could not but leave its imprint on the style and indeed entire argument of these texts. Thus the ultimate goal of the research into the work and careers of some of South Africa's unsung black musicians before the Second World War could not merely be a book about a past that had little bearing upon the country's cruel present. Quite to the contrary, the countless hours of conversation with musicians in Soweto, KwaMashu, and Umlazi, long weeks of reading newspapers, and the many nights spent in workers' hostels in Durban and Johannesburg filled with the most unusual singing and dancing I had ever experienced, involved me deeper and deeper in a search beyond the academic confines of ethnomusicology. Ultimately, this research became a quest for the very foundations of a new South Africa, an exploration of the heritage that the country's workers, artists, and youth are building upon in their struggle for democracy and freedom. The music, life stories, and narratives that emerged from this search brought to life a generation of black artists and performers that has long disappeared but whose struggles, visions, and aspirations were not fundamentally different from those of today's writers, jazz musicians, and actors. In this sense, many of these early performers were in fact themselves leaders in this search, guiding lights, "African stars" who—as one praise poem about one of South Africa's most brilliant black composers during the 1920s put it—"set Africa's great and true distinction."

The book was completed in Berlin. This relocation not only entailed a certain disruption of the routine of writing, but the physical distance from the struggles in South Africa also introduced a more critical perspective into my thinking about culture and social relations in South Africa. Thus *African Stars* does not fit easily into some of the race-versus-class and populism-versus-working-class debates that have been led among intellectuals, workers, and cultural activists about the role of culture and the arts in the process of liberation.[1] As the preamble to the resolutions adopted at the 1987 Amsterdam conference on "Culture in Another South Africa" asserts, in populist and nationalist perspective, art and culture are to be bisected into a "vibrant people's culture, rooted in South African realities and steeped in democratic values" and a "racist culture associated with the apartheid regime" (Campschreur and Divendal 1989:214). A somewhat more isolated socialist or "workerist" perspective, by contrast, posits that true revolutionary art champions only the "objective" cause of the working class, the socialist revolution, and must hence be kept free of "petty-bourgeois" contamination. While this debate admittedly sharpened the eye for the extremely multifaceted nature of the arts in South Africa during a specific period of the antiapartheid struggle, it is beset with the kind of problems that arise when the lofty constructs of pure theory are forced upon the very messy reality of South African society.

African Stars is less concerned with allegedly objective and true causes, and its main theoretical focus lies outside the purview of these debates. Rather the essays in this volume are concerned with the ways in which performance intertwines with the strategies of musicians, dancers, music critics, music teachers, workers, and preachers in a society whose workings they did not control. Thus the history of black popular performance before the Second World War is not simply a narrative about a class society in the making; it is also a commentary on the often obscure, escapist, decidedly undemocratic, and antirevolutionary methods ordinary people have devised in order to make that society work for themselves. These strategies did not generally follow prescribed models of class action and more often than not involved the remaking of fractured worlds in and through symbolic systems whose meaning was not always linked to their broader socioeconomic context.

In this sense *African Stars* is not a social history of South African popular culture as such. Much of the more contextual, broader historical, sociological, and anthropological material, for example, which is presented here will be familiar to the more seasoned travelers in these fields of South African scholarship. Some of it has been masterly unfolded, for instance, in David Coplan's study *In Township Tonight! South Africa's Black City Music and Theatre,* first published in 1985 (Coplan 1985). His was an ambitious attempt to present a narrative about the black experience in South African industrialization and how this has been embodied in performance culture. With its dazzling array of themes and actors that perhaps also inevitably entails a certain lack of attention to specific styles and periods, Coplan's narrative resembles a broad stream whose course is preset by the wider South African sociopolitical landscape and the forces that shaped it. Furthermore, Coplan's book was originally researched in 1976–77, and much new evidence has since come to light. The new South African historiography of the 1970s has largely consolidated itself as a dynamic field in southern African studies, and new theoretical paradigms have emerged.

Given this somewhat-changed academic terrain, this book therefore does not aim at a complete reconstruction of South Africa's black musical history. Rather it brings together a number of case studies that explore some of the more meandering and unexplored backwaters of the historical mainstream. It interweaves episodes into a composite tale that is unified more by approach than by topical continuity, and whose discontinuities illuminate better than coherent narrative structures the different types of experiences and responses to the broader processes of industrialization.

Underlying this common approach in chapters 2–6, the five studies that form the core of this book, is the following specifically ethnomusicological argument. Sociologists and social historians of the South African industrial revolution, it is true, have found much evidence of a growing class differentiation and of the emergence of class-based cultural practices in South Africa. But if we are really to understand the role of popular performance in these broader social processes, cultural analysis can no longer reduce the linkages between social structure and culture, between social process and consciousness in modern South African society to isomorphic relationships and to the opposition between capital and labor. Rather the country's black performance practices during the earlier decades of this century seem to reveal little-known layers and niches of consciousness that help to shed light on the nonmaterial, subjective forces and symbolic processes that have shaped South African society and that sociologists and social historians have found difficult to account for in the often reductionist terms of their own disciplines.

A fuller discussion of the implications of this approach is presented in chapter 1. Chapters 2–6 are thematically linked but also explore—independent of each other—different facets of black popular performance in South Africa between 1890 and 1939. In addition, each chapter takes a particular focus and draws on a different body of evidence. Chapter 2 looks at the South African experience of a particular group of Afro-American performers, based on a detailed examination of the American and South African press of the period. Orpheus McAdoo's concert tours in South Africa were the first link in a chain of continuing black American influences on the culture and music of black South Africans. Chapter 3 is a study of a specific region and city. Durban is South Africa's third largest city and together with its immediate hinterland produced myriad forms of Zulu dances, songs, and instrumental styles that count among the most vibrant and powerful musical traditions in southern Africa.

Chapter 4 explores the transformations of a vibrant form of migrant-workers' dance culture in the crucible of Durban's popular culture during the 1930s and argues that this process was part of the dialectic of hegemony and resistance. Chapter 5 is an attempt—possibly the first—at a serious biography of one of South Africa's most colorful black composers. Reuben T. Caluza lived in Durban most of his life, and the majority of his songs were written during the first three decades of this century and illustrate the dynamics of popular performance culture in its crucial early phase. Chapter 6 examines the early history of a particular style of migrant performance and its transformation in the wider context of social and economic changes in South Africa. The argument here is that this performance genre, while reflecting the increasing articulation of migrants' heterogeneous worlds, served to mediate between disparate social realities and to provide for symbolic spaces in which disjointed social relations were reconstructed. Finally, chapter 7 places the South African evidence within the wider context of popular music on the entire African continent.

While each study can be read on its own, a number of themes, individuals, and sometimes songs thread through all five essays. Thus each of the styles, composers, and locales discussed here is situated in the same historical period between 1890 and ca. 1945. McAdoo's tours, for instance, began in 1890, a year that is regarded by *isicathamiya* veterans as the birth of Zulu male choral singing and that is only five years before Caluza's birth in 1895. Similarly, when Solomon Linda's *Mbube* was released in 1939, Durban's black musical history had reached a watershed year. In a diachronic perspective, numerous cross-references exist between McAdoo, Caluza, and early *isicathamiya*. Thus a continuous line links McAdoo's alma mater Hampton Institute and Caluza's studies there to the role of Negro spirituals in the ideology and social climate of middle-class blacks in the United States and South Africa. Likewise, the *ukureka* or "ragtime" movements popularized by Caluza became a hallmark of rural wedding parties in the 1920s, from where they found their way into *isicathamiya* competitions. There are also parallels in the appropriations of rural dance forms by Durban's ethnic vaudeville troupe Lucky Stars and early *isicathamiya* choirs.

Documenting the unique cultural achievements of black South Africans can be a disheartening enterprise, especially when dealing with those forces of society that regard black people as timeless, ahistorical labor units rather than as bearers of cultural traditions. Here I would like to give mention to two kinds of institutions that have particularly distinguished themselves in this regard. The first group is the recording companies that have been operating in South Africa from at least 1908. Regrettably, the unashamedly public role that these representatives of private capital have played in shaping South African black musical history has not found its equivalent in equally vigorous efforts to preserve the evidence of that heritage. Thus none of the major pioneer record companies in South Africa have found it necessary to maintain archives of the records produced for the South African market. The second institution is the South African Broadcasting Corporation which, through its erstwhile black music director Yvonne Huskisson, has for years denied access to those extensive collections of records and transcriptions that document the profound effect of this institution on black performance in South Africa.

But regardless of such restrictions, few people could have understood better and welcomed more the idea of this book than the musicians it is about. My greatest debt is therefore toward the many musicians whose personal warmth, generous support, and deep knowledge were invaluable resources in researching and writing this book. A full list of their names is found in the bibliography. Here I would like to particularly mention Faith Caluza, Gilbert Madondo, Robert T. Mazibuko, Irene Msane, Paulos Msimanga, Enoch Mzobe, Thembinkosi Phewa, Joseph Shabalala, and Ngweto Zondo.

Technical assistance of various kinds in the field and other services such as translation were provided by the following persons: Lauren Gower, Nana Jali, Luyanda Mahlangeni, David Marks, Mpumelelo Mbatha, Bongani Mthethwa, Naphtalie Morie, Caesar Ndlovu, Charles Ndlovu, Charles Ngema, Thomas Nkadimeng, and Renata Robertson. Archival and related assistance was also provided by Cuthbert Mashego and the staff at the SABC record library in Johannesburg, EMI archives, Annica van Gijlswijk at UNISA, Andrew Tracey and the staff at the International Library of African Music in Grahamstown, Mary Lou Hultgren at Hampton University Museum, Fritz Malval of the Hampton University Archives, Rev. Brutsch at Morija, the staffs of the South African Library in Cape Town and Killie Campbell Africana Library in Durban, and Sandra Fold at the Cory Library of Rhodes University in Grahamstown.

Most of the chapters in this collection went through various stages of maturation and were read and commented upon by many colleagues of whom I would like to thank in particular the following: my former colleagues at the African Studies Institute, University of the Witwatersrand, Johannesburg, Charles van Onselen, Tim Couzens, Paul la Hausse, and Jim Campbell. Doug Seroff has not only been an astute reader, but also generously passed numerous documents, recordings, and references on to me. Dale Cockrell first directed my attention to the Virginia Jubilee Singers and read a draft of chapter 2, as did Helmut Bley of the Department of History at the University of Hanover. Tom Turino helpfully commented upon an earlier draft of chapter 6, while Ken Gourlay, over the years, has been a faithful and most perceptive critic. Rob Allingham, in addition to spending hours of patient reading of my drafts, was an unfailing source of information on South African discography. I also benefited from the discussions and other support I received at various points in time from Christopher Ballantine, Georg Elwert, Robert Günther, Charles Hamm, Heather Hughes, Khabi Mngoma, Artur Simon, and Ari Sitas. By far the greatest debt, however, I owe to Carola Lentz, whose scholarly rigor and remarkable insights into the problems of ethnicity and labor migration were crucial in the final revision of the manuscript.

African Stars

One   # Introduction

For any ethnomusicologist interested in the music of the slums, streets, harbors, and mines of Africa, South Africa constitutes something of an Eldorado. Over little more than a century, the southernmost tip of the African continent has seen the growth of a modern, capitalist society with by far the most advanced economy and probably the most powerful military on the entire continent. As the rise of this giant drew an ever-growing number of people, cultures, and polities into its orbit, the face of the subcontinent was transformed. The culture and music that emerged from this ferment of colonial conquest, dispossession, and industrialization count among the most resilient examples of African urban expressive culture.

But the musicologists among students of South African social and cultural transformation have only haltingly taken cognizance of these changes. Percival Kirby, in the 1930s when most of his studies were undertaken, was mainly concerned with the continuity of African musical practices, and was only marginally interested in the role of performance in situations of culture contact. Westernized African musicians, he later argued, had produced "nothing of lasting value" (Kirby 1967:140), and his famous dictum that the African musician using Western instruments "never performs European music," but instead produces "music designed according to his own principles" (Kirby 1968:257f.), in essence and in practice contained a strong bias against any music that was not based on traditional idioms. As a result, as late as 1954 Hugh Tracey was able to speak of the "drab proletarian gray in imitation of others" that characterized urban black music (Tracey 1954:11), and he thereby indirectly provided the scholarly underpinnings of apartheid cultural policies. These were based on assumptions that, as musical mentor of Radio Bantu Yvonne Huskisson phrased it, a "Western way of life" was but a "surface adoption" and that urbanization would not fundamentally change a persistent "feeling for the 'traditional' " in modern African life (Huskisson 1968:21). David Rycroft's essay on Zulu violin music published in 1977 was the first scholarly attempt to break new ground (Rycroft 1977). Although Rycroft reiterated Kirby's point about the reworking of traditional idioms in Westernized instrumental styles, this study of "town music" was the first attempt at a South African urban ethnomusicology based on solid empirical data rather than on parochial concerns about urban decadence.

The most theoretically grounded critique of the older school of South African musicologists, however, only emerged in the general intellectual radicalization in the aftermath of the 1973 Durban strikes and the 1976 Soweto riots. David Coplan's *In Township Tonight* represented a timely and salutary departure, in methodology, theory, and content, from the narrow paradigms of tribe and tradition. Urban performing arts, he wrote, are not the "disintegration but the creation of a culture" (Coplan 1985:3). Coplan's account is part of a growing literature on performing arts that seriously attempts to place the origins, development, and structure of black urban performance in Africa within the more complex network of social relations, economic structures, cultural traditions, and individual creativity within a particular society (e.g., Bame 1985, Meintjes 1990, Nunley 1987, Waterman 1986).

In terms of theoretical grounding, the present studies further explore some of the issues raised in Coplan's book and at the same time place these on an empirical base that is more focused on specific cases, examples, individuals, and styles. Furthermore, the essays confront a number of issues that have only recently moved center stage in theoretical debates in ethnomusicology and particularly southern African studies. Central among these problems are the dynamics of urban-rural transformation and the articulation of heterogeneous worlds, the dialectical relationship between tradition and modernization, as well as questions of ethnicity and race. However, underlying all these theoretical concerns is one which is fundamental to all analyses of African popular performance and which therefore needs to be addressed here with priority. This deals with the relationship between social structure and culture, between historical process and consciousness as it is dialectically constituted in performance.

Social Structure,   For many students of the South African indus-
Performance, and   trial revolution the preoccupation with social
Consciousness   structure and consciousness has always been of
                        central theoretical concern. For the Marxists
among these scholars this pursuit has frequently also involved an uneasy
encounter between the paradigms of economic class analysis and cultural
analysis. Marxists have generally found it difficult to conceptualize the
relationship between consciousness and society not as a question of
structural correspondence, but as embedded in practice. This is perhaps
most clearly in evidence in the general theoretical trend that has emerged
in South African cultural studies in recent years. Thus the transformation
of South African society and the emergence of new forms of consciousness and urban cultural practices, in the view of a substantial
number of scholars, has to be seen primarily in relation to the broader
process of class formation within world capitalism. The sociologists Mariotti and Magubane, for instance, somewhat summarily assert that the
"class structure of society and the interests of the ruling class are crucial
determinants of the manifestations of urbanization" (Mariotti and
Magubane 1976:252). Third World urbanization, so the argument goes,
is a product of worldwide networks of dependency and underdevelop-
ment, and therefore urban cultural formations and the arts at best *reflect*
the working of these global mechanisms. The pivot of class formation in
South African industrial society is of course the emergence of an industrial proletariat whose sheer size and increasingly central role in the
country's political and cultural scenario are not matched by anything
quite so momentous in other African countries. The road that took and
continues to take South African migrants from the rural periphery to the
gold mines and industries of Johannesburg and Durban leads directly and
mostly irrevocably into the working class (Van Onselen 1982).

The incorporation of this class into a dominant mode of production
and sociomoral relations, as most scholars would agree, has certainly had
a deep effect on its consciousness. But scholars who have charted the
"objective," material parameters of this class in the making have frequently encountered problems in relating its emergent consciousness and
cultural practices to its material foundations. Although consciousness is
now widely considered as existing in a dialectical relationship with society, at once reflecting class formation and acting upon it, this recognition
did not uniformly result in the insight that the symbolic dimensions of
social relations have a certain autonomy. While the debate is increasingly
moving away from the determination of class-based homogeneous cul-

tural practices and consciousness of the nascent black working class in South Africa, it seems that the project of establishing such relationships is still proving difficult for two reasons which are themselves rooted in the very structure of the society under study.

One of the major problems involved in African and especially South African cultural studies lies in the difficulty of determining a class basis of emergent cultures in the industrial era. Industrial expansion in South Africa was breathtakingly rapid and more profound than anywhere else on the African continent. At the same time, however, it was not accompanied by the formation of fully established and culturally homogeneous classes. The cultural practices, including the performance styles, practices, and ideologies of South African blacks, are articulated in multiple, contradictory, and mutually inclusive forms of ethnic pride, regional solidarity, class consciousness, and political ideology. The numerous divisions of language, ideology, and religious traditions cannot be subsumed under class conflicts alone (Bozzoli 1983, 1987; Marks and Rathbone 1982; Barber 1987).

Ethnomusicologists and other students of performance genres have possibly been among the first to become sensitized to the displaced correlation of social structure and practice and to the role of consciousness and symbols in social action. Considerable agreement now seems to exist on the nonisomorphic relationship between song structure and social structure (e.g., Feld 1984). As a result, students of African popular performance in turn have had to realize that performers' and audiences' aesthetic choices can no longer serve as indicators of class position, nor can the stylistic development of genres based on such choices be accounted for in terms of urban adaptation alone (Waterman 1986:25, 28). Conversely, it is equally impossible to deduce an individual's position in the social process, his or her class position, from the musical forms, styles, and genres he or she performs, listens to, or patronizes. A worker who participates in collective performances of rural wedding songs is not necessarily less proletarianized than the one who patronizes soccer clubs and discos. Popular performance in South Africa has enabled migrant workers, teachers, and shopkeepers to express at the same time pan-ethnic African nationalist ideology and Zulu nationalism, pride in status as permanent urban citizens as well as rural nostalgia and horror at the evils of the city. Similarly, songs within the broader genre of *isicathamiya* choral music express working-class consciousness as well as resistance to proletarianization.

The autonomy of forms of expressive culture, the nonreducibility of consciousness to relations of material production, and the linkages between social structure and performance therefore have to be seen primarily as a problem of symbolic mediation and of social action as communicative practice (Comaroff 1985:5; Alverson 1978). Performance, like ritual, is an "emergent social construction" whose efficacy and meaning are created in the relationship between social actors (Schieffelin 1985: 721). At the same time, performance as "signifying practice" mediates between heterogeneous worlds by constructing social spaces in which the coherence of the lived experience is reestablished. The notion of space is crucial here, because it denotes the existence of a sphere of human activity in which the reordering of social relations takes place in nonpragmatic ways. Although these are not unaffected by the participants' general social practice, performance in South Africa offers alternative opportunities of reconstruction in a seemingly intractable and harsh social reality (Blacking 1980b:36).

In the social transformations wrought by the rise of early industrial capitalism in South Africa which form the context of the performance traditions discussed here, the symbolic construction of this space most clearly seems to crystallize around a number of key paradigms. These are perhaps best described by the dual notions rural and urban, tradition and modernity, black and white, and, finally, hegemony and resistance. These are of course not to be understood as dichotomies, but as the outer points of a continuum, as shifting elements in a continuous process of articulation.

Rural-Urban Articulation and the Symbolic Reordering of Heterogeneous Worlds
The changes which the industrial revolution brought to bear upon the rural order and the ensuing articulation of the periphery with the centers of production and political power have long been recognized as central in Third World social transformation. But the dynamics of urban-rural articulation has often been invoked in a rather unilateral, mechanical fashion to account for the emergence of early popular performance and its role in mediating between heterogeneous cultural systems. Thus ethnomusicological studies of African "town" music, in particular, have drawn considerable inspiration from the work of the older generation of urban anthropologists of the Manchester School. Anthropologists such as Max Gluckman and J. Clyde Mitchell saw urban cultural systems as qualitatively distinct from rural systems—Gluckman's dictum "an African townsman is a townsman, an African miner is a miner"—but not as

discrete entities explainable only in terms of their internal structure. Labor migration from the rural context to the urban environment and the resultant economic and cultural linkages between town and countryside were seen as major forces feeding into the social fabric and culture of the cities. Migration involved the selection from a wide range of adaptive strategies, most notably the restructuring and revitalization of rural formations in the town. In fact, the functionality of urban cultures was seen as contingent on the flow of labor, capital, and ideas between town and countryside.

Correspondingly, a number of ethnomusicological studies on migration as a source of musical change stressed the persistence of traditional performance patterns in town where they become encapsulated as affirmations of reconstructed rural identities (Hampton 1977; Koetting 1979/80, 1980; Saighoe 1984). Other authors in turn have underlined the central role of the traditional and popular arts in the formation of specifically urban cultures (Coplan 1981). In the South African context, however, and perhaps elsewhere in the more industrialized regions of Africa, concepts such as "urban culture" or "urban music" may need to be subjected to careful reevaluation. What is therefore argued here is that one of the strongest common denominators in all of the black popular performance traditions examined in this book is not their integrating, adaptive function in town, nor in how far they reaffirm and foster rural social relations in an urban environment. Rather I propose to rethink the process whereby their emergence was determined by, and in turn symbolically reordered, this articulation of heterogeneous urban and rural realities. Rural and urban performance practices are thus seen here as modalities of the same culture that had begun to permeate the whole society. Rural cultural practices depend for their survival, evolution, and functionality on the feedback from the cities, and in certain areas and during specific historical periods are even inseparably enmeshed with urban culture. Conversely, the city is more than a fixed social matrix to which individuals almost passively adjust. Epstein's notion of the town as a "field," a "set of social relations of different kinds, each of which covers a distinct sphere of social interaction" (Epstein 1958:232) and which may have fluid limits and a certain measure of autonomy, not only conveys the more creative aspects of urban formation, but also needs to be expanded to urban-rural heterogeneous spheres of experience as a whole (Coplan 1982a:114).

Given the fluidity of political and economic boundaries between town and countryside in South Africa, both urban and rural cultural formations stretch across a wide spectrum of forms and ideologies that reflect the cultural makeup of sometimes several socioeconomic systems. Particularly during the 1920s and 1930s, in large areas of the South African countryside preindustrial modes of production still existed side by side with a wage economy. From this perspective, the patterning of black musical cultures in modern South Africa needs to be viewed primarily in terms of a restructuring of precapitalist forms of social organization that occurs simultaneously, albeit with varying intensity and significant regional differences, both in the cities and in the countryside. Music and performance are part of a complex network of production and reproduction that spans town and countryside (Coplan 1982b:372). The universality of urbanization, as Philip Bohlman argues, "topples one of the most sacred tenets of folk music theory: the distinction between rural and urban" (Bohlman 1988:126f.). As the distinctions between rural and urban begin to disappear, it becomes problematic to speak of an urban South African culture and its performance correlates. As the countryside becomes urbanized, the particularity of the urban in turn is destroyed by its universality.

An example from the early history of Zulu-speaking migrants' *isicathamiya* choral music illustrates this quite clearly. Although some of its characteristic stylistic features were derived from performance models that were considered as quintessential rural genres, their ultimate origins rested in the urban context. *Isicathamiya* performers pointed to *ukureka* "ragtime" movements and song or *izingoma zomtshado* wedding songs when they wanted to talk about the rural sources of a repertoire which they considered as modern and "civilized." But in the 1920s, performing these allegedly traditional elements was regarded as the most fashionable demonstration of urban sophistication in the Natal countryside. In themselves, these changes in rural culture were of course the result of the beginning of the transformation of the countryside in the 1920s which saturated the rural reserves, farms, and villages with the cultural practices of the mushrooming slums in and around the big cities.

At the same time, to assign a specificity to urban environments in South Africa with their own cultural systems is to ignore some of the abnormalities of South African urban development. During the early phases of South African capitalism, for example, the growth of homogeneous urban communities in South Africa was severely hampered by, among other factors, state policies of urban segregation. Whether the involuntary aspects of township formation, coupled with minimal infrastructural facilities for cultural reproduction, "squashed" classes together or produced further social cleavages remains to be seen (Bozzoli 1987:25–30). The obstacles to, and at times sheer impossibility of, occupying the urban space and to constructing cultural systems based upon a positive identification with these spaces forced black urban dwellers to create, often in opposition to state and managerial intervention, alternative material structures for cultural reproduction.

"Cultural spaces" is what one astute observer and working-class cultural activist calls the physical sites of such cultural reproduction that act as social carriers of events in working-class culture (Sitas 1986b:89). He points out that the term "spaces" is preferable to the notion of institutions which have not resulted in any significant specialization of function. Churches serve both as community halls and for prayer meetings, while the hall of Durban's black trade union ICU in the 1930s accommodated both *ingoma* dances and political meetings. In this sense, the compounds, church halls, open fields, and shebeens of a city like Durban are more specific than the city as an entity (Cooper 1983). In another important sense, of course, the notion of "cultural space" recalls the processes through which black farm laborers, preachers, and dock workers sought to reconstruct a reality by means of symbols in a world marked by disruption and increasingly reduced opportunities for autonomous sociopolitical action. Thus, ultimately the demarcation of these cultural spaces was a question of the power—as Hoyt Alverson says—"to make one's own meaning in the world" (Alverson 1978:280).

Two further points need to be made here about the problems involved in viewing the urban and the rural as discrete social and geographical bases of musical creation. The argument that innovative cultural and performance practices are engendered by a specific and presumably more complex network of social relations in the city presupposes not only a more or less rigid boundary between urban and rural society, but also that rural musical cultures are more homogeneous and therefore less prone to change. Consistent proof exists, of course, in the literature that even changing musical systems display a remarkable persistence of fundamental procedures of stylistic patterning beneath the more obvious changes in surface structure. Thus Robert Kauffman, analyzing the continuity of Shona music in the urban context of Zimbabwe, asserts that "the exact nature of the individual entities is of far less importance than the nature of the processual relationships of these entities" (Kauffman 1972:50). In other words, it is the ordering of performance components such as harmonic patterns, choreography, dress, or lyrics which may be more consistent than each of these parameters in themselves.

But for all the stability of deep structures in African performance under modern conditions, cultural analysts and ethnomusicologists working in Africa must guard against hasty conclusions that "recent rural-traditional music can be made to stand for that of the nineteenth or even eighteenth century" (Coplan 1986:33). South African music, for its part, does not readily support this view. Thus one of the most visible and readily accessible forms of allegedly "rural-traditional" performance, for instance, the male group dances collectively referred to as *ingoma,* can be shown to have emerged only as late as the 1920s. Similarly, just as much as Durban's musical history cannot be written in isolation from the rich cross section of surrounding peoples and cultural traditions of Zululand, Natal, and Pondoland, we cannot assume that any of these rural regions was in any sense less diverse and changing less rapidly than was the Durban music scene during the 1920s. Significantly, it was in a sphere thought to be as resistant to change as "traditional-rural" South African music that the most profound structural changes were wrought and that the trauma of social dislocation was expressed most compellingly.

The tenacity with which scholars have clung to the alleged stability of traditional-rural performance is in part linked to the methodological problems of establishing reliable historical data for a song on the basis of informants' statements or through comparison with "external" historical, anthropological, and other evidence. Within some reputedly older performance genres such as Zulu *amahubo* regimental anthems, for instance, many songs can be identified as having originated during specific periods of the eighteenth and nineteenth centuries. On the basis of structural and textural traits of *amahubo* anthems of reputedly ancient origin, Rycroft was able to establish historical sequences of scales in Nguni music that might serve as a basis of comparison for other songs that cannot be easily dated on the basis of external historical evidence (Rycroft 1971). John Blacking, on the other hand, working with Venda songs of very low topical content, cautions against using scales as clues to musical history. He argues that only by paying careful attention to exact details of performance and to the cultural background can ethnomusicologists compare musical styles (Blacking 1971:212). Blacking's insistence on cultural context points to the need to understand musical history as a process of social construction outside of which no primordial roots exist.

Tradition, Musical History, and the Reconstruction of Popular Consciousness Within the broader context of the cultural transformation of South African society before the Second World War, the fundamental experience of millions of black people has been one of dislocation and alienation. In some cases, such as that of the country's nascent black middle class, this experience involved a twofold process of alienation. First the movement from a marginal position within Zulu precolonial society to its "peasantization" within the colonial economy and the subsequent estrangement from Zulu traditional sociomoral values; and subsequently the increasing marginalization through white settler exclusivism and the turning away from Victorian ideology to Afro-American-derived cultural alternatives (Marks 1986). For the laboring poor dislocation was perhaps a much more radical and brutal experience, less mediated as it was by the relatively more favorable economic conditions of the black elite. In both cases, however, the recourse to tradition and a constant engagement with the past constitutes one of the most crucial mechanisms through which black South Africans reflected and acted upon their fractured worlds. Performers such as the remarkable Orpheus McAdoo, Natal's brilliant "ragtime" composer Reuben Caluza, and *isicathamiya* innovator Solomon Linda, all key figures whose lives and activities are discussed extensively in this book, were in the vanguard of these attempts.

But few notions seem to be have been appealed to with greater frequency and less clarity in South African political and cultural discourse than "tradition." While the term has proved extremely elastic as a tool for political mobilization (Spiegel and Boonzaier 1988), it is in the performing arts that its uses and contradictions become perhaps most obvious. Although a sense of the fragility of such established definitions of "traditional" African music as a predominantly participatory, noncommercial, classless art form of integrated and consensual village, peasant, or pastoral communities has begun to emerge among ethnomusicologists, less clarity seems to prevail about the genesis of musical traditions and the ways in which they intertwine with the construction of tradition in general social practice.

Traditions are not given historical facts that are handed down, as the commonplace label has it, from time immemorial. Tradition has little to do with the persistence of old forms, but more with the ways in which forms and values are linked together. Tradition results from the formation of cultural canons, and is therefore not a matter of ossification, but of change, negotiation, and indeed, as says Stuart Hall, of a "dialectic between text and context" (Hall 1981:236; Bohlman 1988:104–20). Cultural traditions are socially constructed arrangements of behavior that can be reinterpreted, developed, or even "invented"; they are continually constituted in social practice.

But cultural traditions are also a resource which can be drawn upon in situations that have little to do with historical continuity and cultural stability. In Third World social reality, for example, marked as it is by uprooted rural communities, labor migration, and urban mass poverty, tradition occupies a central position in the discourse of social actors. Since the mobilization of the rural poor for modernization and economic advance can only be made in the name of tradition, urban power elites often only invoke traditions in order to legitimize their leadership role. Conversely, for the more marginalized sectors of the urban population, tradition, however reconstructed or "invented" it may be, frequently becomes the only basis on which participation in modernization and development can rightfully be claimed.

Tradition, then, serves to create images of social reality and to construct a discourse that reflects the position of those who refer to it rather than what they refer to. Similarly, as will become evident in the chapters that follow, musical tradition as it was defined in modern South African society from at least 1913 was by no means what its proponents claimed it to be. The creation of a tradition of "Christian Zulu" songs in Durban and Natal shortly before the First World War (chapter 3) was a response by the educated black elite to the penetration of traditional Zulu culture through capitalist modernization and involved the formation of a highly selective canon.

But tradition, however constructed its arsenal of symbols may be, is not only appropriated strategically by opposing social forces in their contest for power. In the black communities of South Africa tradition and its symbols also served as a powerful unifying factor in the evolution of a specifically black identity. There appear to be at least two major reasons for this perspective. The first concerns the nature of musical change and the use of musical symbols in a changing social environment. There is substantial evidence that of all systems of symbolic representation musical symbols are the most resistant to change (Blacking 1977). Thus it is to be expected that shifts in the class structure of a society, for instance, affect its performing activities less profoundly than, say, its political culture.

Surprisingly, it is this stability which in the special context of South African racial and ethnic segregation makes for an interesting deviation from the general picture of the popular arts in Africa. The persistence of old forms furthers rather than impedes the cultural mediation between increasingly heterogeneous social actors. In Durban, for instance, as chapter 3 suggests, the comparatively tardy process of industrialization, the presence of a large migrant work force, and the proximity of the town to densely populated and culturally dynamic areas dominated by agriculture account for a common cultural heritage shared by the entire African community. The class interests of black landlords, squatters, farm laborers, and small peasants may have produced profound internal rifts within that community, but all groupings of Durban's black population ultimately drew on the same set of symbols rooted in the precolonial past.

Thus it is the more tenacious elements of some forms of black performance rather than their heterogeneity and changeability that integrate people. Of course, this is an observation that probably cannot be generalized for all South African music, let alone African popular music as a whole. Here it is the more media- and technology-related aspects of popular performance that enable it to transcend cultural, regional, and class barriers.

If tradition has to do with the construction of images of the past and with the ways in which historical continuity is created in popular consciousness, and if it is in popular performance in particular that such images are expressed most ambiguously, then studies of popular performance offer perhaps one of the most rewarding venues for scholarly inquiry into the workings of popular consciousness. For the analysis of contexts, events, songs, texts, movements, and performance structures gives privileged access to layers of consciousness that are not normally available to scholarly examination. It is for this reason that some social historians of southern Africa recently have made profitable use of song texts in order to reconstruct popular history (Vail and White 1978, 1986).

Similarly, in South African migrant workers' culture the complex and often "contradictory" interplay of modes of dress, body posture, song texts, and sound structure in an *isicathamiya* performance highlights the multilayered nature of migrant workers' consciousness. Nonverbal forms of communication such as dance patterns are useful as sources of popular consciousness because they transmit images of social self-orientation and identity that are not translatable into a literary mode. It is the density of symbolic enciphering in performance, the autonomy of art forms as means of communicating popular consciousness, that illuminate the ambiguities and "dead angles" of popular consciousness and that work against the grain of pure class consciousness. Strikes, manifests, and speeches may be indicators of class consciousness; popular arts and music generally are not. Or as John and Jean Comaroff argue, historical consciousness is not simply a function of industrial capitalism nor is it formed solely in resistance to wage labor. Consciousness is best understood "as the active process . . . in which human actors deploy historically salient cultural categories to construct their self-awareness" (Comaroff and Comaroff 1987:205).

Questions of the construction of tradition through contemporary social conflict are intimately linked to a historical perspective that must lie at the heart of any serious study of black performance in South Africa. In ethnomusicology questions of change have of course traditionally received the most sustained theoretical treatment. One of the most crucial insights that resulted from this focus was the idea that in no known society can musical change be construed as a linear succession of neatly separated performance categories. Musical change is always an uneven process, unpredictable, occurring in some styles, genres, or elements while other musical components of the same tradition remain stable (Nettl 1958:521; Blacking 1971:198–202; Wachsmann 1971; Nketia 1982). But the problem of overlapping strands in musical history also raises a number of methodological issues that need to be discussed briefly here, because they are central to the relationship between structure and practice, between text and process.

Although recorded sound material must form the backbone of any serious study of popular music, it constitutes perhaps one of the most poorly defined categories of ethnomusicological evidence for which analytical criteria of historical interpretation still need to be elaborated. Fortunately, recordings that can be profitably used in reconstructing the history of black South African music are available from as early as 1908. But these vintage recordings are far from constituting "neutral" documentary evidence. Political censorship, marketing strategies, and the interests of intermediaries such as studio staff, talent scouts, and engineers all affected the meaning and content of what was actually being recorded. Thus, these recordings are highly sensitive and fragmentary sources whose interpretation depends on a wide range of ancillary sources such as newspapers, photographs, record advertisements, archival documents, and performers' accounts.

One of the most workable solutions to the problems of documentary reliability of vintage commercial recordings has proven to be the comparative analysis of contemporary performances of reputedly historical material and the corroborative information of performers and others who participated in historical recordings. In addition, the evaluation of surface changes in terms of the "perceptions and patterns of interaction of those who use the music" affords insights into performers' and audiences' sense of history and stylistic change (Blacking 1977:19; Irvine and Sapir 1976). Thus the use of nontraditional musical elements such as electric guitars and new lyrics in contemporary popular performance genres often does not seem to affect in the least their classification as traditional by urban audiences (Zindi 1985; Kubik 1988). Similarly, as John Blacking noted, African performers do not view the alteration of speech tone patterns in urban music as a deviation from traditional practice. Many urban genres are classified as traditional "choruses", in which the speech tone patterns of the words may be ignored (Blacking 1980a:196).

Ethnicity and the Construction of Community in Black Popular Performance   In South Africa as much as elsewhere in Africa, public discourse about tradition rarely goes unaccompanied by its twin notion "community." But just as traditions are constructed, so communities can be "imagined" and become fabrics of "horizontal comradeship" (Anderson 1983: 16). The "invention" of traditions goes hand in hand with the "imagination" and manipulation of communal bonds. It is this aspect of community construction and the ways in which it intertwines with the creation of ethnicity that seems essential in the discussion of the traditional and popular arts in Africa. But before discussing the role of ethnic markers in the making of popular black performance culture in South Africa, it is useful to examine the role of ethnicity in the scholarly discourse about the making of South African society.

Sociologists and social historians of South Africa understandably have been hesitant to acknowledge ethnicity as a key motor of social development and a pivotal point of social conflict for a variety of reasons. Not the least important of these was the fact that apartheid ideology rested on the vision of pristine and distinct ethnic groupings instead of social classes as the structural basis of modern South African society, and it made out ethnic opposition as the major cause of social and political conflict. However, as a number of important studies have demonstrated, under the conditions of the urban ghetto ethnic consciousness among workers was often "manufactured" and manipulated on the basis of divide-and-rule policies and the "invention" of racial categories (Phimister and van Onselen 1979). At the same time, despite such managerial and state strategies of control, the acceptance of ethnic divisions from below is not simply a form of false consciousness (Ranger 1982). The notions of ethnicity and race therefore are not a substitute for class, but important correlates of it. Or as Ari Sitas phrases the matter when talking about different forms of Zulu-speaking workers' ethnic ideology in Natal: different modalities of Zulu ethnic consciousness with varying degrees of availability for ethnic mobilization subsist on different working-class formations, and the "appropriation of this ethnicity by black workers is related to their forms of proletarianization and their responses to a complex system of exploitation and racial oppression" (Sitas 1987:31).

Under certain conditions, then, and particularly in certain areas of Natal, there is no denying the persistence of concepts of ethnic communities and their usefulness to the power strategies of social actors. But ethnicity is woven into the discourse of these actors in a variety of ways. While it is correct that nations are "imagined," in as far as "all communities larger than primordial villages of face-to-face contact . . . are imagined" (Anderson 1983:15), they are not simply the creations of intellectuals and nationalists alone. In Natal, for instance, at least three different sectors of colonial society—the colonial state, the Zulu monarchy and its allies of wealthy black landowners and merchants, and the mass of laboring poor—have been at work to formulate a "Zulu-ness."[1] It would be misleading, therefore, to argue that the local bourgeoisie's use of "Zulu-ness" was false whereas that of the oppositional classes was genuine. Classes, to modify Benedict Anderson's apt phrase, are to be distinguished by the style in which they imagine ethnic bonds that cut across class divisions (Anderson 1983:15).

In much the same way, classes in South African society can be distinguished by the ways in which they "imagine" ethnically based, coherent musical cultures. In other words, the ways in which idealized versions of musically intact communities are imagined make it possible to draw conclusions about the agents of such processes of imagination. Not surprisingly, much of the ethnomusicological discourse is couched in precisely these terms of the "imagined communities." A musical style is defined primarily from the cultural core, assuming a coherent, homogeneous group as social basis of performance. In most cases, a peasant singing about the burden of taxation or a mine worker singing about his kin at home will primarily be seen as a member of the Zulu, Hausa, or Ashanti community, and only in the second place as a peasant or miner. Thus whether a man sings as a lover, miner, father, or migrant, in ethnomusicological perspective, has mostly been subsumed under the fact that he may also be a Zulu or Hausa.

As culture contact becomes a universal fact, the idea of communities with primordial roots as the basis for traditional music becomes one of ethnomusicology's most fragile theoretical assumptions. But the notion of syncretism, once used to denote those sporadic processes whereby cultures in contact produced new practices and expressive forms, also no longer adequately reflects the reality of global cultural evolution where culture contact and homogenization are all-pervasive rather than exceptions. As Karin Barber has rightly stated, syncretism has frequently served as a negative criterion of delimitation: while traditional arts are recognized as objects of study in their own rights, popular arts are seen principally in terms of their deviation from traditional conventions, usually effected by the incorporation of predominantly Western elements (Barber 1987:10).

Contact between Western and African elements is of course only one, historically recent and admittedly especially brutal, phase in the long history of African culture contact. But be this as it may, the central problem for the ethnomusicologist dealing with the communal bases of performance can no longer be the isolation of communities, nations, or ethnic groups with procrustean boundaries, nor in fact, as Klaus Wachsmann has argued, the demarcation of parent cultural traits in syncretic musical systems (Bohlman 1988:120; Wachsmann 1961:148). In contexts such as modern South African society it is the more active, flexible aspects of musical symbols in the formation and negotiation of ethnic boundaries that need to be emphasized. As early as 1956, the role of performance symbols in the situational use of ethnicity was demonstrated by Clyde Mitchell in what must still be regarded as a pioneer work in the Africanist literature on urban popular culture. In his study on the *Kalela Dance* Mitchell showed that by performing the *kalela* dances mine employees in colonial Zambia were making commentaries on the shifting ethnic boundaries that resulted from being classed and from identifying themselves alternately as Africans, workers, or members of would-be ethnic groups (Mitchell 1956).

The situational use of ethnicity is one of the main paradigms in South African black popular performance, the formation of *ingoma* dancing perhaps being one of the most telling examples (chapter 4). The early history of this male dance genre popular among farm laborers and migrants reflects the conflicts between ruling-class notions of *ingoma* as an assertion of age-old tribal identities and working class attempts to use *ingoma* for the ritualized and institutionalized expression of clan antagonisms.

Similarly, the construction of social boundaries through ethnic symbols becomes perhaps nowhere clearer than in the debates surrounding the meaning of the term "black," arguably one of the most sensitive and ideologically charged terms in the South African political vocabulary. One of the central tenets of apartheid ideology has always been the vision of South African blacks as members of a variety of distinct and separate ethnic groups. Such views were of course quoted whenever Afrikaners wished to justify their minority rule, and it is in response to such claims that radical movements from the early 1970s on began talking about South Africa's majority as "blacks" as opposed to the white oppressors. Extending the argument to performance, John Blacking has pointed to the unity of cultural and musical traditions among all South African blacks (Blacking 1980a:199). In fact, for centuries different ethnic traditions have fecundated each other, not to speak of the profound impact that Khoisan musical principles had on the harmonic structure, and hence resultant deep structural homogeneity, of the music in South African Bantu-speaking cultures.

Black music is also a convenient term for the deep bonds that—real or imagined—united African and Afro-American music in the minds of black South Africans. The numerous parallels between black American and black South African humor, folklore, and popular culture were not only the result of concrete historical contact over a period of more than one hundred years. They were also based on similar experiences of racial discrimination and oppression. Long before Orpheus McAdoo and his Jubilee Singers embarked on their landmark tour of South Africa in 1890 (chapter 2), the everyday experiences of blacks in the slaveholding and frontier societies as well as the reality of urban segregation had produced similar patterns of black cultural responses that were to remain significant factors in modern twentieth-century transatlantic culture contact.[2] People of color in the United States, as one black South African columnist noted in 1932, were "Africans in America" and therefore their achievements—musical or other—were a source of encouragement to "Africans in Africa."[3] Infatuation with black American culture, writes Christopher Ballantine, is at the base of "some of the psycho-social dynamics of Africans in South African cities" (Ballantine 1991).

At the same time, as Charles Hamm points out in an important comparative study on *Afro-American Music, South Africa, and Apartheid,*

> most "Afro-American" music imported into South Africa before the middle of the 20th century consisted of "black" music acceptable to white Americans. It was imprinted with white taste and white styles; and in the process of being transformed

into a commodity for white consumers, it had lost much of the
African identity so unmistakable in many forms of Afro-
American music performed and enjoyed only by blacks them-
selves at this time. (Hamm 1988:15)

But Hamm also throws out the baby with the bathwater. Although the
"ragtime" that was popular with black South Africans in the 1920s was
undeniably more "white" than "black" in terms of the cultural source of
its musical components, what mattered was the way in which it was appropriated as an object of black cultural pride in South Africa.

Clearly, on the basis of the evidence from traditional and American-
influenced South African music it would be naive to interpret its blackness and homogeneity in the sense—as Black Consciousness theoreti-
cians have at times argued—that black is everything that is not white.
Such categories ignore the processual character of performance idioms
and the constant shifts in their cultural evaluation. Present generations in
besieged townships seething with discontent may have little tolerance for
the conciliatory, assimilationist worldview of their forefathers, but black
youths of the 1920s had few alternatives other than casting "white" cultural traditions, including music such as minstrel and vaudeville "ragtime" songs, in a black mold.

Nevertheless, despite black-white cultural osmosis and class amalgamation, a strong tinge of the discreteness of black popular performance
pervades most musical genres and musicians' life stories, as well as the
ideological discourse about them. If black South Africans performers
were constantly seeking images to express and make sense of the gulf that
separated black people from a world not their own, they also created alternative worlds and cultural spaces in which blacks could rightfully
reflect upon and direct their own destiny, free of white control. In a society where everything had to be white in order to be of value, these
counterworlds and spaces of necessity had to be black. One of the most
fundamental functions of the performing arts in South Africa, as David
Coplan emphasizes, was therefore to play an "active role in the evolution
of black identity and the internal definition of black aspirations" (Coplan
1985:246).

Thus the term "black music" defies a definition in terms of hard and
fast, essentialist, cultural, ethnic, or racial boundaries. Rather it refers to
the constructs that resulted from the contact of black South Africans with
the culture and music of black Americans, imprinted with white taste
they may have been, and not to any discernible concrete musical substance of an African cultural identity. In fact, one of the recurring themes

in this book will be the hypothesis that in a rapidly changing society such as industrializing South Africa, no "one-to-one equation of musical style and cultural core," no coherent geographic, social, or ethnic basis of style can be established (Bohlman 1988:56).[4]

Hegemony and Resistance: The "Popular" in South African Music

In a country such as South Africa where racial and class barriers in part coincide, it may be tempting to consider black and popular as interchangeable notions for the new forms of musical expression that arose through and in response to colonial conquest, capitalist penetration, and racial domination.[5] But the trajectories of modern urban performance in South Africa, if anything, also serve as a vivid illustration of the constantly shifting boundaries between black and white culture, between popular and elite, hegemonic culture. When so much of black popular culture up until the Second World War was, if not white, at least mediated through white intervention, the notion of some kind of automatic link between the popular class base of culture and its blackness as well as the idea of black popular performance as the most visible manifestation of unwavering popular resistance to class hegemony seems problematic.

The popular art forms in Africa, as Karin Barber has made clear, stand as the central category in the triad "traditional—popular—elite" which Africanists have used to divide African cultures. But it is also a "shapeless residual" and "fugitive" category in that popular art forms "are not elite arts (though they borrow from them, among other sources) nor traditional ones (though they are grounded in them)" (Barber 1987:12). In this sense, the meaning to which the term "popular" has been applied most frequently and perhaps most ambiguously—both in South Africa and in critical accounts of Third World arts—is that of something "of the people," something that stands in opposition to the ruling classes, the government, the officials.[6] As such it tends to dismiss the differences and idiosyncrasies between the popular classes and cultures as insignificant in the face of ruling-class cultural and political hegemony. In this meaning the term has been useful in the formation of Black Consciousness theory of the 1960s and 1970s and continues to occupy a central position in African nationalist discourse.

On the other hand, the vagueness and indeed evasiveness of the term adequately points to the disrespect for convention and aesthetic canons in the popular arts as well as to the intimate links between popular, elite, and traditional arts. As such it helps to uncover the more dynamic aspects of the culture and consciousness of South Africa's majority population. Without blurring the antagonisms and oppositions that exist within black South African society and indeed most industrializing African societies, and without denying the oppositional potential of the popular arts either, the concept "popular" seems to cover the more complex interplay of class dynamics and tensions and the place of performance in the mediation of these social relationships. In the words of Stuart Hall, "popular" indicates the displaced relationship of class and cultures; popular culture and performance are organized around the opposition and consent to the dominant society (Hall 1981:238).

As Jean Comaroff observed in her study of the Tshidi Barolong, the modern world system not only condemned some Third World peoples to live in its shadow, it also produced a corresponding mode of social inquiry that reduces them to mere objects trapped in dichotomous categories of domination and dependence (Comaroff 1985:263). As Comaroff's book and a growing number of studies on the role of peasant resistance and anticolonial politics in southern Africa have made clear, analyses of the role of consciousness in social transformation that are sensitive to the mediating role of symbols in the reconstruction of society must move beyond models of hegemony and resistance as opposing, mutually exclusive forms of social and political action (Beinart and Bundy 1987:27–28). In this sense, black popular music in South Africa during the pre-World War II period is urban music, new music assembled from a wide range of traditional sources. Its evolution is tightly interwoven with the growth of towns and the emergence and nexus of a wide spectrum of social classes within that society, and it is music of opposition to the hegemonic white society. It is all these, but it is also a bridge across class barriers and a way of making elements of the dominant society work for the black laboring classes.

Two

"A Feeling of Prejudice":

Orpheus M. McAdoo and

the Virginia Jubilee Singers

in South Africa, 1890–1898

Prelude   Ever since the beginning of the transatlantic slave trade, contact between Africa and the diaspora, between Africans and the descendants of African slaves in the New World, has influenced the development of black cultures on both sides of the Atlantic. The abolition of the slave trade in the early nineteenth century eventually led to a strong reorientation of Afro-Americans toward their ancestral land and to the beginnings of Afro-American return migration, settlement, and missionization in Africa. Afro-American communities in Freetown, Monrovia, and Afro-Brazilian migration to the Nigerian coast laid the foundations of West African elite cultures that legitimized and defined themselves in terms of their American links.

In South Africa, contacts between black America and Africans were initiated much later and were not the result of massive return migration. But from at least the time of the Boer War these contacts grew into an enduring and possibly the most significant influence on black thinking and cultural development in South Africa, particularly on literature and the performing arts. By about the time of the First World War, blacks and whites in both South Africa and the United States were convinced that "the two societies were traveling along the same road toward a much more competitive and troubled racial system" (Cell 1982:22).

In this chapter, I am concerned with the form that the contact between members of the two societies—the one a colonial frontier society, the other in part based on a plantation economy—assumed in their consciousness. In themselves the two systems, although they may well have contributed to segregation and racism, were quite different. Thus John Cell has argued that "the primary origins of segregation are not in slavery or on the frontier, but in the modern conditions of the 1890s and after" (Cell 1982:4; Legassick 1980). Segregation is "typical of modern, complex, industrializing and therefore increasingly urban societies" (Cell 1982:12f.).

The comparison between the manifestations of the black experience in South Africa and the United States illustrates one of the central methodological premises in this and the following chapters: performance idioms are not to be seen as reflections of social core groups such as classes or tribes but as resources that social actors—be they Afro-Americans, black South Africans, Zulus, or English colonists—mobilize in the construction of the boundaries of self and other. In the particular instance of the century-old discourse between South Africans and Americans which is being examined in this chapter, African and Afro-American identities, in themselves quite separate forms of racial and ethnic classification with their own ambiguous ideological packages and highly contested meanings, have never been givens that could be defined in essentialist terms. Rather, the black popular culture that was in the making in South Africa at the end of the nineteenth century was the result of a process of social negotiation. The creative manipulation of ethnic boundaries as resources in social action, the molding of black transatlantic racial solidarity, and the need for potent symbols as markers of shifting ethnic identities constitute one of the most fertile breeding grounds of early popular performance in South Africa.

Ironically, it was through the tour of a group of young black American performers that this ideological confraternity between blacks in America and in South Africa was inaugurated. The remarkable story of these performers is the subject of this chapter, and it is perhaps best begun by an episode as it was reported by one of those seemingly indestructible and unflagging actors on the South African historical stage, a policeman.

On the evening of March 29, 1898, Trooper L'Estrange of the Natal Police, "on the look out for any criminal wanted," made a routine tour of the Inchanga railway station near Durban. On the platform, near the bar, he encountered Richard H. Collins, a black man, whom he addressed in Zulu, asking what he wanted in the bar. Collins replied: "Who are you talking to? Talk English. I have as much right in the bar as you have." In the argument that followed, considerable confusion arose as to Collins's nationality. It appears that L'Estrange—having dealt on three previous occasions with "dressed natives exempt from native law" who had entered the bar, produced badges of exemption, and asked for a drink—took Collins "for a native of this colony." But Collins, growing increasingly impatient, declared that he was an American citizen and "a professional singer in the McAdoo company" and that he was entitled to get as much liquor as he liked. The trooper then proceeded to arrest Collins, and in the scuffle that ensued the American inflicted a blow on L'Estrange's nose and caught him by the throat. Assisted by the station clerk, L'Estrange eventually managed to pull the vehemently protesting singer in the direction of the police station where he was held for several hours and later released on bail of £5. Court proceedings which were to take place the following morning were suspended following an intervention by the American consul in Durban.[1]

The incident at Inchanga was one of the last chapters in the South African experience of Orpheus M. McAdoo and the Virginia Jubilee Singers, a group of Afro-American musicians who spent almost five years in South Africa between July 1890 and June 1898. While the colonial press was concerned about the effect of the trooper's embarrassing "blunder"[2] on U.S. and colonial diplomatic relations, the historian will interpret Collins's arrest as a significant moment in the emerging American-South African discourse about race relations and segregation of which McAdoo and his troupe became the first and most publicized Afro-American initiators. McAdoo and other members of the company frequently corresponded with friends in the United States and with black newspapers there like the *Southern Workman,* the *Cleveland Gazette, New York Age,* and *The Freeman.* Their reports became the first black American eyewitness accounts of a country whose exacerbating race relations were increasingly to attract the attention of black Americans. In South Africa concerts given by the Jubilee Singers aroused interest in spirituals and Afro-American folk music. But the songs, dances, and sketches that the Jubilee Singers carried into virtually every corner of South Africa also suggested powerful images of race relations in the American South to predominantly white audiences. Moreover, McAdoo's intensive contacts with members of the aspirant black elite of Kimberley, in particular, initiated a specifically *black* dialogue which developed into "a force, from which the oppressed black peoples of diaspora and the fatherland alike could draw intellectual and psychological sustenance" (Cell 1982:22). It was McAdoo's tours that eventually heralded an era of widening transatlantic contacts between white, but especially black, Americans and South Africans.

The Early Years of the
Virginia Jubilee
Singers

Orpheus Myron McAdoo was born in 1858 in Greensboro, North Carolina, the oldest child of slave parents (see fig. 1). The family must have occupied a privileged position among the slaves of the plantation, because they lived in a two-room cottage. Orpheus's mother probably also took good care of the education of her children Orpheus, Fletcher, Eugene, and Bessie Eunice, as she was the only slave on the estate who could read.[3] Around 1872 McAdoo first attended Hampton Institute in Hampton, Virginia, founded in 1868 as one of several institutions of higher education for emancipated slaves. Upward social mobility and improvement were core concepts of the credo that black children like Orpheus were taught at Hampton Institute. McAdoo's own words, written at the age of twenty-four, leave little doubt that for the young teacher "the Indian, like the Negro, has a brain, and if only given a chance of cultivation, he will show his hidden qualities."[4] After graduating in 1876 the young McAdoo taught for a number of years, at the same time devoting his energies to extensive tours with the Hampton Male Quartette, one of the best known Afro-American quartets at the time. In December 1885 the young teacher realized that music was his true vocation and decided to join Frederick Loudin's revived Fisk Jubilee Singers.[5]

The Fisk Jubilee Singers were named after Fisk University in Nashville, Tennessee, which was founded in 1866 as one of seven "chartered institutions" by the American Missionary Association of New York in an effort to provide higher education for the liberated slaves. By the late 1860s the school was already in financial difficulties, and in 1871 George L. White, treasurer and music instructor of the insolvent university, was given permission to take a group of students on a fund-raising concert tour. During their first, seven-year world tour, the Fisk Jubilee Singers introduced American and European audiences to the heart of genuine Afro-American culture: the spirituals, the "sorrow songs" as W. E. B. DuBois called them (DuBois 1903). In 1879, with the situation for blacks rapidly deteriorating, White reorganized the Jubilee Singers, independent of Fisk support, and much against his will and wishes handed over the leadership to Frederick Loudin, a member of the group and by then already a prominent spokesman in the campaign for the Civil Rights Bill of 1875. The bill was conceived to implement the Fourteenth and Fifteenth Amendments to the Constitution that barred states from legalizing racial discrimination. Although Loudin and his troupe managed to generate nationwide support for the black civil-rights campaign,

FIGURE 1. Orpheus M. McAdoo, ca.1897 (The Australasian Stage Annual, January 1900, p. 49)

they could not prevent the Supreme Court from declaring the Civil Rights Act unconstitutional in 1883.[6]

With the floodgates opened to a spate of "Jim Crow" laws, and expecting little sympathy in the United States, Loudin shifted his activities to foreign shores. In April 1884 the new company sailed for England and only returned to the United States in April 1890, after a six-year tour of Australia, India, and the Far East. Somewhere along the way, about October 1889, Orpheus McAdoo and Belle F. Gibbons decided to part company with Loudin.[7] Upon his return to the United States, McAdoo formed his own company, and on May 29, 1890, the Virginia Jubilee Singers, or Virginia Concert Company as the troupe was alternatively called, left New York bound for England. None of the members had been part of the original Fisk Jubilee Singers, and only soprano Gibbons had been part of Loudin's second group. The other members, some of them Hampton graduates like McAdoo himself and his younger brother Eugene, had all been recruited prior to the departure to England. They were the sopranos J. S. Ball and Josie M. Jackson, the contralto Mamie L. Harris, the baritone Moses H. Hodges, and the tenor Richard H. Collins, who became involved in the fight with the Natal trooper eight years later. Lucy J. Moten was their accompanist. In England the troupe was completed by McAdoo's future wife, the "lady tenor" Mattie E. Allen.[8]

After two months the tour ran into unexpected difficulties, but McAdoo, "quite sure of success and . . . not at all discouraged,"[9] decided to sail for South Africa. There, his business success proved to be beyond his "wildest dreams and anticipations,"[10] but the country was to surprise him in another respect. Although Loudin's troupe had not always met with friendly treatment in Australia, the kind of racial bias that awaited them in South Africa upon arrival in Cape Town in mid-June 1890 was without parallel. In one of the first letters McAdoo sent back to his home country from South Africa, he wrote to the head of Hampton Institute, General Armstrong:

> Everyone seemed captivated with the singing; never heard such singing in all their lives, and they said, "and just to think that black people should do it." The latter remark will give you some idea of a feeling of prejudice; well, so it is. There is no country in the world where prejudice is so strong as here in Africa. The native to-day is treated as badly as ever the slave was treated in Georgia. Here in Africa the native laws are most unjust; such as any Christian people would be ashamed of. Do you credit a law in a civilized community compelling every

man of dark skin, even though he is a citizen of another country, to be in his house by 9 o'clock at night, or he is arrested.
. . . These laws exist in the Transvaal and Orange Free States,
which are governed by the Dutch, who place every living creature before the native.[11]

The Virginia Jubilee Singers opened at the Vaudeville Theatre in
Cape Town on the evening of June 30, 1890. On the same night, another
attraction competed for the favors of Cape Town audiences. Lambert
D'Arcs Court Minstrels Troupe promised an evening of "Spectacular,
Music, Drama, Dances, Comedies, Parodies, Reviews, Allegorical, Bom-
bastical, and Comical Burlesques . . . and the Side splitting, and always
Encored Sand and Plantation Dances."[12] McAdoo's own program, apart
from the genuine jubilee hymns, included somewhat similar material to
the one offered by D'Arcs's Court Minstrels. Songs like "Massa's Dead,"
"The Old Folks at Home," and "Old Black Joe" were sung side by side
with the great songs of the jubilee tradition like "Steal Away to Jesus" and
"The Gospel Train." A *Cape Argus* critic identified both categories of songs
as "attributes of the race,"[13] but in reality the former were classics of the
minstrel theater, the most important form of popular entertainment in
mid-nineteenth-century America, in which white performers with blackened faces mimicked and ridiculed blacks.[14]

Interlude: The   Stage impersonation of blacks by whites had
Minstrel Show in   been common in the English theater since at
the United States   least the late eighteenth century. It was, how-
     ever, not until the 1820s and 1830s that
professional American entertainers like Thomas Rice, J. W. Sweeney, and
Bob Farrell began to incorporate an increasing number of songs, dances,
and dialogues portraying blacks in their shows. Rice eventually composed "Jim Crow," a classic of American minstrelsy and "the first great
international song hit of American popular music" (Chase 1966:264). In
other songs, even more popular, like "Zip Coon" and "Miss Lucy Long,"
white Northerners who rarely had any firsthand knowledge of Afro-
American culture portrayed one of their favorite black stereotypes: the
"Dandy Broadway Swell," the free Negro of the Northern cities, who
struts around in flashy long-tailed coats, white gloves, and skintight trousers, boasting of his success with women. Songs like "Jim Crow" and
"Jim Along Josey" mimicked the ignorant "plantation darky," poorly
clad in rags, with ludicrously exaggerated features, and speaking malaprop language.

Such stereotypes became a fixture of the minstrel stage because they reinforced the most cherished beliefs white Northerners held about blacks. In the beginning, minstrel shows consisted of little more than un-related songs, instrumental solos, and dances, loosely tied together by jokes and dialogue. Over the years, however, as minstrel companies grew bigger and accumulated a larger song and dance repertoire, a standard format developed with a clear division of acts and specialty roles. A pi-oneer in forging the new minstrel format was Dan Emmett who presented the first full-scale blackface entertainment at the Bowery Amphitheatre in New York in 1843. In the decade following the appearance of Emmett's "Virginia Minstrels" the American stage witnessed an explosion of "Ethi-opian" entertainments with hundreds of minstrel troupes touring every corner of the country and Europe.

Until the late 1860s a spectator of a typical minstrel show would have witnessed the following scene on stage: seated in a semicircle and performing grotesquely distorted gestures were as many as twenty min-strels, their faces blackened with burnt cork, who sang in unison accompanied by fiddles and banjos. On the ends of the semicircle sat the stars of the show: Brudder or Mr. Tambo, playing tambourine, and Brud-der Bones, playing castanet-like bone clappers. The ludicrous antics and raucous humor of these "endmen" contrasted with the solemn and pom-pous behavior of the "Interlocutor," or Mr. Johnson, the onstage director who held the heavily improvised show together and established a link between the audience and what happened on stage.

A minstrel show typically consisted of three parts: the first featured songs and dances and, above all, the riddles, puns, and "one-liners" of the endmen. The second, the olio, offered anything from acrobatic acts, to men playing combs, to the latest novelty. Its main feature, however, was the stump speech delivered by one of the endmen in malaprop "nigger dialect" on topics such as the "History of England." In the third part, the curtain rose on a one-act skit set on a Southern plantation where happy "darkies" danced "break downs," extolled the goodness of the "massa," and generally seemed to enjoy nothing so much as being slaves. The cast included roles such as Mr. Hide'm, a protectionist, Mr. Flog'em, the slave driver, and the inevitable Sambo, a runaway slave. Until the end of the Civil War this format remained relatively unchanged, but from the 1870s minstrels increasingly introduced variety elements, discarding the old plantation material.

The most profound changes in American minstrel theater, however, were introduced by growing numbers of black professional entertainers who took the stage after the Civil War. Black minstrel troupes soon boasted as members well-known comedians like Billy Kersands and Bert Williams and some of the first black popular songwriters in American music history, like James Bland who wrote "Dem Golden Slippers" and "Carry Me Back to Old Virginny." From the start, black minstrels' attitudes toward racial oppression was marked by ambiguity. Thus Kersands and Williams were extraordinarily popular with black audiences despite the fact that they inherited from their white competitors the images of thick-lipped, boisterous, razor-toting blacks. In the late 1870s when white minstrel groups abandoned the plantation scenes in favor of novelty shows and vaudeville acts, Haverly's Colored Minstrels and the Georgia Minstrels advertised themselves as "natural children of bondage," who re-create in their "naturallist" show "de good ole' plantation" where "de darky will be hisself once more and forget that he eber had any trouble" (Toll 1974:209).

Yet, at the same time the romanticized image of the "darky" was interfused with elements of genuine Afro-American culture and protest against oppression. Inspired by the Fisk Jubilee Singers' revival of authentic slave music, many black minstrels expressed antislavery feelings, while others concentrated on sentimental songs about the black family, one of the strongest emotional refuges under slavery and in post–Civil War turmoil. Black minstrels, then, did not uniformly legitimize whites' distastes for blacks by testifying that blacks, too, shared antiblack feelings. Although black people must have laughed at stereotyped minstrel characters for some of the same reasons whites did, theirs—as Robert Toll argues—was also "in-group laughter of recognition, even of belonging":

> The blacks that attended minstrel shows . . . were probably not concerned with what impression whites would get from the show or with how well blacks measured up to white standards. It was the difference between the black bourgeoisie with their eyes focused on whites and on middle-class standards and the masses of black people whose perspectives were essentially confined to their group and to Afro-American culture. Certainly, all blacks could recognize that Kersands, McIntosh, and Williams performed caricatures—distorted images greatly exaggerating a few prominent features. Unlike whites, they *knew* the diversity of black people; they knew all blacks were not like these stage images. . . . But they also

probably knew black people who shared some of these traits. They laughed at the familiar in exaggerated form. (Toll 1974: 257f.)

However much blacks and whites may have shared some of the same responses to stereotypes of blacks, whites overwhelmingly took delight in finding their worst prejudices confirmed by performers who themselves belonged to the oppressed and ridiculed race. Because audiences were inclined to accept black minstrels as authentic plantation Negroes, one critic was able to argue that Haverly's Colored Minstrels depicted plantation life "with a greater fidelity than any 'poor white trash' with corked faces can ever do," thereby disproving "the saying that a negro cannot act the nigger" (quoted in Toll 1974:202).

Although minstrel shows were first and foremost performed by whites for whites, an influence of slave music on the songs and dances of the minstrel theater cannot be denied. The structures and texts of minstrel songs often reflect key concepts of genuine slave culture, and many early white minstrel performers boasted an extensive knowledge of and sympathy for Afro-American culture. But however many elements of admiration for Afro-American culture the minstrel theater may have contained, it was fundamentally a white institution, while the jubilee songs were deeply anchored in the culture of the oppressed black population.

"Acting the Nigger": In South Africa, the crude racist mockery by
The Minstrel Show white minstrel performers "acting the nigger"
in South Africa was by far the most important ideological rationale of the minstrel show. "Acting the nigger," acting out white fantasies about blacks, was ideally suited as a rationalization of the anxieties of white settlers in South Africa attempting to come to terms with the strength of precolonial social formations and independent African political power.

Minstrel shows had been introduced to South Africa by English colonists as early as the 1850s, soon after the first appearance of the reputedly premier minstrel company, the Virginia Minstrels, in New York. But it was only on August 20, 1862, when the world-famous Christy Minstrels opened a short season in Cape Town, that the stage was set for the rise of a form of popular entertainment which in many ways resembled the development of the minstrel show in the United States (Cockrell 1987). The press stressed the fact that

the fame of the distinguished party who have earned so wide a celebrity as portrayers of Negro character had preceded their arrival in Africa. Besides, the character of the entertainment is eminently suited to the tastes of the people here. . . . Moreover, so essentially true to life—especially African life—in many of its phrases, are the "sketches" of these clever impersonators of Negro character, that they could scarcely fail to please.[15]

In Durban critics were inclined to believe that the "negro oddities" were "as true to life as possible" and expressed astonishment "that so large an amount of local knowledge could have been acquired in so short a time." Moreover, the "coloring of the skin justifies a breadth of treatment in representing the grotesque, which would not otherwise be obtainable. What would seem silly and distorted in an actor of our race, loses its insane aspect when done by a mock ethiopian."[16]

The *Natal Mercury* and *Cape Argus* critics were probably as removed from "African life" and "Negro character" as the Christy Minstrels, but they were certainly correct in predicting that the Christies' "'venture' in coming to the colony is likely to prove the most successful essay of the kind ever attempted here."[17] In the next three decades, blackface minstrel shows became the dominant form of popular white musical and theatrical entertainment in South Africa, perhaps only second in popularity to the public lecture and the circus. Amateur minstrel troupes mushroomed in the most remote provincial towns, and in the major centers of English culture like Kimberley, Durban, and Cape Town, audiences were often able to choose between two minstrel entertainments on the same night. British regiments soon had their own permanent minstrel troupes that enjoyed high patronage from the colonial ruling elite. While minstrels ensured that for soirees under such patronage only cleaned-up minstrel material was presented, working-class audiences soon discovered in minstrelsy one of their most favored forms of releasing racial hatred. On the Kimberley diamond fields, in the twisted logic of racism and confusing the victims of minstrel "humor" with its perpetrators, Africans were frequently abused as "Christy Minstrels" (Matthews 1887:193). Inspired by stereotypes of the minstrel show such as "Jim Crow," white racists eventually came to call their African laborers and servants "Jim."

However, the influence of American minstrelsy was not confined to Anglo-Saxon forms of racist ideology. It also reached deep into Dutch Boer and Cape "coloured"[18] culture and folk song. From at least 1869 the Amateur Coloured Troupe under Joe Lyal presented almost weekly full-scale minstrel shows to Cape Town audiences, nearly two decades earlier than the first "coon" carnivalists marched in the streets of Cape Town on New Year's Day of 1888. By the late 1870s minstrel tunes had become so popular that the well-known Afrikaans folk song "Wanneer kom ons troudag, Gertjie" was sung to the tune of George Frederick Root's "Just before the Battle, Mother," a minstrel tune composed during the American Civil War in 1864.[19]

From the very beginning, African audiences had been introduced to the new entertainment genre. In March 1871 *The Ghost*, one of the most popular "Negro farces" of the day, was "performed for the benefit of coloured people" in Durban. The "several white people" present at the occasion not only took delight in the play, but also in watching the perturbed victims of their laughter. They were intrigued by the "astonishment depicted on the darkie's faces at the wonderful feats of the spectre."[20] One can speculate whether the astonishment might in fact have been due to the shock felt at the crude racist mockery of the show. Be this as it may, by the early 1880s the racial stereotypes of minstrel shows must eventually have become accepted, albeit transformed by the "laughter of recognition," by the growing African urban population. In 1880 at least one black minstrel troupe was operating in Durban, the Kafir Christy Minstrels, which the *Natal Mercury* paternalistically described as "a troupe of eight genuine natives, bones and all, complete who really get through their songs very well."[21] By the late 1880s the minstrel craze had faded and audiences throughout the country preferred more sophisticated forms of entertainment like limelight shows, light opera provided by numerous traveling English companies, and the ever-popular circuses.

In the 1890s both "coloured" and black musicians initiated a process that generations of performers were to continue and to refine in following decades: they not only imitated an American idiom, but they also transformed it creatively into a genuine black South African urban tradition that had ramifications far into the modern styles of the 1920s and 1930s. Cape Town "coon" songs were among the most important influences upon both Reuben Caluza's early "ragtime" songs and on *isikhunzi* (coons), a prototype of present-day Zulu migrant workers' *isicathamiya* music. In both cases, the underlying principle was the reinterpretation of a symbiotic set of black and white musical idioms and possibly even of a dominantly white institution in black South African terms.

"Hopes of Liberty":
The White Liberal
Response

McAdoo's audiences were predominantly white, and their response reflected the whole ambiguity of intracolonial class and race relations. Over a period of more than four decades white South Africans had acquired distorted images of black Americans through an intensive exposure to blackface minstrelsy. The ways in which these images about blacks were built into the discourse of different strata of white colonial society ranged from outright racism to liberal attitudes and paternalism. In Durban, for instance, a few months prior to McAdoo's arrival in South Africa, the amateur conductor Duncan Mac-Coll, who claimed to have seen the original Jubilee Singers in England, presented a concert of "jubilee hymns," including classics like "Steal Away to Jesus," "My Good Lord's been here," and "Turn Back Pharaoh's Army." Especially the last "caused some amusement," when James Watt in the solo part sang "in all seriousness that he's 'Gwine to write to Massa Jesus' ".[22] In Pretoria, one critic felt that McAdoo's performance

> is of the form of the Christy Minstrel entertainments, but [is] devoid of the vulgarities and forced humor of that class. In point of fact, "Christianised Christies" may be taken as descriptive of these performances. Nearly all the pieces sung are deeply imbued with a religious quality, but it is expressed in a way that, although natural under the circumstances, might be considered somewhat irreverent.[23]

The criticism of irreverent expression in the sacred songs of the slaves was typical of the white response. White audiences could not understand that slaves personalized Christianity and could refer to God in no better terms than those of the master-servant relationship of the plantation. Thus, "what whites took for profanity usually was one or another kind of respectful religious imagery" (Genovese 1976:631).

Notwithstanding the initial confusion about the minstrel and jubilee repertoires, audiences throughout South Africa celebrated McAdoo's troupe as one of the finest performing groups that had ever visited the southern part of the continent. "Singing such as given by the Virginia Concert Company," noted the *Cape Argus*,

> has never before been heard in this country. Their selection consists of a peculiar kind of part song, the different voices joining in at most unexpected moments in a wild kind of harmony. . . . it is without doubt one of the attributes of the race to which they belong, and in their most sacred songs they

seem at times inspired, as if they were lifting up their voices in praise of God with hopes of liberty.[24]

The Governor of South Africa, Sir Loch, and Lady Loch attended the opening night in Cape Town, a fact little surprising if one bears in mind that the liberation of the slaves in 1834—albeit not for philanthropic principles, but out of a severe shortage of "free" labor—was one of the ideological foundations of Cape liberalism. Such feelings, however, were not universally shared by a population of white settlers whose ideological frame of reference and "frontier" mentality involved exclusion as well as inclusion.[25] This explains the outright hostility awaiting the Jubilee Singers in places like Worcester, where every performance was "marred by the rowdyism of some of the young men."[26] In Bloemfontein, in a letter to *The Friend*, "Justice" expressed surprise "that a certain sector of our community have shown a disposition to ignore them because their skins are black,"[27] and in King Williamstown McAdoo "had to rebuke the rowdy element."[28] In general, however, such antagonism was the exception rather than the rule, and thus it was somewhat incomprehensible to the *Daily Independent* that, despite the "sanctimonious" character of the program, the Queen's Theatre in Kimberley was not filled with "'goody goody' people, philanthrophists, and negrophilists" but with "audiences of a more mixed character than have perhaps ever been gathered" in Kimberley.[29]

However, the positive reception that greeted the Jubilee Singers throughout South Africa was not only due to the Cape liberal tradition, but also to the ease with which the versatile impresario established communication with virtually any type of audience. The opening night in most towns visited usually concentrated on jubilee hymns such as "Steal Away to Jesus," "Go Down Moses," "I am Rolling through an Unfriendly World," "The Gospel Train," "Swing Low, Sweet Chariot," "Good News, the Chariot's Coming," and others. The second and following nights of an appearance in a town, however, catered more to the colonial taste and featured ballads, glees, songs from the classical repertoire, and somemes even entire "Scottish" programs. The program presented in King Williamstown on October 17, 1890, may be taken as a typical example:

PART I
Glee. . . . ."Jingle Bells". . . . .C. A. White
Virginia Concert Co.
Duett. . . . ."Maying". . . . .A. M. Smith
Misses Gibbons and Allen

Solo. . . . ."Rocked in the Cradle of the Deep"
Mr. O. M. McAdoo
Quartette. . . . ."Moonlight will come again"
Misses Jackson & Harris,
Messrs. Collins and E. McAdoo
Solo. . . . ."Good Bye". . . . .Tosti
Miss Belle F. Gibbons
Medley. . . . ."Popular Airs". . . . .Jubilee Singers
Virginia Concert Co.
Ladies' Quartette. . . . ."Greeting to Spring". . . . .Wilson
Misses Gibbons, Allen, Jackson, and
Madame Ball

PART II

Glee. . . . ."The Bells". . . . .Jubilee Singers
Virginia Concert Co.
Solo. . . . ."We met too late". . . . .King
Miss M. E. Allen
Glee. . . . ."The Moonlight Dance". . . . .White
Virginia Concert Co.
Solo. . . . ."My Star of Eve (Tannhauser)". . . . .Wagner
Mr. M. H. Hodges
Quartette. . . . ."Come, where the lilies bloom"
Misses Gibbons and Allen,
Messrs. Hodges and O. M. McAdoo
Solo. . . . ."La Zingarellas". . . . .Campana
Madame Ball
Glee. . . . ."The Kimberley Band". . . . .Jubilee Singers
Virginia Concert Co.[30]

In later years the program was complemented by lady elocutionist Julia Wormley's "dramatic recitation" of "The Pilot's Story." In 1890 Giuseppe Verdi had visited South Africa with an opera company—a fact which McAdoo could hardly ignore in his attempt to control a sector of the competitive entertainment market—and so his show later included also "30 Minutes of Grand Opera" featuring "Selections from 'Bohemian Girl' and 'Il Trovatore.'"

The Jubilee Singers' first tour of South Africa closed with a performance in Cape Town on January 25, 1892. After a three-year tour of Australia, the troupe returned to Cape Town on June 29, 1895. In addition to Orpheus McAdoo himself, his wife Mattie (née Allen), Belle Gibbons, and R. H. Collins, now transformed into "the only true exponent of American Coon Songs in South Africa,"[31] the new Jubilee Singers included the sopranos Laura A. Carr, Jennie Robinson, and Mamie Edwards, the contralto Marshall Webb, the tenor Will P. Thompson, and C. A. White as accompanist. Until February 1897 the program remained unchanged, but a saturated market must have induced McAdoo to give the jubilee hymns "a well-earned repose"[32] and to restructure the entire show. In addition, since at least July 1896 the impresario had been facing mounting difficulties with some members of his company, most of all with Will Thompson. As a result, the Pittsburgh-born baritone and former member of a jubilee troupe known as the Fisk-Tennesseans left McAdoo's troupe to become manager of the Colonial Concert Company, which presented benefit concerts both for the Perseverance School in Kimberley and for Mamie Edwards, who had also left McAdoo's employ. Apart from brief periods of reconciliation with McAdoo, Thompson and Edwards decided to take up residence in Kimberley, alternatively performing with the Colonial Concert Company and the Philharmonic Society, and directing the Diamond Minstrels.[33]

Will Thompson's and Mamie Edwards's departure caused the impresario considerable chagrin, and in February 1897 McAdoo decided to travel to New York to recruit replacements for the two artists. Upon his return in mid-June 1897, he brought with him eight new artists and named the new troupe the "Minstrel, Vaudeville and Concert Company." In addition to the old audience favorites Jennie Robinson, Belle Gibbons, Mattie Allen, Moses Hodges, and Collins, McAdoo had hired the vocal soloists Dietz and J. Smith, the dancer Louis Love, the banjo soloists Willard Smith and Madeline Shirley, the dancer, comedian, and female impersonator Jerry Mills, the juggler Jose Jalvan, and the "Black Melba" Susie B. Anderson. The success of the new Minstrel, Vaudeville and Concert Company probably persuaded Thompson and Edwards to settle their differences with McAdoo and to rejoin the troupe in August 1897.

Following the broader trends of black minstrelsy in the United States, it was McAdoo's aim to introduce to "the theatrical and music-loving public the genuine American negro as a comedian, singer, dancer, banjoist and general mirth-maker."[34] The new program followed the standard three-part minstrel format. The first part consisted of minstrel tunes such as Stephen Foster's "Massa's in de Cold Ground" and "Home Sweet Home," "I'se Gwine Back to Dixie," and above all the jokes and antics of the "Tambos" Louis Love and Jose Jalvan, and the "Bones" Willard Smith and Jerry Mills. One such joke, a variation of a staple Afro-American joke, shows the parallels in the forms of popular ideology produced by the black experience in the frontier and plantation situations:

One of the corner men asks a brother where he would like to be buried when he died. The brother replied that he would like a resting place in a nice, quiet Methodist cemetery and then asked where his questioner would like to be laid. The latter answered: "In a Dutch cemetery." "Why?" asked the brother. The answer was: "Because a Dutch cemetery is the last place the devil would go to look for a black man."[35]

The second half of the program, the "Grand Olio," consisted of dances and the acrobatic acts of juggler Jalvan. His contortionist act "Ferry the Frog" in particular aroused much admiration, despite the fact that sometimes on the same night and in the same town Frank E. Fillis's Circus presented Jalvan's compatriot and fellow juggler Zarmo, the "£100 per week star and wonder of the age."[36]

The program ended with "America's Latest Novelty," the Grand Cake Walk or "The Negro Minuet." Later this component of the show alternated with the "Negro sketch" "A Theatrical Manager's Troubles with His Office Boy," the skit "Trilby's Wedding, Or, Life on the Mississippi River," or the plantation "drama" in two acts "Good Old Georgia in '49." The latter told the story of the old Negro slave Ephraim Jackson, who "ran away from bondage seventeen years ago, and went to the North to try and earn enough money to buy the freedom of his wife and children. Not having succeeded and feeling that his days were numbered, he starts back to his old Southern home." Tired from the journey, he dies in the arms of his sons, but only after having become reconciled with his young master.[37] Almost four decades after the first appearance of the Christy Minstrels in South Africa, McAdoo's minstrel acts for a short time revived the interest in minstrelsy which had faded since the late 1880s. Even colonial companies such as the white, "respectable" Ada Delroy's Company once again featured minstrel acts such as James Bell's "Senegambian Oddities."[38]

"Kruger's Tears": The "Sorrow Songs" and Boer Paternalism   The changes brought into effect by McAdoo in 1897 must be set in relation to the constraints placed on the effort of making a profit on an expanding entertainment market marked by deep-reaching ideological shifts and rapidly changing patterns of leisure-time activities. The decade between 1890 and 1900 saw some of the most dramatic changes in the history of the subcontinent, and the rise of an industrial giant which increasingly welded the societies of the area into a single political economy serving the interests of a handful of mine magnates. Throughout the 1890s these interests and parallel attempts to gain control of the Afrikaner-ruled republics through the abortive Jameson raid of 1895 and the South African War of 1899–1902 were increasingly legitimized in terms of social imperialism. An ideology of British supremacy and racial segregation came to dominate the consciousness of large sectors of South African society (Marks and Trapido 1979).

The impresario himself and most members of his troupe harbored strong imperial sympathies. When the Jubilee Singers were asked to postpone their appearance in the Queenstown Town Hall in favor of a meeting of the Loyal Colonial League, McAdoo hastened to cable: "Strong sympathy compels the Jubilee Singers to forego concert on Saturday in favor of League Meeting."[39] In 1895 Mamie Edwards, the "Brown Patti," visited some of the mission churches and schools in Kimberley and discovered that the "English people take quite an interest in them." This persuaded her that "of all the people that God in his own divine power ever made, the English people are the people, and surely they must be the chosen ones." Yet Edwards's imperial sympathies also prevented her from understanding the coercive nature of the colonial regime. In Kimberley she visited the compounds, which she regarded as an institution designed not so much to police the work force rather than "to prevent the natives from throwing diamonds out to parties not interested in the mines or fields for any other purpose than stealing." But the men behind barbed wire, despite all the frustration, anger, and revolt, were also "a very good and generous kind of creature," and with most of her English-speaking colonial contemporaries Mamie Edwards shared the myth of the good-natured "native," who "if he likes any one . . . will give his life for him."[40] As such Edwards's empathy with Kimberley's black miners might well have been the result of personal contact and friendliness. At the same time, the image of the good-natured "native" embarrassingly resembles the portrayal of the Southern Negro in minstrel shows such as "Good Old Georgia," revived by McAdoo's company and other black minstrel troupes.

Ultimately, McAdoo's and Edwards's procolonial sentiments were owed to a status unique among black American visitors to South Africa. Earlier, Captain Harry Dean, one of the most colorful black American visitors to South Africa at the turn of the century who was engaged in transporting African laborers by boat between Cape Town and Port Elizabeth and East London, had been "suspected of social climbing when I mixed with the European colonials, and suspected by the government of ulterior motives when I mixed with my own race" (Dean 1929:79).[41] As performers the Jubilee Singers were able to escape Dean's dilemma. They were fluent in their relations with all classes and groupings of colonial society—with the exception perhaps of the African laborers—and in addition to the highest state protection, Orpheus McAdoo at least enjoyed a class position which raised him above suspicions of social climbing or of presenting a threat to the various territorial governments. The description *The Freeman* gave of him shortly after his departure from South Africa to Australia in mid-1898 is indeed indicative of McAdoo's economic success and social position:

> He is prosperous, and an Australian by adoption. He was a classmate of Booker T. Washington. In his accent he is decidedly English. He dresses well in the style of the English upper class. . . . He wears a few diamonds within the bounds of propriety. . . . From all indications he is a thorough gentleman from tip to tip.[42]

But McAdoo was also a professional performer, whose success depended on his ability to cater to a great variety of musical tastes as well as ideologies. To African ears, political comment such as the "Dutch cemetery" joke certainly contained a clear problack message, but for white urban audiences it also expressed strong pro-British and above all anti-Boer sentiments. Far removed from a wholesale adoption of mainstream "white" minstrel ideology irreconcilable with overt problack sympathies, or an unambiguous black nationalist message, McAdoo's show exploited the whole contradictory spectrum of colonial class relations and ideologies. Neither "white" nor "black," the changed emphasis from genuine slave cultural expression to pastiches of deteriorating race relations in the American South in McAdoo's new program reflected at least in part the changing ideological landscape in South Africa toward the end of the nineteenth century.

For very peculiar reasons, the spirituals even struck a sensitive chord with Boer audiences. McAdoo very likely avoided the "Dutch cemetery" joke at a concert at the Huguenot Seminary in Wellington that established cordial relations between the black American artists and the ultraconservative audience. "It is wonderful," wrote one member of the audience, "to see our staid Dutch people to go into ecstasies over them, and our servants who were allowed to go into the anteroom to listen to them were taken right off their feet."[43] The kind of relations the Jubilee Singers established with "staid Dutch people" could perhaps not be illustrated better than by a highly unusual encounter between McAdoo and

the man whose regime was the supreme manifestation of Boer paternalistic ideology. In February 1891 Transvaal President Paul Kruger not
only set foot in a theater, probably for the first time in his life, but when
the Jubilee Singers sang "Nobody Knows the Trouble I've Seen," it is reported, tears ran down "the rugged features of the President."[44] It is
perhaps one of the most peculiar moments in McAdoo's career in South
Africa that the jeremiad of one of the descendants of Ham should have
touched the heart of a man whose rule was built on the firm belief that
these very descendants should be eternal drawers of water and hewers of
wood. But, like slaveholders in the antebellum South, Boer farmers were
capable of deeply rooted paternalistic feelings.

Paternalism, as Eugene Genovese has shown, bound slaves and
slaveholders together in an ideology of superordination and subordina-
tion that, from the slaveholders' point of view, defined involuntary labor
as a legitimate return for protection. But this common ideology also held
its advantages for the slaves. The "impossibility of the slaves ever becoming the things they were supposed to be," Genovese reminds us,
"constituted a moral victory for the slaves themselves. Paternalism's insistence upon mutual obligations . . . implicitly recognized the slaves'
humanity" (Genovese 1976:5). Kruger's agrarian consciousness comprised elements of paternalism that made him, the lord and master,
vulnerable to the assertions of the slaves' humanity expressed in the "sorrow songs."

"Honorary Whites"
The Virginia Jubilee
Singers and Black
Americans in South
Africa

Kruger's tears may have been flattering for
McAdoo, but they glossed over the harsher,
segregationist, everyday practices of Kruger's
bureaucrats. When McAdoo married Mattie
Allen in Johannesburg in January 1891, the
fashionable event was worthy of the attention
of the local press. What bride and bridegroom may have been unaware of
were the inquiries the Johannesburg magistrate made about the legality
of marrying Orpheus McAdoo and Mattie Allen, whom he described as
"almost white—her father is a white and her mother is an octoroon."[45]

Harassment was, however, by no means restricted to officially sanc-
tioned discrimination. On a somewhat less sophisticated level was the
attempt by one Pretoria hotelier to ease the Jubilee Singers of £27.10.0.
Before the Pretoria magistrate, Henry S. Pollington of the Clarendon
Hotel accused McAdoo of welshing on one week's board and lodging for
the entire company. However, McAdoo was able to prove that his com-

pany had not stayed at the Clarendon, and acquittal was given with costs in McAdoo's favor.[46] Five years later, in Middelburg, a resident at the Transvaal Hotel who "never knew that Americans were yellow and black" complained to the local magistrate "that coloured people were staying at the same hotel as white persons." Yet, here as in Pretoria, the courts ruled in McAdoo's favor.[47]

McAdoo must have greeted this fact as a pleasant change from practices in some regions of the United States, but in reality he had to ascribe it to his status as an "honorary white" which the English colonies and the Boer republics were prepared to grant to all black American citizens (Keto 1972; de Waal 1974). Although the number of black Americans in South Africa, according to Clement Keto, never exceeded one hundred at any given time during the 1890s, their presence was a source of constant worry for the Boer and colonial governments, and frequently an embarrassment for American representatives in the country. However, desirous to foster friendly relations with the United States, the Kruger regime made several attempts to negotiate an agreement with the United States regulating, among other things, the status of black American citizens. Negotiations were slowed further by an incident in 1893 which involved a black American named John Ross, who worked on the Delagoa railway. Ross had been brutally assaulted by a white policeman after answering back to verbal abuse by a white coworker. Memoranda flew back and forth between the American representatives and authorities of the Transvaal Republic, and Ross, supported by the U.S. Department of State, eventually filed a lawsuit against the Kruger Republic for damages totaling $10,000. Although in the end the American government "made the Boers pay"—as AME Bishop Henry M. Turner later put it—friendly relations were soon restored, and all black Americans resident in the Transvaal were required to register at the Consular Agency in Johannesburg and to be issued with special passes identifying them as black American citizens (Keto 1972).

This arrangement probably not only relieved the U.S. Consul of the burdensome duty of having to protect his black countrymen, but also suited Ross's own efforts to maintain a fairly privileged status with regard to his African brothers. When the Volksraad passed Law No. 31 in 1896 requiring all blacks seeking employment in the mines to wear a metal badge, Ross, who was now working as an engineer with the Netherlands Railway Company, feared that coloured persons "would be placed on a level with the raw, savage, totally uneducated aborigine" (quoted in de Waal 1974:54).

Soon after his arrival in South Africa, McAdoo had addressed a personal letter to Kruger, requesting protection for himself and his company as "citizens of a Sister Republic."[48] With the support of Transvaal prime minister General Joubert, who impressed on Kruger McAdoo's intention of "founding churches and schools,"[49] the request was granted. George F. Hollis, the U.S. Consul in Cape Town, later boasted that his letter to Kruger had "paved the way for courteous treatment among a people prone to despise the blacks." His hopes, however, that "this visit will have its effect on colonial feeling"[50] were somewhat premature, for the high protection sometimes failed to produce the desired immunity. In following years, McAdoo and other members of his company like Collins were arrested. As the first black American to protest the pass laws, the annoyed impresario eventually voiced his rejection of the inferior status of blacks in the Transvaal from the stage of a Johannesburg theater, in the presence of officials of the Transvaal government. The inopportune publicity strained relations with the U.S. Consular agent in Johannesburg, who reprimanded McAdoo that

> there was no truth in his statement [and] that he had no case whatever. I further told him that I considered him entirely in the wrong in bringing those men here from the States without bringing Passports with them and . . . calling upon me immediately upon his arrival to know if it was necessary to have any protection for them in order that they would not be stopped or molested in any way by Police Officials.[51]

After the Boer War, the Milner regime abolished the "honorary white" status, and black Americans deluged the American consulates with applications to defend their rights. Some of these applicants were more concerned about the fact that they were made to "wear a pass" like a "native in his barbarous state"[52] and saw no link between their own inferior status and the oppression of their African brothers.

"When Will Africans Stop Being Slaves?" The Black Response

For black South Africans the identification with the American artists was complete. Predictably, Africans had to content themselves with separate shows in church and community halls, and the few town halls and theaters which municipalities like Kimberley and Pietermaritzburg occasionally opened to segregated black audiences. It was here, among the small urban black communities, that McAdoo and his troupe were received with undivided enthusiasm. The admiration must have crossed internal class divisions within the African community of an Eastern Cape frontier town such as King Williamstown, even if it was somewhat hampered by problems of communication. During the Jubilee Singers' visit to the town in October 1890 some obviously more rural contemporaries

> could not quite understand what sort of people they were. Some of them hesitated to class them as Kafirs, as they seemed so smart and tidy in appearance, and moved about with all the ease and freedom among the white people that a high state of civilization and education alone can give. Occasionally, however, a Kafir would salute a "Singer" in his own language, and when he failed to get a reply he would look puzzled, exclaim *Kwoku!* and walk away wondering how his "brother" did not return the salute.[53]

Education and a "high state of civilization" were the unshakable ideological foundations of African petty bourgeois political and social involvement within the established colonial structures. For Kimberley's black clerks, preachers, and artisans as much as for emancipated slaves and the Fisk students who had formed the Fisk Jubilee Singers two or three decades earlier, the solution to racial oppression and segregation lay in increased social mobility through education. Apart from McAdoo's musical abilities, it was his reports on black educational achievements in the United States that left the deepest impression on young and aspiring Africans such as Josiah Semouse, an employee in the Kimberley post office. Personal contacts with members of the troupe and McAdoo's short lectures on Afro-American history and culture that frequently opened the show provided valuable points of reference for self-conscious young Africans. Thus it is little surprise that it was Semouse who wrote the first African eulogy of the Jubilee Singers. McAdoo and his troupe performed in the town between July 31 and August 16, 1890. Semouse, and some of his friends like Patrick Lenkoane and possibly Solomon Plaatje,[54] were in the audience in the Kimberley Town Hall when the Jubilee Singers, on the last day of their stay, presented a concert for "Natives and Coloured People."[55] A few weeks later Semouse's enthusiastic article on the "Great American Singers" appeared in the Morija-based mission monthly *Leselinyana:*

> Gentlemen, I do not find the words to describe the way in which these people sang. Unless I am mistaken, I can say that they sang like angels singing Hosannah in heaven. All the people on the diamond fields agree that they sing better than anybody else, white or black.[56]

Semouse's article, after a lengthy outline of slavery and emancipation, culminates in an ecstatic description of Afro-American achievements and in a passionate call for national emancipation:

> Hear! Today they have their own schools, primary, secondary, and high schools, and also universities. They are run by them without the help of the whites. They have magistrates, judges, lawyers, bishops, ministers, and evangelists, and school masters. Some have learned a craft such as building, etc. When will the day come when the African people will be like the Americans? When will they stop being slaves and become nations with their own government?[57]

Semouse's feelings were echoed, if somewhat more eloquently, by John Tengo Jabavu, editor of *Imvo Zabantsundu* and a leading African politician of the time:

> It would strongly savour of presumption for a Native African of this part to venture a critique on his brethren from America, who are now visiting this quarter of their fatherland, and whose position, socially, is being deservedly pointed at on all hands as one that Natives here should strive to attain to. As Africans we are, of course, proud of the achievements of those of our race. Their visit will do their countrymen here no end of good. Already it has suggested reflection to many who, without such a demonstration, would have remained skeptical as to the possibility, not to say probability, of the Natives of this country being raised to anything above remaining as perpetual hewers of wood and drawers of water. The recognition of the latent abilities of the Natives . . . cannot fail to exert an influence for the mutual good of all the inhabitants of this country. The visit of our friends, besides, will lead to the awakening in their countrymen here of an interest in the history of the civilization of the Negro race in America, and a knowledge of their history is sure to result beneficial to our people generally.[58]

In the African communities of Durban and Pietermaritzburg, the sites of extensive American missionary activity since the mid-nineteenth century, McAdoo's visits evoked no less enthusiastic responses, and African correspondents of the Edendale-based Protestant mission paper *Inkanyiso Yase Natal* celebrated the Jubilee Singers as "our music heroes."[59]

The reception was equally warm among "coloured" residents of Kimberley, where the "coloured" *South African Citizen* was not averse to testifying that "Mr McAdoo's Minstrels . . . showed the superiority of the American coloured people over the South African."[60] The strong statement may in part be due to the fact that during their second tour McAdoo and the Jubilee Singers, apparently anticipating a prolonged stay and involvement in South Africa, had founded *The Citizen,* the first known "coloured" newspaper and precursor of the *South African Citizen.*

In agreement with the prevailing optimism reigning among African shopkeepers, clerks, preachers, and large landowners, Semouse and Jabavu may have overestimated the role of education in removing class and racial barriers. They were correct, however, in predicting the beneficial effects that were expected from McAdoo's tour. Visits to Adams College and Lovedale, the "African Hampton," had persuaded McAdoo and his brother Eugene that the "Kaffir race is the most powerful in this part and the most intelligent," and McAdoo informed General Armstrong of his plan to offer a seventy-dollar scholarship to "an earnest Christian boy" to take up studies at Hampton Institute.[61] While at Hampton the news was greeted with "gratification," the announcement caused some disturbance in South Africa. McAdoo found himself summoned to appear before a committee of unsympathetic whites who inquired whether he was "singing to educate Negroes" or for his own business. One angry minister bluntly declared that "if it is to educate the Kafirs and Zulus, you will never succeed in Africa."[62] McAdoo's reply that it was his own enterprise and that he could do with his money as he liked seemed to have settled the dispute, for a few weeks later Titus Mbongwe embarked on the trip to Hampton.

Titus Mbongwe was a young clerk in Kimberley when he heard the Jubilee Singers in the concert in the town hall that had left such a deep mark on the minds of many of his African friends. McAdoo found him "unusually intelligent"[63] and offered him the passage to Hampton and a scholarship. After a fitting send-off party and concert in the Beaconsfield Town Hall, Mbongwe left Cape Town on October 23, 1890, equipped with "a lot of information about life and educational progress in Africa" and a paper on the "Natives of Cape Colony" that McAdoo had asked him to prepare for Hampton. On November 12 the train that was taking him from Plymouth to London collided with another train, killing Mbongwe and a large number of other passengers.[64]

The tragic news had not yet reached South Africa, however, when five young men in King Williamstown, inspired by Jabavu's column, decided to demonstrate their "interest in the history of the negro Race in America" and applied to Hampton Institute for admission. William W.

Stofile offered himself "as a scholar who is desirous to be educated in the American Institutions,"[65] while K. Charles Kumkani and Samuel Cakata wrote that

> from the year 1889 we was desire to be, are in the college, unfortunately we were on account of being very poorest because our perrents they are on a position red Blankets. Will you please grant our petition which we required, we want you to receive us to candidature, my Lord we are very poor, but we desire the educational. . . . Mr. Orpheus M. McAdoo he gave an interesting account of your educational, and we ask him if we must start away with him, and he said we must send our application.[66]

Armstrong's positive response was motivated by considerations of a broader political nature, for he held that "it might be a good thing to help some over for the sake not only of themselves but to show the unbelieving Dutch boers and other colonists what American practical education can do for the natives to-day as in the past."[67]

However, Stofile's and his friends' hopes failed to materialize as did those of Isaiah Bud-M'Belle, a young teacher at the Wesleyan School in Colesberg. Bud-M'Belle saw the Jubilee Singers during their two-day stay in Colesberg in August 1890 and asked McAdoo for a bursary. McAdoo, having stretched his purse to the limit by supporting Mbongwe, encouraged the teacher to approach General Armstrong directly. Bud-M'Belle's credentials and his complaint that "in South Africa a coloured man gets no sound education,"[68] were certainly not lost on the General, but nothing further came of his application. He was soon to move to Kimberley where he eventually became an influential member of the Kimberley African community and a close friend and brother-in-law of Solomon Plaatje. Many years later, as a court interpreter, he renewed his contacts with the Jubilee Singers. In 1897 he formed the Philharmonic Society together with Sol Plaatje, H. R. Ngcayiya, and Will Thompson, and soon afterward—again with the indispensable Thompson—joined the white Diamond Minstrels, certainly a novelty in the usually segregated musical circles of the town.[69]

Ethiopianism, the African Methodist Episcopal Church, and the Jubilee Songs   Of all the young aspiring Africans in Kimberley and other towns, perhaps none was more determined to obtain the benefits of an university education in America than a young woman from Fort Beaufort named Charlotte Manye. At the time of McAdoo's visit to Kimberley, Charlotte taught at the Wesleyan School. Her debut as a soloist in the Beaconsfield Town Hall on September 8, 1890, proved to be Mbongwe's farewell concert, in which he himself ominously sang "You Can't Always Tell."[70] Mbongwe's admission and imminent departure to Hampton not only infused Charlotte with greater determination to pursue her ambitious goals, but the concert also inspired Albert Walklett, a minister with some musical talent, to form a group of African musicians modeled on McAdoo's Jubilee Singers. This was Charlotte's chance, and when the "African Jubilee Singers" or "South African Choir," under the direction of two white musicians, Walter Letty and J. Balmer, embarked on a tour of England (see fig. 2), Charlotte felt closer to her dreamed-of education than ever. The fate of the South African Choir caused a considerable stir in South Africa and London and was given extensive coverage in the white and black press of the time. A number of British publications such as the *Illustrated London News,* the *Review of Reviews,* and *South Africa* carried photographs of the choir and interviews with some of its leading members, while South African mission papers such as the *Christian Express* and the independent black weekly *Imvo Zabantsundu* proudly reported the choir's latest moves. The Morija mission paper *Leselinyana* even carried full-page reports by choir member Josiah Semouse.

The enterprise ended under disastrous circumstances when the white promoters Balmer and Letty abandoned Semouse and some choristers in London. But this fact counted little in the eyes of the energetic Charlotte. In Sheffield she had met the Bohee Brothers, a black American minstrel troupe, whose leader George Bohee persuaded Charlotte that "England was a godforsaken country, but America was God's own country."[70] And so Charlotte did not think twice when Balmer and Letty made plans for a North American tour in February 1893. After a successful tour of Canada and the East Coast, the adventure again ended in a fiasco, and the entire choir, deserted by Letty and Balmer in Cleveland, Ohio, was offered shelter by the African Methodist Episcopal church (AME) official C. Ransom (Ransom n.d.:73). Charlotte was soon admitted to Wilberforce University, from where she wrote glowing letters to her sister Kate, who in turn showed them to her relative, Rev. Mangena M. Mokone, by then a leading figure in the emerging Ethiopian church. Mokone's church affiliated with the AME and Charlotte Manye returned to South Africa, where she played a prominent role in the women's branch of the South African Native National Congress (SANNC), and until her death in 1939 as a social worker in the AME church.[72]

FIGURE 2. The South African Choir in London, 1891 (Review of Reviews [London] IV/21, 1891, p. 255)

Time and again, students of the black American experience in South Africa have stressed the role of black American missionaries in shaping nascent African political consciousness, and it is tempting to assume a direct link between the jubilee tradition and the Ethiopian movement in South Africa.[73] Not only were the Jubilee Singers, through Charlotte Manye and the South African Choir, instrumental in establishing contact between the AME and the Ethiopian church in South Africa, but McAdoo's troupe had also lent some publicity to AME Bishop Henry M. Turner's tour of South Africa in 1898 by welcoming the Bishop at the Johannesburg railway station "in a manner highly complimentary and even flattering."[74] Furthermore, within the young church spirituals were vigorously promoted by senior AME officials. Mokone himself had heard the Jubilee Singers in Pretoria and in Kimberley. Simon Hoffa Sinamela, who was directing the Presbyterian choir when McAdoo arrived in 1890, eventually trained the African Jubilee Singers before their departure to England and subsequently organized the church choir in Mokone's Ethiopian church. Mokone was apparently satisfied with Sinamela's adoption of Afro-American models and wrote to Turner in 1896: "Our teacher, the Rev. Simon Hoffa Sinamela, sings nearly as those Jubilee Singers of 'Virginia.' "[75]

AME ministers clearly viewed the spirituals as the appropriate expressive idiom for a church based on a specifically black reading of the gospel. But AME church leaders soon also set out to reshape the Afro-American idiom and to mold it into a new African church hymnody that was relatively free of European influences. Sinamela composed a series of hymns including "Kgoshi Sekukuni," a hymn which blended Afro-American material with traditional Sepedi praise poetry (Mokone 1935:3). Eventually some black students who had followed Charlotte Manye to Wilberforce, among them Jacobus Xaba and J. Z. Tantsi, translated American jubilee hymns into the vernacular.

Notwithstanding such African reinterpretations of the Afro-American musical heritage, some members of McAdoo's troupe had previously expressed doubts about the wisdom of the emigration schemes advocated by Turner. In 1890, to McAdoo's tales about slave trade, slavery, and dreams of an Afro-American Zion, enthusiastic black audiences in the Kimberley Town Hall exclaimed: "Come back! Come back to Africa, the country of your forefathers!"[76] However, such displays of pan-African solidarity failed to persuade Mamie Edwards, for instance, who believed that "there are quite enough blacks out here now"[77] and that black and white cooperation would have a deeper impact on African political emancipation than black American mass immigration.

Irrespective of such ideological discrepancies, Afro-American and African expressions of Christianity paradoxically differed in one other fundamental respect. However unambiguously Josiah Semouse, Tengo Jabavu, and Charlotte Manye praised the musical abilities of the American visitors, the evidence does not indicate that they were sensitive to the political significance of the slave songs to any marked degree. As a system of collective repression, slavery in the American South was probably many times harsher than racial exploitation in South Africa, even if significant differences in individual suffering could be observed in both countries. What is perhaps more relevant in this respect, however, is the fact that blacks in the American South and South Africa also responded in different ways to their inferior social position, most notably perhaps in their use of religious ideology. Although Christianity, as Genovese has argued, internalized relations of lordship and bondage and therefore served as the perfect legitimization of the slaveholding society, the slaves, in embracing the Christian faith and worldview, at the same time had forged their "most formidable weapon for resisting slavery's moral and psychological aggression" (Genovese 1976;659, 167). Spirituals such as "Go Down, Moses" were both the ritual balm on the wounds of dehumanization and the battle cry of that resistance:

> When Israel was in Egypt's land,
> O let my people go!
> Oppressed so hard they could not stand,
> O let my people go!
>
> No more shall they in bondage toil,
> O let my people go!
> Let them come out with Egypt's spoil,
> O let my people go!

In South Africa, African resistance to domination and oppression, up until the early twentieth century, had at its command a far wider arsenal of weapons, including open armed revolt. Thus for the African elite, rooted as it was in strong, independent peasant communities of the Eastern Cape and Natal, Christianity was primarily a premise of their involvement in colonial society and only rarely a weapon against its unpleasant side effects. But it was never the spiritual foundation for the struggle of an entire class against its total submission.

Finale: The Jubilee Songs in South Africa after 1898   The year 1898 witnessed the first rumblings of a storm that was to transform the face of the subcontinent: in 1899 a war broke out between Britain and the Boer republics that was to last until 1902. For the Jubilee Singers the year 1898 signaled the end of nearly six triumphant years of concert tours. The first omen of a more troubled future appeared in January 1898, when Will Thompson again decided to leave the troupe. In a last, ill-fated attempt to compete against McAdoo on the highly volatile colonial entertainment market, Thompson joined the Cape Town-based, predominantly "coloured" Buffalo Glee and Concert Company with I. Bud-M'Belle, who by now may have become a close business associate of his. Things took a turn for the worse with Collins's arrest on March 29, 1898, and on the night of April 4, 1898, for the final time, the curtain in the Durban Theatre Royal rose on McAdoo's minstrel entertainment presented by a somewhat depleted company. The reason for this "awkward predicament" was that Messrs. Willard Smith, Joe Jalvan, and Louis Love and Miss Shirley had been offered one pound a week more by a "rival manager" and declined to appear "unless their

present engagement was made equally remunerative."[78] This was re-
fused, and the dissatisfied singers decided to form their own "Coloured
Minstrel Company."[79]

These difficulties and looming Anglo-Boer hostilities expedited
McAdoo's decision to leave South Africa with the rump of the Minstrel,
Vaudeville and Concert Company, thus concluding one of the first and
one of the most fascinating chapters in the history of the black American
experience in South Africa. McAdoo sailed for Australia and soon formed
a new company, the Original Alabama Cake Walkers. But even in Australia, as lessee of the Palace Theatre in Sydney, stiff competition with rival
American minstrel troupes and mounting difficulties with his employees
made his life uncomfortable. Orpheus McAdoo died in Sydney on July 7,
1900.[80]

Irrespective of divergent black readings of the gospel in both countries, the Jubilee Singers' legacy lived on in South African black performing arts. After the First World War, spirituals became increasingly popular
among the urban elite as a moral bulwark against the rising tide of working-class forms of musical expression. The "sorrow songs" transcended
the boundaries of the AME church and were warmly received within
other independent black churches that were equally struggling against
European dominance and that had particularly strong black American
links. Thus Enoch Mgijima's Israelite movement in the Eastern Cape
fused Xhosa words and melodies with spirituals introduced by black
American missionaries of the Church of God and Saints of Christ (Edgar
1977; Lea 1925:15f.).

But predominantly white missions such as the American Board of
Missions only remittently gave recognition to black sacred songs. The
reasons for this reluctance are not only to be looked for in white attitudes
toward the Afro-American heritage. Not all sectors of the black Christian
community attached the same political significance to the message expressed in the slave songs. Other churches that were groping toward
African expressions of Christianity such as Isaiah Shembe's Church of
Nazareth in Natal relied more on the symbols of Zulu political autonomy,
and they remodeled autochthonous, traditional musical systems for their
liturgical purposes.

By the early 1920s the AME was firmly established as one of the
strongest black churches, but its image with white officials had changed
from that of a seedbed of nationalist agitation and sedition to "far and
away the most respectable" of South Africa's black churches. Charlotte
Manye and other students had returned to South Africa where they

helped to implement black American educational goals. In 1921 James E. Kwegyir Aggrey arrived in South Africa with the Phelps-Stokes Commission to persuade public opinion of the beneficial effects of racial peace.

Black newspapers such as *Umteteli wa Bantu* carried articles on the "Original Jubilee Singers" by Henry H. Proctor, and on "The Miracle of Negro Spirituals" by famed Afro-American educator James Welden Johnson. Spirituals, he wrote, transcended the "barbaric and martial cries" of African rhythms. The American Board of Missions' Rev. Ray Phillips contributed columns on Roland Hayes and Harry Burleigh. In Durban, W. Temple presented a concert of spirituals in the "white" town hall in 1923 that possibly inspired Reuben Caluza and the Ohlange Choir to try their hand at "Peter Go Ring Them Bells" the following month. At the opposite end of the class spectrum, the *Workers' Herald,* organ of the militant Industrial and Commercial Workers' Union (ICU), published the words of spirituals and underlined their African roots.[81]

But it was only in 1927 that spiritual singing became accepted as an integral part of South African black musical performance culture. In 1918 Charlotte Manye had founded Wilberforce Institute near Johannesburg. The musical activities at this high school soon came under the hands of the energetic Dr. Francis Herman Gow. Of Jamaican descent, Gow was born in South Africa in 1887 and received training at Wilberforce University in Ohio. At one time a music master at Zonnebloem Training College in Cape Town, the young teacher not only wrote and produced a show entitled "Up From Slavery" in 1925, but in April 1927 his Wilberforce choir gave a live broadcast of jubilee songs from Johannesburg.[82] Finally, in 1930 Columbia recorded his choir singing four spirituals including "Mary, Don't You Weep" (Regal GR7) and "It's Me, O Lord" (Columbia AE 3). These recordings constitute the earliest recorded evidence of spiritual singing in South Africa and share many of the stylistic features of the older American university choirs and quartets.

Gow's recordings had a far-reaching effect on the popularity of Afro-American sacred music in South Africa and led to the formation of a new South African school of quartet singing. Two of the leading quartets in the country were the Wesley House Quartette of Fort Hare and the Bantu Men Social Centre Quartette. The latter emerged from the Glee Club, the first male quartet to perform jubilee songs in South Africa. Initiated by Ray E. Phillips in 1924 and superseded in 1934 by the BMSC Quartette, the Glee Club consisted of A.S. Vil-Nkomo, J. Radasi, J. R. Rathebe, and Hlubi. Both Rathebe and Vil-Nkomo belonged to the AME church and took an active part in black Johannesburg's social life with its dance clubs, Order of the Elks, and Literary Debating Societies.[83] The Wesley House Quartette of Fort Hare was based at the University College there, the country's oldest high school for blacks. The quartet consisted of W. Nkomo, T. G. Ngcwabe, G. Bikitsha, and O. Mdala and eventually became the first male quartet to record spirituals in South Africa (Gallo GE 180).

Radio broadcasts by both quartets in 1937 were among the first by black musicians. Such recognition of Afro-American culture not only spread official, ruling-class notions of "civilized" black culture, but also imbued black listeners with racial pride, "because they have shown the white population what Africans could do once they are given the chance."[84]

While the role of quartet singing in South Africa remains confined to the aesthetic and ideological models of the African elite, the jubilee legacy reemerged one more time among migrant workers on both sides of the Atlantic. In the industrial centers of both Alabama and South Africa, workers created vibrant vocal styles that are indebted to the jubilee tradition. Among steel mill workers in Birmingham, Jefferson County, a male gospel quartet style emerged (Seroff 1985), while Zulu migrant workers in Johannesburg and Durban beginning in the early 1930s developed a male vocal style called *isicathamiya* (chapter 6).

Three   Cultural Osmosis,

Ethnicity, and Tradition

in Black Popular Music

in Durban, 1913–1939

The cities of Africa are arguably among the most powerful and restless motors of modern African musical development. The continent's major urban agglomerations like Kinshasa, Johannesburg, Douala, Ibadan, and Accra generated exhilarating musical styles such as *Kongo Jazz, kwela, soucous, makossa, juju,* and *highlife,* and many of the world's leading black entertainers—Myriam Makeba, Fela Anikulapo-Kuti, and Manu Dibango, to name but a few hail from some of these cities. Although it comprises more than 2,000,000 inhabitants, Thekwini, as the seaport city of Durban is known to its Zulu-speaking inhabitants, ranks considerably low on the list of African megalopolises. But despite its limited geopolitical role, Durban harbors a complex network of rich, intersecting black musical traditions that deserve closer scholarly examination. Yet in terms of scholarly output and ever since Johannesburg, the country's premier musical workshop, has recently come under more rigorous scholarly scrutiny,[1] Durban has clearly been the Cinderella among South Africa's musical centers. Only one study, George Jackson's *Music in Durban* (Jackson 1970), seems at first sight, to break the academic monotony, but on closer inspection the book proves to be little more than a minute account of Western classical and popular music in Durban. While Jackson's research produced an abundance of data on massed-choir performances of Handel's *Messiah,* the author remains remarkably silent on the black traditions of Durban.

This essay will unfold those pages of Durban's musical chronicle that were written by black musicians and artists, and it will take the reader along the more inconspicuous and dusty alleys of South Africa's black musical history—the dance clubs, factory compounds, union halls, and dance arenas—that musicologists and social historians like Jackson ignore in their search for the scant traces of the country's European heritage.

The focus on a city as locus of musical history may seem artificial. But in reality, of course, Durban as much as any other city in South Africa was never sealed off from its rural hinterland and the country at large. But what gives Durban its specificity as a discrete entity is the unique way in which local social stratification, politics, and the Zulu cultural heritage intertwined in the making of its black musical history.

On a more theoretical level, this essay is concerned with the social, cultural, and political factors that influenced the evolution of black popular performance in Durban. It is argued that in the decades between the turn of the century and the Second World War, Durban's black musical history was marked by a great diversity of performance traditions, but that urban growth, industrial expansion, and socioeconomic class differentiation did not divide these traditions along class lines. Rather, a deep-reaching osmosis of forms and styles seems to characterize early black performance in the port town, one that renders the determination of homogeneous class cultures and performance idioms in class terms difficult for at least three reasons.

First, industrialization in Durban proceeded at a much slower pace than elsewhere in South Africa, and with an elaborate system of organized migrant labor effectively blocking permanent black urbanization, Durban's black population maintained strong links with the rural hinterland. Teachers, ministers, and traders, but also stevedores, shop assistants, and domestic servants, to varying degrees and in different ways, depended on a rural support base for their social and cultural reproduction. Thus people who might have otherwise experienced quite diverse work situations, living conditions, and patterns of cultural reproduction in town were by and large bound together by common cultural roots in preindustrial Zulu society.

Second, up until the Second World War, the black sector of Durban's total population of an estimated 151,000 was relatively small compared to the vast army of black workers toiling in the mines and other industries around Johannesburg. Until 1939 Durban's black elite never numbered more than a few thousand people, while the harbor and railway workers, traditionally one of the strongest sectors of Durban's black industrial proletariat, still counted no more than 30,000 employed in 1935. In addition, this black urban population was fragmented into small occupational groups whose members rarely, if ever, perceived themselves as part of social classes. Whereas the upper strata of the city's black community had been shaped by several decades of exposure to and absorption of a uniform Western mission culture, the social and cultural fragmentation of the city's laboring masses clearly militated against the evolution of a homogeneous working-class culture.

Third, none of the numerous group cultures evolving in Durban was in itself sealed off from the other surrounding cultures. Thus it is questionable to speak of a homogeneous Zulu musical culture. Zulu-speaking Africans throughout Natal have always perceived finer regional and stylistic shades in their music than the commonplace label "Zulu music" seems to imply. For not only did Zululand traditions and South Coast idioms differ, but in time each of these became infused with non-Zulu elements such as Bhaca dancing and the Sotho *isiRashiya* concertina style.

Furthermore, between the wars the boundaries between Durban's black strata were blurred not only by the shared experience of abject poverty, human degradation, and intensive interethnic contact. In contrast to the huge numbers of black miners who were cooped up in the compounds on the Witwatersrand and isolated from black urban communities, dock workers in Durban's harbor area, the Point, lived within walking distance from the city center where dance halls, churches, and soccer fields provided a fertile ground for the fusion of elite culture and working-class dance and music. Thus the popularity of Reuben Caluza's "ragtime," the hymnodial roots of *isicathamiya* male choirs, and the hammering out of *isicathulo* boot dancing between docks and missions were the result of this intensive contact.

At the same time, communication within Durban's wider black community was guided by at least two broader mechanisms in the dialectic of power relations. As a result of mounting political repression, urban segregation, and oppressive labor legislation, the position of the city's black intermediate classes increasingly became a precarious one. To secure their privileges, black intellectuals and large landowners played the role of self-appointed spokesmen of their communities in negotiating minor concessions for the laboring poor while offering a check on black popular militancy to the white bourgeoisie at the same time. But speaking for the black majority also meant speaking in their language. The political hegemony of Durban's black leaders therefore always involved an integration of mission, rural, and urban working-class cultural elements.

Second, the integration of workers, domestic servants, and stevedores into Durban's labor market was uneven and therefore provoked heterogeneous responses to proletarianization. At the very least, working-class cultures in the city constantly oscillated between two poles. Those workers who were more firmly and securely incorporated into the urban work force identified with and at least partially accepted Western cultural models, while the more vulnerable sectors, the unemployed and the day laborers, rallied around the symbols of the countryside. Thus working-class cultures in Durban differed markedly in their susceptibility to elite cultural hegemony as well as in the depth of their anchorage in vigorous, autonomous rural cultures.

A further line of argument here is that as a result of the blurred class and cultural contours among Durban's black population and often as an impedance to the formation of distinct class cultures, the persistence of ethnicity and ethnic cultural traditions remained determining factors in urban cultural development. But neither of these were unshakable constants; ethnic boundaries and traditions were continually being negotiated in the social process, and their continuous redefinition was contingent on the position of social actors as well as on the historical moment. Portrayals of Zulu rural customs by urban, mission-educated vaudeville troupes in 1904 differed significantly from those in 1936. In addition, at each stage the interpretation of ethnic heritage by elite audiences proceeded from a different angle than that by migrant workers. Similarly, the reception of images of black identity and modernity that were being spread among black South Africans by means of minstrel and vaudeville shows produced differing South African versions of the "coon" among literate performers and early protagonists of migrants' *isikhunzi* music.

But for all the ambiguity of urban class relations and the opalescence of ethnic traditions and cultural dynamics, the decades between 1913 and 1939 afford unique insights into the making of Durban's early black musical history. This period stands out as one of the most turbulent phases in the annals of Durban's black population and was marked by an unprecedented acceleration of urban growth and by a dense sequence of milestones in the political history of African resistance. Parts of Natal's African population had already been drawn into marginal sectors of the urban economy well before the beginning of the twentieth century, and by that time the sharpening class contours and conflicts of the metropolis had left their indelible mark in the city's annals.

In 1913, one of the great watershed years in South African history, the Native Lands Act dealt a mortal blow to the independent African peasantry. But the same year also marked the first anniversary of the South African Native National Congress (SANNC) which later became the African National Congress (ANC). The effects of the Act and the First World War drew increasingly larger numbers of dispossessed rural Africans into the Durban labor market and heralded a new era of large-scale industrial expansion, urban growth, and political unrest. In contradistinction to Durban's still minute class of black entrepreneurs, priests, teachers, and clerks, the percentage of workers in the city had reached unprecedented numbers. The number of Africans living in Durban had escalated from an estimated 20,000 in 1918 to 29,000 in 1921. The vast majority of these Africans, 59%, had found employment as workers in the chief industries. The 1921 census revealed that there were nearly 9,000 domestic servants, almost 6,500 railway workers, and some 1,500 shop assistants.   •

For most of these people living conditions were steadily deteriorating after the war, and with falling wage levels Durban's growing black laboring classes found themselves caught in a web of disease, hunger, crime, and large-scale liquor consumption. But the war also had a profound effect on Durban's black middle class. While sectors of the laboring classes like the dockworkers resisted increased economic hardship in a rash of strikes in 1918–19, black shopkeepers, teachers, and petty traders, as elsewhere in the Union, were becoming increasingly radicalized. The reasons for this intensification of black popular struggles must be sought in the changed sociopolitical climate in South Africa after the war. The stark reality of urban segregation had been enforced in the Urban Areas Act of 1923. Followed by a barrage of repressive laws aimed primarily at securing a stable supply of cheap African labor, the new legislation increasingly confronted Durban's black middle strata with the danger of proletarianization.

Among the most serious forces to challenge exploitation and oppression during the 1920s was the Industrial and Commercial Workers' Union (ICU) led by Clement Kadalie. In 1928 A. W. G. Champion and the Natal branch of the ICU seceded from the organization to form the ICU Yase Natal. This organization had a membership of 88,000 and in fighting a number of significant bread-and-butter issues soon became a serious threat to white rule in Natal. In 1929 a boycott of Durban's municipal beer halls spilled over into a riot that was only stamped out by the hitherto largest police operation in South African history. The years until the outbreak of the Second World War were marked by a decline in popular resistance and a further deepening of mass poverty as a result of the Depression.

But long before that, in 1913—the beginning of the period under discussion—it was the teachers, clerks, ministers, and shopkeepers that formed the culturally most visible sector of the still minute black community, and it is to their musical traditions that we have to turn first.

"I Wish My Colour Would Fade": The Reworking of Afro-American Music and Musical Comedy

The "prehistory of popular performance in Durban's middle classes is inextricably wedded to the rise of land-owning peasant communities of *amakholwa* (believers) in Natal in the mid-nineteenth century. For most of these Christian farming communities the identification with Victorian, Christian cultural models had never been an easy process. Prosperous African farmers who had grown up with the firm belief in the superiority of individual property rights and hard work over traditional communal land-tenure found it increasingly difficult to reconcile these essentials of Victorian ideology with a social reality in which these very rights came under massive pressure from white settlers who wanted to expand their political and cultural hegemony. A combination of factors, not the least significant of which was the white settlers' hostility to a successful and independent Christian black peasantry, "made it far more difficult for Natal *kholwa* to model themselves on an idealized perception of imperial middle-class society in the way that the African intelligentsia in Kimberley . . . were able to do" (Marks 1986:58). Perhaps nothing better conveys the contrast between white-settler exclusivism and African identification with Victorian ideology, and the resultant cultural crisis in Natal's black elite, than the words of Johannes Khumalo, spoken in 1863 at Edendale in protest of the exclusion of Africans from civil law:

> We have left the black race and have clung to the white. We imitate them in everything we can. . . . Look round you. You have an English house, English tables, chairs. . . . everything round us is English but one, and that is the law.[2]

For Zulu speakers up until the turn of the century, the prevailing category of music that symbolized the identification with English values was *imusic.* It was the least politically overt musical category and as such included predominantly Western classical music, hymns, English ballads, and part songs such as "The Lass of Richmond Hill," as well as Anglo-

American ballads such as "They Grew In Beauty Side By Side" and "The Little Brown Jug."[3] *Imusic* constituted the bulk of the repertoire of most mission-based Durban choirs of the period such as the popular Thulasizwe choir under J. P. Mahlobo and the Flying Birds under Littin Mthethwa. Ultimately, the genre as well as the names that choirs like the Motor Car Choir, Steam Roller Choir, and Electric Light Choir had chosen for themselves signaled confidence in "progress" and "improvement," keywords of the educated black elite.

Largely because of the prevalence of American Board of Missions activities in and around Durban, urban revival hymns of the Sankey school occupied a special place within *imusic* and in the sacred repertoire of black Durbanites. From as early as 1876, Durban shops had been selling *Hymns in Kafir, From Sacred Songs and Solos, By J. D. Sankey.* In 1905 the Durban paper *Ilanga Lase Natal* (Natal Sun) published a Tonic Sol-fa score[4] of "Just As I Am," and in the same year a quartet under G. Radebe performed Root's "Along the River of Time." By 1906 *Ilanga* had complemented the repertoire of printed hymns by "Abaqubi Bevangeli," the Zulu version of a Sankey hymn.[5]

Although *imusic* was essentially grounded in European and American music, it was not simply a black imitation of metropolitan elite culture. Despite the indebtedness of many Sankey hymns to genuine jubilee songs, *imusic* lacked the qualities that were needed to satisfactorily express the growing resistance to declining black political autonomy and deteriorating class privileges toward the turn of the century. It is for these reasons that it is not really possible to speak of an "elite" culture—in the sense that Karin Barber has given to the term—in the upper strata of Natal's black society at the turn of the century (Barber 1987). Although the landowners of Edendale may have been conversant with the full repertoire of metropolitan culture, they were at the same time groping toward alternative forms of cultural and political expression. By the turn of the century various forms of Ethiopianism, Afro-American ideas of self-advancement, and embryonic African nationalism had become powerful alternatives to colonial ideology and major forces in the intellectual climate of Natal's *amakholwa* communities. It is the role of defense against white exclusivism and racism that accounts for the early impact of Afro-American music and minstrelsy together with a variety of other forms of musical comedy and black humor on the evolution of black popular music in South Africa, particularly in Natal and Durban.

Durban audiences had first gained experience of Afro-American culture through the visits of Orpheus McAdoo and his Jubilee Singers between 1891 and 1898 (chapter 2). McAdoo's concerts of jubilee hymns as well as his minstrel shows were the first representations there of black life and living conditions in the United States. *Amakholwa* audiences throughout Natal celebrated the descendants of former slaves as their "music heroes" and by the turn of the century, minstrelsy had reached even the remotest rural areas in Natal and elsewhere in southern Africa. Mission school graduates formed minstrel troupes modeled on McAdoo's company and the numerous white blackface troupes. In Durban itself, groups like the Brave Natalian Coons operated, while the Western Minstrels under Rev. Sivetshe's son B. M. Sivetshe were based at Adams College near Durban.[6]

Admiration for Afro-American values ran particularly high at Ohlange Institute (see fig. 3) a private college outside Durban, founded in 1901 by SANNC president John L. Dube as a South African counterpart to Booker T. Washington's Tuskegee Institute in the United States. Musical performance formed an integral part of Ohlange's educational program,

FIGURE 3. Ohlange Institute, ca. 1904

and some of Durban's finest choirs emerged from the school overlooking the hills of Inanda. Apart from a brass band conducted by Clement Tshabalala, one of Ohlange's first boarders, the school boasted the Nightingales Choir conducted by Isaiah Ngidi and the G. T. V. Dum Choir under Walter Dimba, a future official of the ICU. The regular Ohlange Choir was under the batons of Charles Dube and Ngazana Luthuli. In addition, "coon" groups like the Highland Coons under D. H. Opperman and the Inanda Native Singers under Alfred J. Ncamu were particularly active in performing minstrel songs and other Afro-American-derived material. The latter group's repertoire included such Stephen Foster classics as "Old Folks at Home," "Gentle Annie," "Some Folks Say That a Preacher Won't Steal," C. A. White's "I'se Gwine Back to Dixie," and "coon" songs like "Who Stole My Chicken Away" and "Oh, Gloriam."[7] Fashionable wedding parties of mission converts were treated to solo performances of minstrel songs like "Good Old Jeff" and Henry C. Work's "The Kingdom Is Coming," while church and mission-school choirs tried their hands at J. Bland's "Dem Golden Slippers," the Haverly's Minstrels tune "Irene, Goodnight," and vaudeville, music-hall comic ballads like "Cock of the North" and "Hold Your Hand Out Naughty Boy."[8]

Until at least 1915, ragged minstrel outfits as well as cork-burnt faces were regular sights at mission-school concerts,[9] and minstrel bone clappers became integrated as *amathambo* into the repertory of Zulu traditional musical instruments (Kirby 1968:10f.). As late as 1918 scenes like the following, reported from a rural mission night school in Umzumbe, south of Durban, were not uncommon:

> One of the items was a march across the platform of all the urchins with a bone clapper, at the head of the line . . . and to the astonishment of all, one of the most heathenish boys stood up and sang "Tiperary," keeping time to his singing by the twirling of an invisible mustache. (Bridgman-Cowles 1918:7)[10]

Apart from "Tipperary," bone clappers, and such perfectly innocent numbers as "Good Old Jeff," minstrel shows also included more sensitive items. One of the English "coon" songs that was remembered by Robert T. Mazibuko, Mariannhill graduate and veteran of the vaudeville troupe Hiver Hyvas, as a popular tune in Durban before the First World War ran as follows:

> Coon, coon, coon.
> I wish my colour would fade.

I wish I were a white man
instead of a nigger coon.[11]

A song such as this illustrates the ambiguity inherent in images of
Afro-Americans that were mediated by white stereotypes. A symbol for
the successful and self-conscious urban black and as such abused by
white racists, the "coon" could also be a positive hero for blacks. Thus it is
debatable whether "few black South Africans could understand the
crude sexual or racist lyrics" and whether hence the appeal of "coon
songs" "was not in what they said, but in the rhythm and swing in which
they said it" (Coplan 1985:71). Certainly, "Coon, coon, coon" was sung
in English, and its meaning was therefore not easily accessible to more
rural audiences. Furthermore, some "coon" songs were translated into
Zulu, a process that clearly toned down some of the shriller racist over-
tones.[12] The mainstream minstrel material, however, that over time had
become standard fare at black minstrel shows in the United States, was
generally regarded by black audiences as inoffensive. Thus an all-time favorite of both Afro-Americans and black South Africans for the better
part of the late nineteenth century and into the 1920s, Foster's "Oh Susanna," with its mildly derisive portrayal of the ignorant country bump-
kin and of courtly love, was probably understood more as a mockery of
rural blacks than of blacks as such (Austin 1975:27–40):

I came from Alabama wid my banjo on my knee,
I'm g'wan to Louisiana
My true love for to see.
It rain'd all night the day I left,
The weather it was dry,
The sun so hot I frose to death,
Susanna don't you cry.
  Oh, Susanna, oh!
  Don't you cry,
  I've come from Alabama,
  wid my banjo on my knee.

I jumped aboard de telegraph
And trabbelled down de riber,
De Lectrie fluid magnified,
And killed five hundred Nigger.
De bullgine bust, de horse run off,
I really thought I'd die.
I shut my eyes to hold my breath,
Susanna, don't you cry.
  Oh, Susanna, oh . . .

"Oh Susanna" provided the archetypal symbolic structure in which black intracommunal differentiation could be dealt with in a humorous way. In South Africa the song was interpreted more specifically in the sense that those who failed to understand the signs of the time and spoke but an imperfect English clearly demonstrated the need for some "enlightened," "progressive" leadership in the black community. But there were also other songs, such as "Some Folks Say That a Preacher Won't Steal," another Foster tune of 1855. With its jibes at preachers and any other exposed members of the community as could be mentioned in add-on stanzas in actual performance, the song could in fact be read as a critical view of black leadership from the lower ranks of the black community and as such must have been ideally suited to South African conditions:

> Some folks like to sigh,
> Some folks do, some folks do.
> Some folks long to die,
> But that's not me nor you.
>
>> Long live the merry merry heart
>> That laughs by night and day.
>> Like the Queen of Mirth,
>> No matter what some folks say.
>
> Some folks fear to smile,
> Some folks do, some folks do.
> Others laugh through guile,
> But that's not me nor you.
>
>> Long live . . .
>
> Some folks say a preacher won't steal,
> Some folks do, some folks do . . .

From these examples of American minstrel songs it seems clear that in the hands of early black South African performers, the characters of the minstrel stage become central tools of black intracommunal criticism. Minstrel humor closed the ranks of the black community and ultimately helped to restore racial confidence. Thus it is a perfect illustration of the effects of minstrel performances that as early as 1904 the Inanda Native Singers persuaded doubtful concertgoers who "did not think there is anything worth seeing which could be done by blacks," of the viability of black values.[13]

The legacy of the minstrel theater is even more clearly mirrored in the rise of two genres of stage performance, musical comedy and drama, in and around Durban. Immediately after the war, students at Mariannhill monastery outside Durban began experimenting with one-act dramatizations of folk tales and social topics. The productions were inspired by playlets written by Father Bernhard Huss on biblical themes and school life and by some of Reuben Caluza's dramatized songs such as *Isangoma* (Witch Doctor) (HMV GU 73), in which the versatile composer had first combined dance, action, and song in a coherent stage presentation with props and sets.[14] The result was plays like *The Egg Thief* and *The Inspector.* Most of the plays have survived in the *Dramatisation Book,* a collection of manuscripts which was compiled after 1919, possibly by Benedict Vilakazi's sister, and which is presently kept in the archives of Mariannhill monastery.[15] Others, such as the immensely popular pantomime *The Barber Shop of Olden Times,* were possibly indebted to early American minstrel skits such as Dan Emmett's playlet *German Farmer or The Barber Shop in an Uproar* (Nathan 1962:220). The skit depicts the melee caused by a maladroit apprentice in a barber shop:

> Apprentice enters with broom, sweeps, cleans chairs with duster, puts them in order. Client enters, kicks apprentice who makes a bow, takes umbrella and hat, shows client a chair. Just when client is going to sit, apprentice takes chair away, client falls, gets angry, runs after apprentice who puts chair down. Client sits, apprentice sweeps.
>
> Fat baron enters. Apprentice takes overcoat and stick, shows baron second chair. He refuses it and sits on the breakable chair decorated with nice cloth, breaks it, falls down. Apprentice wants money, baron gives, sits on second chair.
>
> Visitor enters, falls over broom of sweeping apprentice, wants to strike apprentice who dodges. Client receives blow, jumps up, presses visitor firmly on chair. . . .

The Mariannhill plays and Caluza's song-dramatizations and sketches were staged in the hall of Baumannville location[16] as part of classical concerts and, like Dube's Ohlange brass band and Mthethwa's Zulu Union Choir, enjoyed the financial support of the town council (see fig. 4).[17] The municipal interest in African recreation came in response to the rapid transformation of Durban's black urban population and the emergence of forms of urban culture that were potentially in opposition to white rule. It was inspired by the reform initiatives of the American Board of Missions Rev. Ray E. Phillips in Johannesburg that were aimed at "moralizing the leisure time of natives" (Phillips 1938:58; Couzens

FIGURE 4. The Brass band at St. Francis College, Mariannhill, ca. 1900 (Mariannhill Archive)

1982). In Durban it was Phillips's ABM colleagues James Dexter Taylor
and J. McCord, and the Catholic priest Bernhard Huss, who spearheaded
this movement toward social control in using drama as a means of defus-
ing black militancy. Indeed, for Mariannhill graduate and poet laureate
Benedict Vilakazi "the birth of a *Zulu Drama*" was directly linked to the
"ebb of the political upheaval of 1920" (B. Vilakazi 1942:272).

Leaving aside the sheer naïveté of these precursors of modern black
South African theater, their importance lies in the "rapid dramatic effect
with which the movement and change of scene" were realized on stage
and in "their later effect on the minds of students" (B. Vilakazi 1942:273).
One of these students was Nimrod Makhanya (see fig. 5), one of the earliest black musical comedians in South Africa. Nimrod Makhanya was
born in the Transvaal, son of Jan Makhanya and Kate Manye, an extraor-
dinarily musical woman who had traveled to England as a member of the
South African Choir in 1891 (chapter 2). From 1920 Nimrod attended St.
Francis College at Mariannhill and the Ohlange Institute where he came
under the influence of Reuben Caluza.[18] In 1930 he formed the Bantu
Glee Singers, a highly popular variety troupe modeled on Caluza's Double
Quartet, which recorded more than forty records for His Master's Voice in
Johannesburg in 1932 and undertook extensive tours of the country until
well into the 1950s.[19]

Makhanya shared with his teacher Caluza a remarkable talent for dramatic effects and comedy. Rooted as they were in Afro-American minstrel theater and British music hall skits of the Harry Lauder variety, Makhanya's sketches portrayed social misfits and the "evils" of "detribalization" and proletarianization. One of these and among his best known comical numbers was "Ndiyi Traveller" (HMV GU 78), a song about the vagrant George, composed around 1926:

Manene namaLedi alapha klendlu . . .
zintombi nezinsizwa zendawo ngendawo . . .
Ngiyabona ukuba aningiqondi.
Kusukela kulemini seningiqonda.
Ngingu George mina!
UGeorge omkhulu ka Maqanda.
Nginjenje ngenziwa ukunxila.
Phansi eMdubane bayangazi.
EKapa bayangazi.
ELusuthu bakhala ngoGeorge.
EMapondweni bakhala ngobuti.
Eshowe bakhala ngoGeorge.
Yimi lowo osho njalo ngenziwa ukunxila.
Angisi mfundisi natishela.
Ngiyinto ezinxilelayo.

FIGURE 5. Nimrod Makhanya (Zonk [Johannesburg], August 1951, p. 28)

Ladies and Gentlemen in this hall . . .
Boys and Girls everywhere . . .
I can see you don't know me.
From this day on you will know me.
I am George . . . myself!
I am big George, son of Maqanda.
I am like this because I am a drunkard.
Down at Durban they know me.
At Cape Town they know me.
In Baustoland they yearn for George.
In Pondoland they yearn for brother George.
At Eshowe also they yearn for George.
It is I who say so because I am drunk.
I am neither a minister nor a teacher.
I am just a "thing that drinks"![20]

Makhanya's appearances as the ragged, ne'er-do-well George set standards for what was to grow into one of the greatest fruits of Zulu musical creativity: musical comedy. The line that links Caluza, Makhanya, and other Zulu-speaking comedians such as Ndaba Majola, Victor Mkhize, and Petros Qwabe belongs to one of the proudest traditions in South African performing arts, and—to vary the words of Lawrence Levine—no inquiry into the consciousness and inner resources of black South Africans can ignore the content and structure of black humor (Levine 1977:300).

Among the numerous functions of black laughter, the one that seems the most pervasive under the conditions of racial oppression in South Africa is to provide some measure of control over the seemingly inescapable tyranny of racism. The most frequently applied method was not so much by the classical method of role inversion but by evoking black solidarity through intracommunal criticism. Certainly, a song such as "Ndiyi Traveller" served to distance the mission-educated elite from the "uncultured" urban laborers and therefore legitimized leadership claims. But the laughter about George was also a laughter of recognition: blacks knew that in the final analysis the vagrants and unemployed were part of the same community. Seen from the bottom end of the social ladder, however, the victims of black laughter were often those who had carved out a niche for themselves in the upper echelons of society, the preachers and policemen, the clerks and *indunas,* rather than the Georges whose social mobility proceeded in a more downward fashion. For instance, an early recorded version of the well-known work song

"Nyikithi" (Lift Up) is more than a satire of the black assistants of labor repression:

Oz' uphelele!
Hiya sesimphethe!
Sikhuluma nobani?
Sikhuluma nephoyisa elesab' insimbi!
O sigubu mbambe!
Simthi: Nyikithi!
Ayivumi yithele amanzi!

All together now!
Hiya! Hold together!
Whom do we address?
We address the policeman who fears the handcuffs!
O! Heave, hold!
Lift, up together!
If it sticks, try water![21]

Like migrants' representations of the "coon" in early *isikhunzi* choral music (chapter 6), songs such as this provide clues to the perspective on black solidarity from below. "Nyikithi" reminded black policemen—a privileged social position at the time—that they, too, were black and like migrant workers victims of racial oppression. Thus in spite of a perceived common black identity the forms and direction of black intracommunal criticism as well as the specific ways in which American popular culture was transformed were always a question of social position and negotiation. As we shall see in the following section of this chapter, the construction of a black identity through the medium of song, dance, and musical comedy involved at least as many contradictions and ambiguities as the evolution of Zulu ethnic traditions in modern Durban.

The Invention of a Tradition: From "Zulu Christian" Songs to "Splendid Savage Grandeur" Afro-American cultural models, however diluted by minstrelsy they may have been, clearly provided black alternatives to a "civilization" that was increasingly resented as being exclusively "white." At the same time they lacked the ethnic components that rural Africans could readily identify and use in expressing widespread anticolonial sentiments. But ethnic traditions, in the hands of the black cultural elite as much as for white liberals, white capitalists, and the state, were a double-edged sword. The central ambiguity in ethnicity in southern Africa and elsewhere in Africa was the fact that it could be "created" from above in an attempt to hamper unified political resistance against colonial subjugation (Vail 1989). At the same time ethnic consciousness served in many cases as a powerful focus of popular opposition, and frequently coexisted with other forms of consciousness, whether national, racial, or worker (Beinart 1987:307).

It is this ambivalence that is reflected in the evolution of Zulu performance genres in Durban and Natal between the turn of the century and mid-1930s. Naturally, it was within the Christian churches that the frictions between precolonial cultural traditions and modernity first became apparent. The missionaries, one *Ilanga* correspondent complained, had "naturally discouraged and tabooed" traditional culture, but failed to put anything "in the place of old heathen songs of the Natives."[22] In parts of Natal rural Christians had therefore begun to replace the blunt Victorian type of Christianity by their own African Christian church repertoire. In Inanda, only a stone's throw from Dube's Ohlange Institute, Isaiah Shembe had founded the Church of Nazareth in 1911 and composed an extensive body of liturgical songs, in part based on traditional genres such as *isigekle*. To complement the notion of a truly African form of Christian worship, Shembe also created a new type of ritual dress combining traditional Zulu regalia with white colonial uniforms called *amaScotch*, and a religious choreography (*ukusina*) that drew extensively on traditional *isigekle* dance patterns.[23]

Others who could not be concerned with the intricacies of black Christianity contented themselves with more worldly, satirical songs. One of these, "Inkomidi Isesikoleni" (The Committee Is at School), was popular in Ndwedwe District among John Dube's clan of the Qadi people:

> *Inkomidi isesikoleni,*
> *Sihlushwa amakholwa.*

> The Committee is at school.
> We are plagued by Christians.[24]

Clearly, against the dwindling resonance of Christian and Victorian values and notwithstanding the popularity of minstrel music with urban and mission audiences, the spokesmen of the Christian elite of black landowners had to consider more effective ways of securing their hegemony over the black laboring masses. In addition, the larger *amakholwa* landowners at the turn of the century found their position increasingly undermined by war, drought, and rinderpest, and finally by the Native Lands Act. As a result of weakening prospects of accumulation and of integration into the colonial bourgeoisie, landowners increasingly came to the insight that they "would need to seek a larger constituency to help protect the gains they had made so far, if not to expand them. And this meant forging links with the wider African community" (Marks 1986:59). John Dube himself, although opposed to non-Christian "tribal" customs such as *lobola* (bridewealth), had very clear ideas about this dilemma: "It is under the tribal system that the land is hel[d] by our Natives and, if I want land, I cannot get away from it. If I want land, I must associate the occupation of the land with the tribal system."[25]

Getting the land meant to sing the song of the land. Performance offered ideal ways of symbolically linking the values of the past with the experience of the new society. Whereas previously *amakholwa* and traditional peasantry each belonged to mutually exclusive classes with their own diametrically opposed cultures, early music competitions organized by Dube before and during the war featured sporadic performances of dance songs such as "Umfazi Umaqed 'Isikhwana" (My Wife Is Wasting Money) accompanied by traditional drums and reed flutes.[26] Together with Zulu versions of Western part songs and choir arrangements of Zulu folk tunes, traditional musical genres constituted *isiZulu*, a musical category whose popularity sometimes exceeded that of *imusic*. Although *isiZulu* and traditional dances were usually shunned by white missionaries as "heathen," traditional performance idioms provided a common, genuine framework for the expression of Zulu ethnic identity in opposition to the virulent racism of Natal's white settlers.

But what thus became defined as "traditional" of necessity had to be based on elite notions of a "purified" cultural heritage. Clearly, when the rural and urban black masses drew on vigorous precolonial cultural practices to define and make more secure their situation under the new economic order, such continuity frequently threatened the position and leadership claims of Natal's black elite based as it was on assimilation into the hegemonic European life-style. What was thus discarded as outmoded or simply declared as non-Zulu in the name of a "Christian Zulu" culture in most cases did not accord with the strategies of Dube and his allies to advance their acceptance in white colonial society.

Critics of the concept of "invented tradition" are right, of course, that traditions are always invented ones. But it is the appropriation of peasant traditions by urban elites and the subsequent myth of cultural continuity that make the notion of "invented tradition" particularly useful within the South African context. It is the invention of an entirely new body of "traditional" songs and dances for which the term "folk music," faute de mieux, seems to be appropriate. Folk music, in South Africa, is the product of a culturally and politically conscious reworking of "traditional" performance styles by the black intelligentsia under the conditions of the urban ghetto. As such it is distinguished from popular music which, although equally grounded in traditional music, is the product of a much greater amalgamation of styles from a much wider range of cultural and class sources in which the laboring masses have a far greater stake than in folk music.

Interestingly, it was outside South Africa, at the black American Hampton Institute in Virginia, Orpheus McAdoo's *alma mater,* that the arguably first experiments in a redefined Zulu folk idiom took place. Madikane Cele, a young Ohlange pupil and a relative of Dube's, attended the Hampton Institute from 1907 to 1913 and acquainted his teachers and fellow black American students with Zulu folklore and music. The highlight of Cele's studies was the presentation of "For Unkulunkulu's Sake," a pageant depicting the salvaging of positive, traditional, rural values through missionization (see fig. 6). Two decades before "ethnic" vaudeville shows by the Lucky Stars and the Amanzimtoti Royal Entertainers in South Africa, the Hampton play featured traditional songs and dances in village settings and performers in traditional garb.[27] Toward the end of his studies Cele recorded a number of cylinders for the eminent folk song collector Natalie Curtis.[28] The recordings included regimental anthems, love songs, and light dance songs and were subsequently transcribed and published by Curtis in her *Songs and Tales from the Dark Continent* (Curtis 1920:57–61, 133–49).

That some of the earliest recordings of traditional Zulu music should have been made in the United States is by no means accidental. Cele enrolled at Hampton at a time when American composers were engaged in a controversy that had been raging for several decades over an American national music. Hampton Institute played a key role in nurturing the Afro-American cultural heritage through its journal the *Southern Workman* and the work of pioneers such as R. Nathaniel Dett, but among middle-class Afro-Americans the legitimacy of the black musical heritage was frequently contested (Levine 1977:162–69). It was scholars such as Natalie Curtis whose vigorous support for American folk music prepared the ground for white middle-class acceptance of "the Negro's influence, at least, on the music of this country" (Curtis 1913:661).

At home in South Africa, and coinciding with Cele's efforts, Dube and his wife Nokutela, a music teacher, in 1911 published *Amagama Abantu,* the first collection of African secular songs (Dube and Dube

FIGURE 6. Madikane Cele in "For Unkulunkulu's Sake" at Hampton Institute
(Hampton University Archives)

[1911]). The booklet contained Tonic Sol-fa scores of thirty-one Zulu
wedding songs, love songs, and *umqumqumbelo* dance songs cast in Western four-square, choral harmonic structures. Together, Cele's and Dube's
activities helped to fill the void created by missionary cultural indoctrina-
tion, thus defining middle-class notions of the Zulu musical heritage and
providing the foundations of a repertoire that was distinct from "Zulu
songs which are of a very poor quality and thus cannot be sung in front of
the educated audience."[29]

That the revitalized and domesticated traditions of the precolonial
countryside could be used to check the resonance of anticapitalist ideologies and militancy among the urban masses, as well as the rural labor
tenants and reserve dwellers, became clearer after 1918. The war had
restructured Durban's black society profoundly. The city witnessed a period of unprecedented expansion, and thousands of workseekers fleeing
desperate rural living conditions swelled the ranks of Durban's black residents. To counter increasing outbursts of popular discontent, the Durban
municipality devised a set of reform programs such as improved housing
and recreational facilities. On a more general level, the postwar period
saw a more sustained effort by the state to influence black political thinking by a restoration of Zulu tribal authorities and a strengthening of
ethnic consciousness. Thus Shula Marks has shown how in the hands of

the state, Zulu history, the Zulu monarchy, and the symbols of Zulu ethnicity became a crucial part of the strategy of social control. The foundation of Inkatha in 1922–24, an organization aimed at gaining state recognition for the Zulu monarchy, was an important component of this
strategy (Cope 1985:154–234; Marks 1986:112; Marks 1989).

Within popular performance the resurgence of Zulu ethnicity
among shopkeepers and stevedores was the product of an even neater
meshing of various class initiatives. Already prior to the First World War,
as we have seen, for more conservative nationalist leaders such as Dube,
Zulu ethnic consciousness and traditionalism had served as a base for
broadening their ideological hegemony and for buttressing their class
position, and had found expression in the performance of traditional music belonging to the *isiZulu* category. Such attempts reached grander,
commercial dimensions when the first gramophone recordings appeared
on the Durban market. In 1927 James Stuart recorded some twenty records of royal *izibongo* and other traditional lore, and in 1929–30 Simon
Sibiya and John Matthews Ngwane followed with a further thirty-four
records which not only included traditional songs but also "comic songs"
like "Ngi bonelen' amapoyisa."[30]

Certainly, such recordings invoked in town audiences images of
rural harmony and helped to discourage permanent urban residence as
viable lifelong alternatives. But to ascribe the popularity of Zulu lore and
royal symbols to the working of some ideological strategy of the state or
entertainment industry alone would be to underestimate the popular acceptance of traditional power structures. Among rural Africans, the loss
of independent African power, the destruction of gender relations, and
the patriarchal structures of the Zulu kingdom nurtured a strong and genuine anticapitalist ideology tempered by traditionalist sentiments, the
focus of which was the Zulu king. The affairs of the Zulu royalty therefore
resonated deeply with rural Africans, and the fact that royal political
maneuvers became topics of songs is more than the result of some ideological strategy from above. A song such as "Inkosi Bayibizile Eshowe"
(The King Has Been Summoned to Eshowe), now widely considered a
genuine, "traditional" song, commemorates Solomon ka Dinizulu's frequent bouts of ill feeling vis-à-vis the white administration in Eshowe,
then administrative capital of Zululand:

> *Inkosi bayibiza Eshowe.*
> *Siyofika kusasa.*
> *O bayibiza kwaNongoma.*
> *Zinsizwa salani ngoxolo.*

The king has been summoned to Eshowe.
We will get there tomorrow.
O, they have summoned him to Nongoma.
Gentlemen, remain calm!

Interestingly, these words have been set to a number of different tunes, one of which shows strong "traditional" roots. It is in this form that the song surfaced during the upsurge of black union militancy in the late 1970s and early 1980s when it was recorded by Jessica Sherman (see example 1).

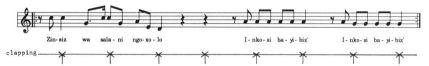

EXAMPLE 1. "Inkosi Bayibizile Eshowe" as performed by trade unionists during the 1970s.

The need to "invent" traditions, born as it was from the social, political, and ideological dilemma of Natal's and Durban's black urban elite, was absent among the rural population. The fact that traditions could be integrated almost seamlessly into a changing social environment and be adapted without black-elite intervention is demonstrated by a variety of concertina, guitar, and violin styles which Zulu migrants and laborers on white farms in the Natal hinterland had created from traditional instrumental genres. German Valantino concertinas, for instance, had been introduced to South Africa as far back as the mid-nineteenth century, but it was only after the First World War, due to the import ban on German products, that the Italian Bastari counterpart caught on with rural Zulus and became known as *Ibastari*. But the concertina was not confined to farms and reserves, and "nerve recking concertina playing"[31] and singing gangs of *amalaita*, youthful criminals, were early audible signals of an increased working-class presence in Durban. J. Clegg identifies two major concertina styles. *IsiChunu* originated from the Chunu clan in Msinga and incorporates the chordal structure of traditional girls' *imfilitshi* mouthorgan music. *IsiNdwedwe*, on the other hand, comes from Ndwedwe district and draws heavily on girls' *umakhweyana* bow music. Although initially scorned by missions as *izibambo zika Satan*, "Satan's handles," the *ikhostin* (concertina) eventually became a symbol of rural stability and intact family structures.[32] On at least one occasion, although not without causing considerable debate, concertina playing even formed part of an *amakholwa* wedding, and even thoroughly elite composers like Durbanbred Alfred Assegai Kumalo began their musical careers as concertina players.[33]

Closely linked to concertina music is a complex repertoire of guitar styles that emerged from within the ranks of young migrants and domestic servants. Much of the descriptive metaphors of guitar playing and guitar competitions derive from stick fighting, and both the styles and contents of guitar songs relate Zulu migrants' guitar music to the experience of farm laborers. Equally condemned by mission and petty bourgeois ideologues as an enemy of homemaking (*Isiginci asakh' umuzi*, A guitar won't build a homestead), one of the earliest guitar styles is called *ukuvamba* (strumming) and might be anchored in Western, and particularly Boer, guitar techniques. Although *ukuvamba* remains important as an accompaniment to *isicathulo* gumboot routines, the early 1920s saw the emergence of numerous other novel styles named after and related to *isishameni, isikhuze,* and *umsanzi* dance styles (Clegg 1981b). The early history of these guitar styles is difficult to reconstruct from the evidence available on gramophone records, as the recording companies did not become interested in guitar music until the late 1940s.

Even less documented but equally rooted in the flux of migrants to and from Durban's labor reserves around the time of the First World War is violin playing. The history of Zulu violin idioms remains fragmentary at this stage, but present-day usage of the violin in *ingoma*-related styles such as *isishameni* suggests a parallel development with guitar styles. Alternatively, it does not seem unreasonable to assume a direct relationship between the violin and the *igqongwe,* a tin-resonated guitar which David Rycroft traces to the *ramkie* (Rycroft 1977).[34] Either way, one may speculatively derive the Zulu technique of bowing with a straight bow from practices introduced by Afrikaans farmers, while the introduction of the violin—as Rycroft suggests—can be related to Wild West films which had been presented by ABM missionaries to migrant laborers and slumyard residents in Clairwood from at least 1924 (ibid.).[35]

If the acceptance of ethnic traditions among black cultural leaders before the war and during much of the 1920s was never more than halfhearted, the 1930s saw significant changes in black attitudes toward tradition and ethnicity. Thus in 1932 Mark Radebe, leading musical ideologue and Johannesburg music critic, argued that a genuine national musical idiom had to be "based on the only real Bantu music, namely, its folk music."[36] Radebe's folkloristic stance grew out of the gradual shift of liberal positions and urban reform projects toward an acceptance of territorial segregation and the idea of African reserves as viable repositories of black development. In Natal an ideological alliance between Dube, sugar baron Heaton Nicholls, and Senator Edgar Brookes exerted a strong influence on African thinking about ethnic tradition; and both the Ohlange Institute and Adams College were instrumental in bringing the educated elite into tune with the new policy (Rich 1984). Thus it is by no means accidental that in terms of musical performance, the shift toward traditionalism first took shape at Adams and Ohlange. Brookes was principal at Adams, and the most influential "ethnic" vaudeville troupe, Mthethwa's Lucky Stars (see fig. 7), was largely composed of teachers trained at Adams.

The Lucky Stars had been founded in 1929 by Esau Fika Mthethwa, a teacher at Amanzimtoti. On his death in 1933, the troupe was taken over by his younger brother Isaac Layton Mthethwa, a teacher born at Inanda in 1913, and Joseph Nkunzi Zubane, born in 1896. Isaac Mthethwa first became involved in such solid middle-class enterprises as the Mendi Memorial Club, but also in the ICU. In addition to Mthethwa and Zubane, the Lucky Stars consisted of eight members, most of them young graduates of Adams College. The troupe quickly made a name for themselves through appearances at the Bantu Social Centre, Durban's Town Hall, and eventually tours of the Union. Esau Mthethwa had been a skilled performer on violin, piano, guitar, and concertina, and this mixed heritage was partly reflected in the shows. Apart from such European classics as "The Sea Hath Its Pearls," the Lucky Stars gloried in "scenes of native domestic life with a realism which would be otherwise unobtainable" (Lloyd 1935:3). These scenes were fully developed one-act skits modeled on the Mariannhill plays of 1919 which concentrated on themes like *Umthakathi* (witch doctor) and *Ukuqomisa* (courting).[37]

The show impressed white liberal audiences and evoked in impresario Bertha Slosberg the desire to "salvage from European influence the remaining power, the native simplicity, the splendid savage grandeur of a dying pagan land" (Slosberg 1939:192). However, plans to take the Lucky Stars to Europe failed to materialize, and the troupe continued to play to mixed audiences throughout the Union until shortly after Isaac Mthethwa's death in 1937. Among black audiences, as D. Coplan pointed out, the dramatizations of an idealized cohesive and culturally integrated society were all the more appealing for their remoteness from the insecurity and alienation of urban life (Coplan 1985:126). And though elite critics such as Herbert Dhlomo mocked the show as "exotic crudities,"[38]

Durban working-class audiences "perceived finer shades of relevant ethical significance, and relished the skillful dramatization of a double-barreled purpose in each play" (Gérard 1971:197).

The resurgence of ethnic pride, as Shula Marks has shown, was coupled with a growing patriarchal concern over the "proper" conduct of Zulu women. For not only had the 1930s drastically increased the number of workseekers in urban areas, but for the first time nearly 50 percent of all African employees in Durban were women (Marks 1989:220). But dominated as it was by men, Durban's black performance culture reflected the conservative and chauvinist underpinnings of Zulu nationalism. If, in the eyes of conservative black leaders, men had but to choose between a criminal career and allegiance to traditional chiefs, the rightful place for a woman was in the rural homestead. Thus, "E Zintsukwini Zo Tshaka" (In the Days of King Shaka) (Columbia YE 12), a tune recorded probably in 1937 by music critic Radebe, laments the changed sex roles in the urban context and declining male and conjugal authority:

> *Ezinsukwini zawoShaka sasihleli.*
> *Ezinsukwini zawokhokho*
> *sasingahlushwa yilutho*
> *ngoba sasibuswa indoda endala uShaka . . .*
> *Wathi lapho mhla efayo*
> *wathi thina maZulu siyosala singahlangene,*
> *siyofana nezinyoni.*
> *Kodwa ke nempela siyabona*
> *ngokusuka ezintabeni amakhosikazi ashiya amakhaya.*
> *Eza lapha ayokwenzani?*
> *Ayonyathela njengezintombi*
> *bese ekhohlwa ngabantwana.*

In the days of King Shaka we were rejoicing.
In the days of our forefathers
nothing was troubling us,
because we were ruled by a wise ruler, King Shaka . . .
When he died,
he said that we Zulu shall never be united,
and that we shall live scattered like birds.
We have already experienced this
through the moving away of married women from home.
What are wives doing here in the urban areas?
They behave like young girls
and forget about their children.

FIGURE 7. The Lucky Stars, 1937 (Ilanga Lase Natal [Durban], May 1, 1937)

The reworking of ethnic traditions from above was embedded in a process of much grander dimensions that aimed at the complete restructuring of social relations in urban South Africa in the wake of the Great Depression. This process, however, was never simply a one-way street and involved more than plain coercion. It resulted from the complex interplay of social actors mobilizing a wide spectrum of sometimes conflicting cultural resources, and is perhaps best illustrated by the evolution of popular dance in Durban (in particular *ingoma* dance; see chapter 4) and by the reshaping of Durban's cultural geography during the 1930s.

The Struggle for the City: Social Control and Popular Consent in Black Performance during the 1930s By the late 1920s and early 1930s Durban's black cultural leaders had found it increasingly difficult to defend the notion of an ideal urban, black citizen in middle-class ideological terms. The 1920s had seen the rise of vibrant popular dance forms like *indunduma* and *thula ndivile*, and with the growing popularity of concertina, guitar, vernacular songs, and action songs, the fine line between middle-class notions of "uplifting entertainment" and forms of backyard amusement was effectively breaking down. Already in 1917 cultural leaders had deplored the lack of differentiation between "good" music and what they perceived as low and degrading performance styles. Lowered admission fees, "Sentinel" argued, "would perpetrate bad music."[39] The poet and journalist Rolfes R. R. Dhlomo, echoing apprehensions in the United States about ragtime, pointed to its effect on working-class, leisure-time activities and called for initiatives to stem the tide of the "dancing craze." In the same vein, one *Ilanga* correspondent perceptively identified action songs as "a type of performance which may degenerate easily into what is silly and vicious."[40] Other cultural leaders, teachers, and clergymen also deplored the mushrooming of dance halls.[41] But the threat these spokesmen perceived was not so much directed against Christian morals as against their credibility with white officials as leaders of submissive black communities.

The osmosis in Durban's black class and cultural relations is also mirrored in the role of the city's black population had been playing form the mid-1920s in shaping the city's "cultural geography" through the creation of a network of cultural "spaces" that cut across class boundaries and were largely independent of white benevolence and support. The network spread concentrically from Cartwright's Flats, the most strategically situated and the busiest site of working-class, leisure-time activities during the 1920s and early 1930s. Slightly to the east of the Flats were located three important areas of black housing: Msizini Barracks, Baumannville location, and the Greyville South African Railways Barracks. This residential complex was catered to by a dense network of beer halls, shebeens, and dance halls in the surrounding smaller streets and lanes.

One of these was Fountain Lane, a favorite gathering place for Durban's black workers, and as such was not held in high esteem with the police. The chief constable deplored the fact that the street "required more police attention and supervision than any other thoroughfare in the vicinity."[42] The degree of attention it had received in little less than twelve months in 1932–33 is clearly evident in the more than 260 arrests made there, which are partly due to the presence of C. D. Tusi's dance hall. This venue enjoyed considerable support from Durban's intelligentsia, but also attracted a good deal of illicit liquor consumption and "rowdyism." Equally popular was an establishment run by one Mrs. Phillips that offered liquor and commercial sex. The only social activity in Fountain Lane that the town council viewed benevolently took place in no. 40 in a house that throughout the 1920s had served as the headquarters of the Mendi Memorial Club. This was an association that was concerned primarily with the commemoration of the sinking of the troop carrier Mendi in 1917 that cost the lives of 615 black soldiers.

Only a stone's throw away from Fountain Lane was John Nduli's African Social Club at 117 Prince Edward Street, established in 1933 as a "depot of female impersonators." But the African Social Club was only one of at least two clubs in Prince Edward Street. At no. 71, the African Workmen's Club chaired by James Ngcobo counted some 800 domestic servants as members and conducted a lively business.

One of the numerous lanes that connects Prince Edward Street and those running parallel to it is Etna Lane, an area that until the mid-1930s was populated by a number of shebeens run by "coloureds" as well as the International Amusement Club. In the eyes of police officials, the Club was a "most unsavory place" that served as a meeting place for homosexuals, possibly domestic servants and compound residents. In 1933 the Club was closed down, and the managers may have shifted their territory to Nduli's African Social Club. Further away, at the northern end of the recreation grounds, was Alpheus Seme's dance hall in Umgeni Road, a very popular den that had attracted the attention of the police right from the opening night on February 7, 1931.

Among the dances that took place in places such as Seme's Hall were *indunduma* and *thula ndivile*.[43] The latter had emerged in Durban in the late 1920s as a result of the marked shifts in the ethnic composition of the migrant work force. Growing numbers of poverty-stricken Africans from Transkei and Basutoland traveled to Durban in search of work and brought with them a repertoire of performance styles that carried strong Xhosa and Sotho connotations. The original tune of *Thula ndivile* has been ascribed to the Durban composer Willie Mdholzini,[44] but it was not until 1930 that it was first recorded by Caluza's Double Quartette in London (HMV GU 37). As yet little is known about Mdholzini's biography, but during or shortly after the Second World War he was busy leading the Clermont Township Lads and Lasses as well as the African Babies. The latter choir recorded two of his songs for His Master's Voice (JP 7), and the lyrics of two of his songs were published by Hugh Tracey (1948:43, 67). Together with other examples, Mdholzini's songs appear to demonstrate that as a genre *thula ndivile* concerned itself primarily with the collapse of traditional value systems under the constraints of urban living. Mdholzini's song "Ikhiwane Elihle," for example, blames the alcoholism among urban slum dwellers on the breaking up of family ties:

Zintombi zinsizwa niyakhalelwa emakhaya.
Linigwinyile iTheku.
Abanye bashiya omakotshana nabazali bekhala emakhaya . . .
Kwathi enye insizwa ibungukile.
Yafika ekhaya sokwasala izindonga zodwa.
Yaswela ukuthi izolalaphi-na,
yasukuma yayakocela indawo komakhelwana.
Yathi: "Yeka ithemba ngokuba alibulali."
Yathi: "Yeka ikhiwane elihle linomkhuba."
Yeka ukukhonza isishimeyane.

Girls and young men, you are needed at your homes.
You are swallowed up by Durban.
Some of you left your wives and parents crying at home . . .
Once a young man went away from home.
He returned and found it in ruins.
He needed somewhere to sleep,
so he bestired himself and went to his neighbors.
He said: "But hope does not kill."
He said: "But a good-looking fig is bad inside."
O, the vanity of worshiping [*shimeyane*] liquor . . .[45]

Another *thula ndivile* tune, "Ulixoki Lomfozi" (This Woman Is a Trouble-maker) (HMV GU 140), recorded in 1932 by Nimrod Makhanya's Bantu Glee Singers, criticizes the decline of traditional gender roles in the urban environment:

Ulixoki lomfazi.
Uchitha umuzi kababa.

This woman is a troublemaker.
She is scattering my father's family.

Far more sophisticated and ethnically less unambiguous than *thula ndivile,* and more directly perceived as an imitation of ballroom dances unknown in traditional Zulu dance styles, was *indunduma* (mine dumps), the first truly urban dance form in Durban after the war.[46] Usually performed on keyboard instruments and tin shakers, *indunduma* was connected with *marabi,* a style that originated in Johannesburg, and it is through returning Natal migrants that *indunduma* possibly filtered back to Durban.[47] We owe a description of *indunduma* music, albeit tinted with middle-class snobbery, to Herbert Dhlomo:

The people danced to the accompaniment of an organ and a most cacophonic "orchestra" of small tins filled with pebbles. The atmosphere was obscene. For the first time in the history of Bantu entertainments liquor was introduced. The functions were like night-clubs of the lowest order. And yet what naturally talented players the ragtime and the Ndunduma concerts had! Vampers (as they were called) who improvised many, "hot" original dance and singing numbers at the spur of the moment, and who play or accompany any piece after hearing the melody once, and do so on any key; fellows who played music not because they were taught or paid or because it was fashionable, but because they were born musicians.[48]

In addition to entertainment, Durban's black dance halls also accounted for a significant portion of the city's limited black entrepreneurial activities and provided income opportunities for semiprofessional and professional performers. Seme's hall, for instance, attracted such a numerous clientele that its proprietor was able to hire the services of the resident pianist Mathwica.[49] Instrumental performers like Mathwica were few and far between in Durban's dance halls and shebeens, but some achieved legendary fame. One of these musicians was MaReyiza, a violinist. MaReyiza was the first to introduce *marabi* to Durban, his most popular tunes of later years being "Silele KwaBhanki" and "Sohamba noMaReyiza, Sohamba Kuze Kuse" (We Will Accompany MaReyiza until Daybreak).[50] MaReyiza's favorite haunts were the shebeens in the less built-up areas of Mkhumbane where he was active until the 1950s (Moloi 1987:27). Mkhumbane was the name Zulu inhabitants had given to Cato Manor, until 1960 one of South Africa's worst slum areas outside Durban, before its residents were removed to the modern township of KwaMashu. In Mkhumbane enthusiastic shebeen patrons accompanied MaReyiza by playing the *marabi* percussion part, traditionally performed with pebble-filled milk tins, with sticks rattled along corrugated iron sheets. In the more densely populated areas of Mkhumbane, not to mention Durban's inner-city district, such vigorous musicmaking usually ran the risk of attracting the wrath of landlords and burgesses. At the shebeens in the Samseni area, *isicathamiya* groups "would sing in hushed voices, because they were afraid the Indian landlords would call the police."[51]

But Samseni not only had the advantage of offering a wide range of alternative, illicit alcoholic drinks; at the same time it was conveniently linked to the Victoria Street beer hall in town by a direct bus line. This beer hall was one of the oldest in Durban and was especially popular with early *isicathamiya* performers. Although more restricted in the freedom they offered to workers who wished to create their own forms of entertainment, municipal beer halls like the one in Victoria Street were nevertheless important venues of working-class recreation and musical creativity. They were complemented by numerous less auspicious halls, back rooms, and sheds that workers managed to transform into relatively uncontrolled spaces. Typical of these was *Ematramini,* the disused tramway sheds in Alice Street, that among other purposes served as a rehearsal ground for *isicathamiya* groups such as the Evening Birds.[52] It is in this sphere of intense experiment and cross-fertilization that blacks in Durban were struggling to defend their autonomy as urban dwellers. The urban space thus because the most hotly contested sphere of black cultural transformation in which both the local black elite and the state had a stake.

The resilience of black urban politics and the threat it posed to white hegemony were most forcefully brought home to Durban residents by the outbreak of the Durban riots in June 1929 when thousands of harbor workers decided to mount a systematic boycott of Durban's beer halls. The campaign, halfheartedly backed by Champion and the ICU, was smashed by an unprecedented use of police force that left eight people dead. Among the more material losses sustained by the ICU was the hall and the brass band, which fell victim to looting white crowds. In the wake of the riots, Mark Radebe's elite group African Male Voice Choir recorded "Namhla Siyahlushwa" (Today We Are Troubled) (Columbia AE 37), one of the popular protest songs that emerged after the riots:

> *Sizokwenzenjanina thina?*
> *Namhlan siyahlushwa.*
> *Sitheliswa imali engasisiziyo thina.*
> *Abakhokheli bethu babanga izikhundla,*
> *asisaqondi ukuthi sozoshonaphi thina.*
> *Wafa uMakhalempongo obeligugu lethu.*
> *Wafa nempi yakhe, umntakaBulose bo!*
> *Balweli spesheli nepasi lomzimba.*
> *Asisaqondike thina ukuthi soshonaphi.*

> Whatever shall we do?
> Today we are troubled.
> We are made to pay money that does not help us.
> Our paymasters strive for honors,
> while we do not know where to go.
> Our precious Makhalempongo died.
> He died with his men, son of Bulose!

They fought against the Special and Registration passes.
We don't know where to go.[53]

Interestingly, the words of this song capture more of the black grassroots militancy and disenchantment with a conciliatory leadership than its hymn-like, staid tune would seem to indicate. This procedure is typical of much South African black political song and represents a deliberate attempt at blending a rather varied set of symbols through the use of communicative channels with different "messages." As will be seen in the work of Reuben Caluza (chapter 5) and in the contrasting metaphors used in the audio, kinesic, and visual components of *isicathamiya* performance (chapter 6), such seemingly contradictory statements are not an expression of a diffuse or false popular consciousness. The heuristic methodological value of such overlapping layers of text and music in a song such as *Namhla Siyahlushwa* lies precisely in the fact that they provide realistic models of the complex nature of popular consciousness.

One of the official responses to black militancy during the watershed years 1929–30, apart from the use of tanks and guns, was a more carefully designed strategy to determine the scope and character of black urbanization in much more clearly defined segregationist terms. This strategy involved among other things, a number of "welfare" schemes such as the provision of sports grounds. Looked at from a broader perspective, however, such official benevolence was in fact only part of a package of much harsher measures aimed at a tighter control of alternative, autonomous forms of popular entertainment. Thus in February 1932 the town council passed regulations for the control of halls and meetings. The draft rules met with the strongest protest from Durban's black leaders, because not only did the leaders envisage a de facto closedown of Durban's inner-district black entertainment facilities, but the rules placed every black political meeting under white supervision. In any case, the sudden vacuum created by this move probably not only benefited the shebeens on the outskirts of the city, but it also, at least partially, had the opposite effect of driving frustrated workers into the less-controllable niches of black entertainment. At the very least, the antiliberal measures reinforced the widening gap between black dockworkers, domestic servants, preachers, teachers, and white society, and destroyed middle-class hopes of urban "civilized" status.

A sketch by Lindi Makhanya and Company entitled "Ikonsati eBantusport" (The Concert at Bantu Sports) (Gallo GE 879) that is worth quoting at length describes the frustrations of a young sewerage worker from Durban's Point, aptly called "Reserve," who left Durban "because places like Tusi's and Mini's have all been closed," and who subsequently is attracted to *isicathamiya* competitions in Johannesburg.

> A: Did you get the news that there is a music extravaganza at Bantu Sports today? Linda's group [Solomon Linda's Evening Birds, V.E.], Mchunu's group, and the ICU group [Mkatshwa's Choir, V.E.] will be there . . .
>
> B (Reserve): You know very well that I don't want to move around here in Johannesburg, and you also know that people tend to stab each other in gatherings like music competitions.
>
> A: Hey, go away! You always beat about the bush when people are inviting us. Let's go man!

The sketch then describes how the young migrant "with the five shillings which I earned after hard labor at Point by carrying human excrement" gets involved in the bidding process that rapidly heats up to a general tumult:

> C: *Order please, order please,* be quiet. With this ten-cent piece, I am saying you do not know anything about music.
>
> B: Sis, this is no music at all, is this the way how you sing in Johannesburg? With my penny I am saying that they must sit down, they do not know music. I do not want to see them here, they must sit down.
>
> C: *Order please, order please!* You do not know music. Someone has paid a penny instructing you to sit down. Let us now give that Durban lady and her boyfriend "Reserve" a chance to sing so that we can listen to their music.
>
> B: They are fighting. Stop it! I told you that I do not want to attend such gatherings. Just look now, we will be arrested during the very first days of our arrival here in Johannesburg.

Apprehensions that the city council's antiliberal measures would help to foster an oppositional subculture outside municipal control rather than to eliminate an existing one in its midst had of course been articulated by Durban's black elite from as early as 1930 and are well documented in the minutes of the Native Advisory Board. However, rather than these more verbally articulate forms of discourse that make for the historian's daily bread, the representation of popular ideology by members of the black intelligentsia in forms of expressive culture such as this sketch as well as in previously mentioned examples serves as a useful methodological device in deciphering the more subtle, inner workings of popular culture and power politics. For not only does *Ikonsati eBantusport* reveal more about underlying class interests than overtly political discourse, the skit—more than complex political statements—provides everyday images of power, authority, and order, fittingly couched in the language of the dominant culture ("order please, order please") that were designed to become accepted as the normal way of life by urbanizing migrants such as "Reserve."

With the suppression of the 1929–30 riots, the closing down of dance halls, and the institutionalization of *ingoma* dancing, Durban's political climate was clearly beginning to be determined by much less stormy-weather conditions. As communist and ICU activist Gilbert Coka acidly remarked:

> Indoor entertainments were confined to concerts. Ragtime comic songs provided the usual programmes. Dancing had already claimed adherents when the Town Council closed dance-halls. The native press echoed the sentiments of its subsidizers. It appealed for moderation and constitutionalism. (Coka 1936:317)

The new phase of political acquiescence is reflected in the activities of two institutions designed both to represent and spread ruling-class notions of black urban culture and to organize a popular constituency for black elite leadership: the Bantu Social Centre and Champion's Workers' Club, popularly known as ICU.

The Ambiguity of Class: The Industrial and Commercial Workers' Union (ICU) and the Bantu Social Centre Six years after its foundation, the Durban branch of the ICU opened the African Workers' Club at 11 Leopold Street in December 1925. This was succeeded by the Natal Workers' Club in May 1928, shortly before A. W. G. Champion and the Natal branch seceded from the parent body to form the ICU Yase Natal. Although after 1930 Champion's ICU Yase Natal had ceased to exist as a political force of any importance in Durban's black popular resistance, for more than a decade the union club played an important role in the construction of a politically conscious, popular cultural alliance in Durban.

Some scholars have pointed to the class discrepancies between ICU leadership and the rank and file (Bradford 1987; Marks 1986; la Hausse

1984, 1987a), but as a result of the meshed musical and symbolic heritage of Durban's black strata, and the fragmented and ambiguous nature of class formation and class consciousness in the town, these distinctions were not translated mechanically into union cultural and musical activities. During the worst years of the economic recession, the structure and content of ICU concerts graphically illustrate the meshed cultural traditions of Durban's black strata and Champion's attempts to reconstruct a popular alliance around the symbols of African nationalism and Zulu ethnicity.

Champion wished ICU concerts to be "indistinguishable from those of whites" (Bradford 1987:141). As a result, ICU hymns, apart from "Nkosi Sikelel iAfrika" (God Bless Africa), included Mazisa's "Vukani Mawethu" (Awake My People), the "Red Flag," and other hymn-based songs. In the Natal countryside ICU branches, somewhat incongruously, even organized weekly fund-raising concerts featuring organ playing by well-dressed officials (Bradford 1983:10; 1987:142). A brass band and the ICU National Choir completed the regalia that publicly signaled the union's claims. Brass bands were not only an important instrumental tradition among black South Africans, but also lent themselves to the expression of very diverse class ideologies. Thus Ohlange Institute and Mariannhill both supported brass bands whose repertoires consisted of tunes like "Hiawatha's March." The ICU band concentrated more on union songs of British provenance.[54] In 1931 the Durban branch also had the violinist Tommy on their payroll, but here as with most ICU symbols the violin could have been the source of quite a diverse set of meanings attached to repertoires such as classical music and Zulu violin styles.[55]

ICU concerts in 1932 quite vividly illustrate the varied fare and usual round of cultural activities that characterized the ICU in Durban after the riots (see fig. 8). "Stage Manager" H. Msomi was able to present the Sunbeams, the Dem Darkies from Pretoria under James D. Mogaecho, the Blue Ham Bees from Durban, and the Mad Boys from Johannesburg on three consecutive nights in April. The ICU Hall, he claimed, attracted choirs from all over the country "because peace prevails in this place." In June under the motto "The more we are to-gether, the happier we will be," mission school tap dance troupes such as the Midnight Follies and the Famous Broadway Entertainers appeared along with A. A. Kumalo's Zulu Male Voice Party, J. P. Mahlobo's Thulasizwe Choir, and the Moonlight Six of ICU led by Gideon Zonke Masinga (b. 1913), an Inanda-born composer and entertainer. Masinga's activities also involved vaudeville shows with the Masinga Minstrel Strutters and the Broadway Entertainers, one of the best-known tap dance groups in Durban during the late 1930s.[56] The year was rounded off with a "unique entertainment" by the Dixies Raglads from the Amanzimtoti mission school and the Apologise Voices from Izingolweni College.[57]

As Helen Bradford correctly points out, "in a dehumanizing environment largely lacking in venues for legal entertainment, the ICU's cultural events fostered cohesion, afforded collective enjoyment and reaffirmed blacks' right to shape the world for themselves" (Bradford 1987:141). But despite the focus on "peace" and "happiness" the basis for such black collective identification was thin when so much of it was modeled on white hegemonic culture. Furthermore, the attempts of political leaders such as Champion to shape union cultural activities according to their own class-based preferences were constantly kept in check by the strong working-class element in their constituencies. For Champion's largest following had always been drawn from the ranks of Durban's estimated 9,000 domestic servants, and hence ICU events featured much *ingoma* dancing. Pairs of ballroom dancers that "moved slowly and decorously and exactly on European lines" under the gaze of less sophisticated onlookers were somewhat exceptional fare at the Natal Workers' Club. But *ingoma*—in Champion's view—was "the real thing" (Perham 1974:198).

In the rural hinterland the union had already sponsored traditional dancing, and in Durban concerts at the Workers' Hall contained a strong admixture of black working-class elements. From at least 1932, *isicathamiya* groups like the Evening Birds also had regular appearances on the ICU stage. Apart from songs about the rural homestead, performances at the ICU hall above all featured songs promoting Champion and his organization. Thembinkosi Phewa recalls that the Evening Birds

> sang for Champion. This was a special request. Then spectators paid to enter the hall and watch us. This was just for entertainment over weekends. He did not pay any money. We did not expect money, in any case, because we were actually enjoying ourselves. . . . Champion would buy food, cakes, etc. There was food for the singers which they had for a song, and the rest of the food was sold to the spectators. It worked the same way as the *stokfel.* . . . There is a song about Champion, a complicated one. We did not compose it. It was composed by the Shooting Stars. . . . The words went like this: "Thank you for your kindness, Champion. We thank you for your kindness, Mahlathi [praise epithet for Champion],

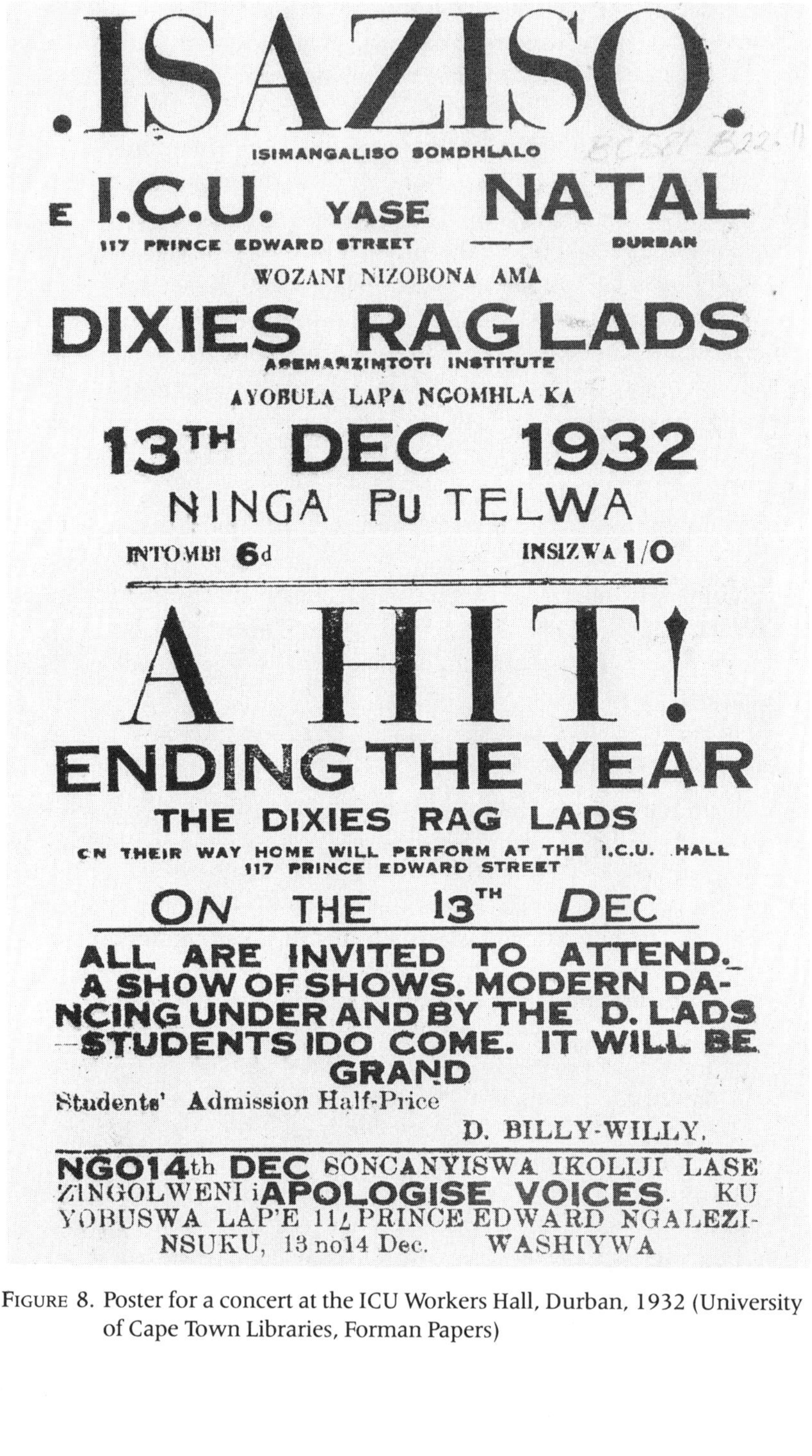

FIGURE 8. Poster for a concert at the ICU Workers Hall, Durban, 1932 (University of Cape Town Libraries, Forman Papers)

the good that you have done for the Zulu. May God bless
you." It was in praise of Champion. It was just like an *imbongi*
[Zulu traditional praise poem], but we used to sing it.[58]

"Traditional" praise poetry notwithstanding, the proximity both in perception and style of middle-class and working-class backgrounds was
inscribed into the very musical repertoire of *isicathamiya* choirs (chapter
6). In fact, the symbiosis cannot be better illustrated than by an ICU-sponsored competition in 1938 which brought together *isicathamiya* choirs
such as Mzobe's Crocodiles and the Evening Birds and Johannesburg's
elite tap dance troupe the Darktown Strutters.[59]

If Champion's cultural initiative reflected the revised ICU policy of
acquiescence and accommodation, the Bantu Social Centre represented a
more openly defined attempt at co-opting Durban's black urban dwellers.
The Centre opened its doors to the public in 1934, and the list of paid-up
members included the pinnacle of Durban's black society, names like
Frank Caluza, W. F. Bhulose, J. Dube, Ngazana Luthuli, Jack Malinga,
William Mseleku, Benedict W. Vilakazi, and others. It was directed by the
composer Alfred Assegai Kumalo (1879–1966) who, like Caluza, was
born in Edendale. Kumalo's professional career oscillated between such
diverse occupations as transport rider between Charlestown and Johannesburg, municipal clerk, and building contractor.[60] In 1929 Kumalo
had formed the Zulu Male Voice Party, one of the best-known classical
choirs in Durban. This group concentrated almost entirely on *imusic* and
Kumalo's own compositions which—as one *Ilanga* critic remarked—
were different "from the one[s] which set young feet and legs, to sway up
and down the stage howling and yelling (or crooning) on top of their
voices."[61]

Throughout the late 1930s the Centre attracted an increasingly
larger sector of Durban's black population, of a more heterogeneous class
composition than its elite leadership would seem to suggest. For the
16,000 visitors that attended bioscope evenings in 1938 were certainly
not all drawn from the ranks of the literate minority of urban blacks. Nor
were the 2,500 and 5,500 visitors who were entertained by *ingoma*
dances and boxing events respectively in 1935. Concerts were by far the
most popular single category of activities offered at the Centre, but even
these were not uniformly sedate affairs, as far as can be judged from the
"rough usage" to which the concert piano had been exposed.[62]

But however popular *ingoma* and *isicathamiya* choirs may have
proved, it is Durban's restrictive urban cultural policies that can largely be
blamed for a gradual decline in black performance activities in the port

town after 1933. This is exemplified by both the development of black jazz and professional performance in Durban. From the late 1920s, dance bands modeled on whatever glimpses black South Africans could catch of American, preferably Afro-American, performers had been emerging in South Africa.[63] But the radius of action of these bands—the Merry Blackbirds, Jazz Maniacs, or Merrymakers—was Johannesburg and the smaller towns along the Rand. Similar bands did not exist in Durban, and prominent Durban-born or -bred performers such as Ndaba Majola and Nimrod Makhanya had migrated to Johannesburg—possibly as a result of Durban's restricted entertainment venues.

But there are deeper reasons for the decline of popular performance in Durban. Although the Natal metropolis experienced explosive growth and further industrial expansion, the development of South African manufacturing industries, and its concomitant social differentiation during the mid-1930s, was a process concentrated on the Rand. In 1935 the strongest portion of Durban's working class was still the domestic servants with 14,000 employed as opposed to a mere 4,731 merchants and 352 policemen. Durban's intermediate stratum, then, was clearly too small to support full-time professional bands. Against this weak middle class in Durban, the 23,000 property holders that populated Johannesburg's suburbs Sophiatown, Martindale, and Newclare in 1938 clearly represented a more formidable support base for a dense network of cinemas, dance clubs, and jazz bands. Conversely, with a 6d. to £1.6.0 admission to the ICU hall and an average monthly wage of £56 in Durban in 1931, the city's working class hardly represented a stable base for such dance bands either.[64]

The dilemma is exemplified by the career of William Mseleku, one of Durban's younger black entertainers during the late 1930s and perhaps one of Caluza's most promising disciples. A Mariannhill graduate and Amanzimtoti teacher, Mseleku had been experimenting with traditional dance and music genres tied together in a coherent stage presentation from at least 1932. Mseleku was born in 1912 near Amanzimtoti, and like many of his contemporaries was rooted both in Western traditions and Zulu rural and semiurban styles. William's musical socialization took place with the help of a homemade tin guitar before he took up violin and saxophone. In 1932 Mseleku formed a group of musicians and actors, variously called Amanzimtoti Players, Amanzimtoti Zulu Choir, or Mseleku's Party. The troupe recorded almost thirty records for His Master's Voice and consisted of Mseleku's siblings Mavis and Alfred, his wife Elvira, and the students Victor Khumalo, Siberia Chamane, Raymond

FIGURE 9. The Amanzimtoti Royal Entertainers in typical ragtime pose, 1937. From left; victor Khumalo, Siberia Chamane, Raymond Dladla, Alzena Sishi, Elvira Mseleku, Lulu Msome, Mavis Mseleku, Alfred Mseleku, William Mseleku. (Bantu World [Johannesburg], March 5, 1938)

Dladla, Alzena Sishi, and Lulu Msome.[65] In 1935 the group was renamed the Amanzimtoti Royal Entertainers (see fig. 9), and recorded further records for Gallo (GE 135–38).

Despite Mseleku's popularity, Durban's black community could not support a group like the Amanzimtoti Royal Entertainers on a professional basis. Typically, Mseleku's Royal Entertainers tried to solve the problem by constantly locating new audiences of diverse social backgrounds and by negotiating the whole range of musical styles available at the time. While most other black entertainers never left the orbit of the mission schools to become semiprofessional entertainers, Mseleku combined tours of the white coastal resort hotels with concerts to raise funds for his studies in England.[66] Performances by Mseleku's troupe featured sketches, action songs, and "ragtime" songs of the Caluza variety coupled with a choreography such as is visible in illustration 9.[67] As an active ANC member, Mseleku also enlarged the repertoire of "sweet, patriotic songs" with tunes such as "Izizwe Ezimnyama" (The Black Nation) and "Vulani amaSango maDoda" (Open Up the Gates, Men). Like Caluza he also harbored strong proroyal feelings, and ethnic nostalgia is evident in songs such as "Umukile uSolomon" (Solomon Has Disappeared) and "UTshaka" (Shaka).[68] However, among Mseleku's innovations one must also credit the popularization of Zulu yodeling. From the late 1920s Durban's record shops carried numerous Jimmie Rodgers records on the Zonophone label. In 1932 William and his brother Wilfred recorded some songs directly modeled on Rodgers' "Blue Yodel" series of songs (HMV GU 80).

Conclusion   There can be little doubt that Durban and its rural hinterland have played a crucial role in the history of black popular music in South Africa. For at least two reasons Durban is distinguished from Johannesburg, Kimberley, or Cape Town by the uniquely colorful threads of musicians, regional styles, and ethnic traditions which it wove into the magnificent tapestry of South Africa's black music.

First, the presence of remarkably prosperous mission stations from as early as the mid-nineteenth century in Natal enabled a minute, but culturally vibrant, community of black landowners, merchants, teachers, and artisans to steep itself in British and Afro-American musical traditions, at the same time maintaining numerous links with the wider rural periphery. Reuben Caluza and his action songs are a classical product of this juncture as is the emergence of a black musical theater from the Mariannhill plays and Mthethwa's Lucky Stars.

Second, the syncretic blending of musical styles and performance practices has always been one of the strongest motors of urban musical change in Africa, and in this regard the industrial heartland around Johannesburg is beyond any doubt the main laboratory where migrants from throughout the subcontinent appropriated each other's repertoires of cultural symbols. In contrast and irrespective of the finer regional and stylistic shades of "Zulu music," Durban and Natal stand out as a musically relatively homogeneous area and the home to one of the most distinctive dialects within South Africa's black musical languages.

Durban's black musical history during the earlier decades of the twentieth century also serves as a reminder that musical history in South Africa and probably in Africa in general cannot be "read off" from abstracted social relations. Rather, black popular performance in Durban between 1913 and 1939 has structured social relations in the port town in ways that frequently work against an analysis of Durban's social history in class terms alone.

Four   "Horses in the Race Course":

The Domestication of

Ingoma Dance, 1929–1939

Riots and Dance Championships: The Meaning of Popular Culture

On a Saturday night in January 1930 several thousand African men clad in loincloths and the calico uniforms of domestic servants thronged a concert in the Workers' Hall of the Durban branch of the Industrial and Commercial Workers' Union (ICU) in Prince Edward Street. To the pounding sounds of hundreds of sticks, successive teams of dancers, some of them trained by union officials from the rural hinterland, rushed on to the stage and performed the virile, stamping _ingoma_ dance. The Zulu term _ingoma_ (literally, song) covers a broad range of male group dances like _isikhuze, isicathulo, ukukomika, isiZulu, isiBhaca, umzansi,_ and _isishameni._ The kinesic patterns of _ingoma_ are inseparably linked to choral songs in call-and-response structure, and as such constitute a complex statement of the unity of dance and song in Zulu performance culture.

The peak of Zulu-speaking migrants' dance culture, _ingoma_ evolved out of the profound transformation of traditional rural Zulu culture through impoverishment, dispossession, and labor migration around the time of the First World War. But on that night in January 1930, at the climax of the spectacle, the _ingoma_ dancers struck a particularly defiant note. British traveler and anthropologist Margery Perham, who had visited Durban to probe the prospects of liberal reform in South Africa, was shocked to hear an _ingoma_ song whose Zulu lyrics were regrettably not handed down, but which cannot have been any less belligerent than the English translation ICU leader A. W. G. Champion was whispering into her ear while the spectacle was in full swing:

> Who has taken our country from us?
> Who has taken it?
> Come out! Let us fight!

The land was ours. Now it is taken.
We have no more freedom left in it.
Come out and fight!
The land is ours, now it is taken.
Fight! Fight!
Shame on the man who is burnt in his hut!
Come and fight!

(Perham 1974:196)

The angry mood was fueled by a wave of protest that had been sweeping through the port town and the Natal countryside for several months. As we have seen, in June 1929 the unrest had culminated in a boycott of Durban's beer halls, which were controlled by a municipal brewing monopoly and had become widely resented as symbols of state oppression. Finally, on June 17 the campaign spilled over into open revolt when an angry mob of white vigilantes besieged a group of black protesters inside the ICU Workers' Hall and 6,000 Africans—many of them *ingoma* practitioners—came to their rescue. In the ensuing clashes between vigilantes, Africans, and police eight people were killed and more than 120 injured. Like all burghers startled by a sudden outburst of urban popular protest, the local authorities swiftly blamed the riots on ICU "agitators" as well as on a number of practices such as *ingoma* dancing not in favor with white Durbanites. In order to counter further unrest, A. W. G. Champion was deported from Durban, and a ban was ordered on, among other things, carrying sticks and *ingoma* dancing.

Almost to the day nine years later, in June-July 1939, the first "Natal Native Dancing Championships" were staged in Durban in which more than fifty *ingoma* teams participated. In his opening remarks the Administrator of Natal mused over three decades of "thought on the organised development of Native dancing," and evoked the day when *ingoma* competitions would be "conducive to the inculcation of that team spirit and healthy rivalry which we all know to be so valuable." The Chief Native Commissioner of Natal praised *ingoma* dancing as a "healthy form of exercise," and a lavish brochure persuaded the spectators that there were "no war dances today in Southern Africa," and that to call an *ingoma* dance a war dance would be "the equivalent of calling football military training."[1]

What had happened in the decade between 1929 and 1939 is the story of a remarkable transformation, of the domestication of *ingoma* dancing from a militant, oppositional, and suppressed form of popular culture to a tourist attraction. As such this metamorphosis occupies but a brief moment within the wider context of popular cultural dynamics in South Africa. But at the same time the role of *ingoma* in the 1929 riots touched one of the nerve centers of capitalist cultural transformation, and as such, perhaps not surprisingly, produced an extraordinary amount of official correspondence and documents.[2] What is to be gained from an examination of this material together with a number of other ancillary sources such as vintage gramophone records, oral testimony, and newspaper reports is an insight into the intertwining of socioeconomic change, political power, and popular culture during the turbulent early phases of capitalist development in South Africa. The transformation of *ingoma* was not simply the result of the working of some strategy of "social control" from above, nor indeed a question only of the wholesale acceptance of ruling-class cultural hegemony by the masses below. Together with other analyses of urban cultural dynamics such as Terence Ranger's landmark study on the East African *beni* (Ranger 1975), the early history of *ingoma* serves as a striking illustration of the processual and dynamic character of popular culture in Africa.

Migrant Laborers, Criminal Gangs, and the Transformation of Traditional Zulu Dance   Although the contours of Durban's popular performance idioms after the war and during the early 1920s are blurred by the lack of sufficient numbers of sound recordings from before 1930 as well as written and oral evidence, we can safely assume that rural dance forms continued to occupy a great deal of the leisure time of newly urbanized domestic servants and dockworkers. In order to understand the transformations that occurred in those ten years between 1929 and 1939, it is therefore necessary to direct our attention to African male dances in particular, one of the most powerful and most prominent symbols of working-class identity.

The majority of traditional Zulu dances were group activities that were embedded in and reflected the social and gender divisions within precapitalist Zulu society (Krige 1950:340–44; Rycroft 1975). The dances that white colonists tended to notice most were *amahubo* regimental dances, the most powerful expression of Zulu military might and group identity. One *amahubo* anthem that was sung shortly before the outbreak of the Anglo-Zulu War of 1879 must have so alarmed white settlers and officials that an English translation was even published in official colonial documents:

> There are the white people,
> let us fight them,
> let us commence first.
> Why should we look at them,
> and wait for them to begin.
> Let us Zulus commence.
>
> (*Further Correspondence*, 1879:74)

Although by the 1880s Zulu independent political power had been broken, the songs and dances still rang with antiwhite feelings and violence. Once removed from their precapitalist context and transformed into assertions of new regional or ethnic identities in the cities, these dances were received with considerable anxiety by white colonists. In particular, it was the alleged military connotations of the urban dancing collectively referred to as *ingoma* that stirred up white fears.

But the *ingoma* dances of the 1920s represented less the continuity of traditional performance genres within precolonial Zulu expressions of power and warfare than the complex interaction of traditional dance forms, labor migration, and missionization. In particular, *ingoma* is a product of the dramatic socioeconomic changes in Zulu society after the final downfall of the independent kingdom. In precolonial Zulu society the patrilineage was the main unit of production, and it was to a large extent self-sufficient. But these units also stood in a competition to each other which resulted from the independence of the self-reproducing homesteads and their organization in potentially opposing larger units, the districts. But this horizontal structure and its susceptibility to tensions was also subjected to a vertical system of age regimentation and loyalty to the king. While this system could not prevent the outbreak of horizontal, territorial conflict, it was able to mitigate such competition to a certain degree. In other words, the combination of interlineage and interdistrict opposition with vertical hierarchy in the precolonial Zulu kingdom was ultimately an element of social cohesion.[3]

But when the Zulu kingdom was finally destroyed in 1879, the age-regiment system lost its former function, and as a result it was no longer able to counteract the horizontal oppositions and territorial conflicts. With increasing dispossession and scarcity of land, what was once an element of precapitalist political cohesion could no longer be expressed and contained in legitimate ways. The traditional territorial tensions spilled over into so-called "faction fights" that pitted families and clans against each other in grim battles. It is under these circumstances that in parts of Zululand a mechanism was developed whereby this interdistrict tension was defused and channeled into a form of ritual expression called *umgangela*. This was an interdistrict competition of playful stick fighting (*ukudlala ngenduku*) staged by returning migrants and governed by a strict set of rules that, among other things, prohibited stabbing and other potentially lethal war techniques.

In the white farm areas adjoining the Msinga reserve, the situation was somewhat parallel, except that here new territorial boundaries had been drawn which in no way respected those of the traditional districts. These only survived as "phantom" districts in the minds of reserve dwellers who now derived certain rights such as grazing or simply employment on white farms from their belonging to one of these phantom districts. As a result of this, ferocious armed conflicts were not uncommon between workers on a farm which overlay two or more opposing phantom districts. In this situation a self-policing institution such as *umgangela* increasingly turned into an occasion for serious confrontation. And it is in yet another attempt to control such conflicts, Jonathan Clegg argues, that *ingoma* dance competitions arose in the Natal midlands (Clegg 1982:9).

Whether stick fighting or *ingoma*, these forms were essentially associated with migrant workers. It was they who also transported these ritualized conflicts into the cities where they automatically became what they were on white farms: expressions of competition by rural territorial units and districts for resources under the conditions of the urban labor market. Farm laborers in the Natal midlands such as Jubele "Lumbu" Dubazane, young migrants in Johannesburg, and dockworkers in Durban were responsible for redefining the group alliances, oppositions, and conflicts of the countryside as expressed in dances such as *umqonqo, indlamu, ingadla,* and *inkondlo* wedding dances in ways more congruous with the harsh realities of rural dispossession and proletarianization.

In their search for aesthetic models and expressions of self-conscious urban status, workers first became interested in the dances and songs developed in and around the mission stations. Interestingly, it was on rural mission stations that *isicathulo,* one of the first urban working-class dance forms, developed. Hugh Tracey maintains that the original *isicathulo* dance was "performed by Zulu pupils at a certain mission where the authorities had banned the local country dances." The name *isicathulo,* "shoe," reflects the introduction of footgear at the missions, the sharp sound of boots and the clicking of the heels contrasted with the muffled thud of bare feet in more rural dances such as *indlamu* (Tracey 1952:7).

Isicathulo dancing was featured regularly at mission and school concerts, and as late as 1916 "ragtime" composer Reuben T. Caluza enjoyed a particular renown as a skilled *isicathulo* dancer. Regardless, however, of such early evidence of the presumably middle-class origins of *isicathulo,* the determination of an exclusive class basis of this dance form is problematic. Rather, *isicathulo* offers an example of the intermingling of rural, urban, mission, and working-class performance traditions around the time of the First World War. As a step dance, it was closely related if not identical with other dance forms that had evolved earlier among farm laborers and inhabitants of the rural reserves. Foremost among these was *stishi* (stitches), a ragtime-inspired dance that spread from the Reef towns into rural areas as far afield as Paulpietersburg and influenced present-day dance routines also known as *stishi.*[4]

To the south of Durban, in Pondoland, Bhaca migrants developed a similar step dance, called *isiBhaca,* that some dance researchers alternatively regard as the prime source of either tap or gumboot dancing after the war. Clegg, for instance, maintains that as early as the 1880s Bhaca migrants brought the style to the Reef mines from where it filtered back to Durban. From the 1920s Bhaca workers also constituted an increasingly larger percentage of Durban's migrant labor force. Either way, it seems clear that around the time of the First World War, *isiBhaca* was danced in Durban's docks by stevedores and workers with rubber Wellington boots, and became generally known as "gumboot" dance.

Present-day *isicathulo* consists of routines like *Amaphoyisa* (policemen) and *Salutho* (salute) that mimic the behavior of black policemen and "boss boys," while patterns like *Benoni* or *Maritzburg* are named after their city of origin. In addition, *isicathulo* dancers frequently indulge in sophisticated solo stepping, prototypes of which had been available to migrant workers from the mid-1920s through Charlie Chaplin and Fred Astaire movies as well as touring black tap dance groups.

Another form of *ingoma* that arose from the experience of colonial conquest and police repression in town was *ukukomika.* Probably not unlike some *isicathulo* routines, it consisted of pantomime-like movements imitating and ridiculing Western army drills, and as such may have been inspired by *beni* in East and southern central Africa (Ranger 1975). Early in 1930 Margery Perham witnessed a display of *ukukomika* in the Durban Workers' Hall:

> One team did a dance founded on the British Tommy . . .
> They marched in ranks, formed fours, saluted, bringing their
> hands down with a resounding smack on their bare thighs,

carrying their sticks like rifles, whistling famous half-remembered tunes of the war. (Perham 1974:196).

But *ukukomika,* despite its comical component, also represented a more serious effort at appropriating the symbols of imperial warfare for the expression of Zulu workers' resistance. In any event, both aspects of *ukukomika* were two sides of the same coin and as such too sensitive to be acceptable to white residents. Thus when ICU leader Champion organized a display of *ingoma* for whites in December 1929, only a few months after the Durban riots, the military *ukukomika* was substituted with a more innocent satire of a tennis match! (Bradford 1987:333). But in general such smoothing over of the rougher manifestations of Zulu dance could do little to dispel white fears that the "dangerous" side of *ingoma* by far outweighed its "beneficial", self-policing effects.

The *umzansi* dance originated in the Ndwedwe and Mapumulo areas on the coast south of Durban and is often referred to as *isiZulu* or *indlamu*. Its aesthetic, like that of other group dances, is permeated with the tensions between dancers from different regions. These are given powerful expression in individual dance solos called *One-One* and contrast with the opening collective statement by the entire dance team moving in file. *Isishameni,* by contrast, favors vertical movements. A typical product of the *amagxagxa,* people who are neither traditionalists nor Christians, *isishameni* was the creation of a timber worker named Jubele Dubazane from near Colenso in Natal. Jubele combined the vertical body postures and stamping movements of *umqonqo* with *isicathulo* routines, at the same time introducing a new song style that incorporated the Wesleyan hymns used at weddings (*izingoma zomtshado*). *Isishameni* dancers consider themselves as soldiers (*amasoja*), and a great deal of the ethos of a performance is couched in military terms.[5]

The competitive dance events the labor migrants constructed around these genres not only helped to make sense of the experience of labor migration, but at the same time afforded an opportunity to assert ties of solidarity based on common regional and ethnic origin. As such, competitive dance performances contained both stabilizing and labor-disrupting elements. The opposition between sections of the work force based on ethnic or regional affiliation, for instance, could be effectively used to block collective identification as workers. Mine owners, the Witwatersrand Native Labour Association, and some large Durban employers therefore organized spectacular dance competitions from at least 1921 (see fig. 10). On the other hand, violent opposition remained an impor-

Figure 10. A dance competition organized by the Witwatersrand Native Labour
Association, 1921 (Johannesburg, Africana Museum)

tant component of competitive *ingoma* dancing that was difficult to
control from above. Public opinion on clashes between rivaling *ingoma*
teams was usually divided. One missionary, who only desired "the best
things possible for the native," reasoned that "native dances, combined
with strong drink, battle axes, and other dangerous instruments form a
combination which the natives themselves and Europeans should fear."[6]
The Director of Native Labour, for his part, denied that "native dances are
in themselves bad," adding that some mine compound managers were
"decidedly against the system of visiting teams and competitive dances as
tending to give rise to too much rivalry and excitement and resentment at
being adjudged losers in competitions."[7]

The point, however, that both the missionary and the Director of
Native Labour were missing is that *ingoma* dancing was the cultural cor-
relate of the "political economy of tribal animosity" among migrant
workers (Phimister and van Onselen 1979). The conflicts between dance
teams, in ritualized competitive performance as well as during the ensuing violent clashes, were not the result of age-old clan and tribal antagonisms, but rather stemmed from the mobilization of networks of kin and
regional solidarity under the highly competitive conditions of the urban
labor market. Thus the violent aspects of *ingoma* dancing which some

nervous burghers attributed to the combined effects of liquor and "excitement," to more perceptive observers of African leisure-time activities more accurately appeared as the result of the military and criminal aspects of urban forms of youth organization and their cross-linkages with *ingoma* dancing.

In fact, analyses that trace the origins of *ingoma* to *umgangela* stick-fighting rituals of rural youths (Clegg 1982, 1984) are congruous with attempts to understand criminal organizations among domestic servants in terms of struggles over employment opportunities. From the turn of the century, Durban's African migrant population, numbered at 18,000, increasingly produced a stratum of young migrants who were the most vulnerable and hence least successful sector of the nascent working class in adapting to the capitalist socioeconomic order. Many of these newcomers, variously called *abaqhafi* or *amagxagxa,* translated the trauma of proletarianization into a set of rigid organizational patterns whose focal points were the *amalaita* gangs.[8] *Amalaita* gangs specialized in theft, robbery, and attacks on white residents and recruited their members predominantly from the ranks of young domestic servants, the "kitchen workers," whom J. M. H. Nyandeni, a prominent dance leader of the 1930s, identified as the main adherents of *ingoma* dancing.[9] Mainly operating after hours and without the slightest suspicion on the part of their "madams," during the day *amalaita* signaled their presence in the streets of Durban by defiantly carrying sticks and wearing bright uniforms and by frequent public displays of *ingoma* dancing.

Thus if official suspicions that *ingoma* dancers were little more than disguised *amalaita* were probably overstated, they correctly assumed the cultural continuity between rural forms of socialization among youths and expressions of ethnic group rivalry in the countryside and within the evolving urban work force. Although by no means all *ingoma* amateurs were *amalaita,* the group activities of gangs and *ingoma* dancers shared a common set of mostly military symbols inherited from the precolonial past and the experience of impoverishment, emasculation, and intraclass antagonisms.

But *ingoma* not only formed the core of migrants' leisure-time activities and overlapped with the group symbols of criminal gangs. Long after the destruction of the Zulu kingdom and when independent African power had become but a distant memory, these dances continued to resonate in the minds of dockworkers, domestic servants, and farmhands with the glory of the Zulu heritage. Above all the songs articulated the most deep-seated desires of the expelled, dehumanized, and dispossessed black masses: the cry for land, the longing to regain the land the fore-fathers had lost to the white settlers. And it was precisely these thousands of landless from the reserves, the "yawning crack that empties forth human beings,"[10] that formed the rank and file of the ICU. It was the dockworkers and 9,000 domestic servants in the port town who by dancing *ingoma* demonstrated that they wished to be subjects of chiefs rather than "boys" "nagged in the kitchen by white housewives" (Perham 1974:200).

The Union, "The Real Thing," and a Sunday Outing   The ICU had been founded in 1919 by Clement Kadalie as a dockworkers' union in Cape Town. By the late 1920s it had grown into the first black mass organization in South African history whose Natal branch under the leadership of A. W. G. Champion alone claimed a membership of some 50,000 Africans.[11] For such an organization it was natural, therefore, that the cultural background of its rank-and-file membership should have strongly conditioned its cultural activities and made it into one of the strongest motors of black South African popular culture. *Ingoma,* in particular, seemed to be the supreme embodiment of these class and cultural backgrounds; it was indeed, as Champion acknowledged, the "real thing" (Perham 1974:198).

At the same time, as an intellectual whose family boasted of having long adopted European standards, Champion had his own views about a modern, black urban culture, and hence ICU activities also reflected the salaried leadership's own class-based preferences. ICU-sponsored cultural events in Natal and Durban featured hymns and organ playing by well-dressed officials, ballroom dances, *isicathamiya* choirs, and brass bands. These genres and symbols, then, were not narrow, class-linked institutions, but reflected the cultural osmosis among South Africa's black strata and the fragmented and ambiguous nature of class formation in the port town. At the same time, the fusion of cultural symbols helped to strengthen black political cohesion, as well as the ideological hegemony of union leaders over the rank and file by suggesting their own cultural practices as models for the successful black citizen.

But both working-class unity and upward social mobility also conflicted with white notions of the ideal black subject. Certainly, the Durban riots had turned a new page in the history of Durban's working-class struggles. But they also brought into sharper relief the contours of a substantial and permanently urbanized working class, whose forms of cultural expression were increasingly being perceived as potentially detrimental to ruling-class hegemony. As a result, the riots also ushered in an era of increased attempts to mold the emerging working-class cultural practices in ways more attuned to ruling-class notions of popular urban culture.

Among the lighter tasks completed by the Commission on Native Riots investigating the disturbances in Durban was a Sunday afternoon outing at Cartwrights Flats and an evening at the ICU Hall in Prince Edward Street. Champion had invited the members of the commission to persuade themselves of the harmless character of *ingoma* dances and to get the local authorities to lift the ban on *ingoma*. [12] The Sunday tea party probably contributed to the insight that *ingoma* was one of the core leisure activities of Durban's laboring poor and as such contained both labor-disruptive elements as well as stabilizing components. In its final report the De Waal and Native Affairs Commissions recommended a more refined strategy to diffuse popular discontent by appointing a Native Welfare Officer and channeling substantial funds into African welfare.

The recommendations were part of a package of much harsher measures aimed at tighter control of alternative, autonomous forms of popular entertainment. Thus in February 1932 the town council closed down, inter alia, all dance halls, drinking dens, and meeting places in the inner-city district and at the same time decided to lift the ban on *ingoma* dancing events "on condition that they were held at a venue to be decided on by the Town Council, and that regulations were drawn up governing the conduct of the persons taking part, and appointing the dates and times that the various participants were to perform."[13] Dance teams greeted this change of attitude with some satisfaction, and some leaders eagerly if somewhat prematurely anticipated the creation of a special dance site with floodlights and a neatly cut lawn. Provision was also to be made for admission fees, a measure, so team leader J. M. H. Nyandeni assured the town clerk, which would keep undesirable spectators out and help "to have rowdyism put to an end in Durban."[14] By February 1932 Durban's Native Welfare Officer Sidney Shepstone was able to report that the "experiment" had been successful, dancing having been organized on most Sunday afternoons on one of the football fields at the Native Recreation Grounds in Somtseu Road. Finally in June, on Shepstone's initiative, the dance teams held a meeting at the Snell Parade Police Station that led to the formation of an association of dance teams presided over by a disciplinary committee and the team leaders (*amagoso*).[15]

Notwithstanding some minor incidents of violence, by 1933 relations between dance teams and the police had reached a previously unknown height, for some teams were happy to rehearse and perform in front of the adjoining Native Police Barracks! Crowds of up to 3,000 spectators were regularly drawn to the spectacle, and what in previous years might have appeared to paranoid burgesses as an intimidating gathering of bellicose men in "traditional" garb was now clearly and much to the relief of the chief constable "having a beneficial effect in drawing Natives away from the centre of the town during week-ends."[16]

Yet if the chief constable was looking forward to a "white" city center, the dance teams were not uniformly prepared to accept the domesticized format that had been grafted onto workers' traditional expressive forms of group rivalry. On October 7, 1934, the teams of Mameyiguda Zungu, a stevedore at the Point and leading *ingoma* dancer, and Makulesekopo Shandu clashed violently in a dispute over access to the dancing ground. Shandu's men, apparently trying to settle old scores with Zungu from the previous weekend, forced their way onto the ground where they got locked into a fierce stick fight with their opponents. Shandu's dancers were eventually driven off the field only to return moments later, bombarding Zungu's group with stones that left two spectators seriously injured.[17] Dances were only resumed on November 4, but by this time the "Regulations Governing Ingoma Dances" had specified further restrictions including the prohibition of marching in formation, singing *amahubo* regimental songs, and performing the challenging *giya* steps.[18] As late as 1935 *ingoma* performances were treated as potentially dangerous whenever they involved the display of allegiance to traditional chiefs. Thus Champion's intention to stage an *ingoma* dance as a welcome to Chief Mavutwa Gumede was viewed with disfavor unless conducted under police supervision at the recreation grounds.[19]

The fact that *ingoma* had become officially accepted as a legitimate form of black urban recreation by no means pleased all sectors of the black elite in like manner. *Ingoma* dancing was still viewed by many as a vestige of the "uncivilized," "heathen" past that stood in the way of a full integration into modern South African society. Black intellectuals, artisans, school teachers, and other educated black urban dwellers rightly suspected that by testing the acceptance of "traditional" and "non-Christian" forms of cultural expression among Durban's middle strata, the philosophy behind the new urban political line in reality was to check black cultural assimilation and to demonstrate the possibilities of racial and cultural segregation. Thus while one black critic applauded the respect the mining industry was giving to "tribal custom and traditions in the compounds,"[20] another bemoaned the fact that "stark-naked men are to be seen in the streets strutting about, with as much unconcern, as if they were in the reserves." The solution, according to the latter observer, was that there was "no objection to war dances, provided they are staged by the enlightened Bantu. When they are staged by the uncivilized, it is a sign of retrogression, because finding his performances so patronised, he has no inducement to progress."[21]

But regardless of the fact that the city council had been able to register such partial victories in domesticating *ingoma,* and unmoved by middle-class apprehensions about stark-naked men, *ingoma* dancers continued to express in submerged form the animosities of the countryside as, for instance, in *Sokushaya Isangquma* (You Will Be Struck by Hailstones), a faction fighting song by Inkumba Emfece led by Mnandi Zama:

Imikhombe iyenanana.
Sokushaya isangquma.
Lezonduku zonanana.

A bad turn deserves another.
You will be struck by hailstones.
These sticks of yours will meet ours stroke for stroke.[22]

Nor were *ingoma* protagonists such as Mameyiguda impressed by black middle-class models of cultural assimilation. Although *ingoma* songs were indebted to Christian wedding hymns, Mameyiguda's song *uSatane uyangilandela* (Satan Is Following Me) (HMV JP 12), for instance, ridicules the hymns of Durban's black Christian community:

USathane uyangilandela.
Nangu naye eduze!
Ho, Nkonyane yendlovu.
Nangu naye eduze!

Satan is following me.
Here he is near me.
O, Calf of the Elephant,
Here he is near![23]

Durban's white councilors were probably not equipped to understand such subtle working-class critique of their black middle-class allies. But the more experienced engineers of "social control" such as the NWO Shepstone might have discovered yet another, less obvious advantage of domesticized *ingoma* performance. For the provision of separate forms of recreation—*ingoma* for "the Tribal Native" and football for "the de-tribalised Native"[24]—reinforced existing class distinctions within Durban's black strata. Parodies such as Mameyiguda's song distanced Durban's laboring masses from the ideological hegemony of the black intelligentsia, and expressed the real obstacles to a black, popular class alliance.

The domestication of *ingoma* dancing was the overture to much more concerted and comprehensive attempts by the local government and some Durban companies at a complete redefinition of the terms of reproduction of the labor force. Bakers Bakery, for instance, supported soccer and *ingoma* teams, and after 1931 maintained a recreation hall. This venue—thus Native Commissioner H. S. Fynn in his opening address—promoted "good fellowship" and "pleasant rivalry," and offered concerts by comedian Ndaba Majola, bioscope shows, and *isicathamiya* competitions.[25] But the domestication of *ingoma* and other forms of popular entertainment was by no means complete until the end of the decade. Since at least 1938 plans to build an *ingoma* arena had been mooted by NAD officials and Broadcasting Director Hugh Tracey,[26] not without causing some disquiet among a great number of *ingoma* dancers led by Mameyiguda (see fig. 11). Apart from being an acknowledged dance leader, Mameyiguda was much in demand with the Durban broadcasting studio, and in 1932 he had recorded a whole range of traditional and *ingoma* songs for His Master's Voice.[27] He was thus well aware of his own commercial prospects and suspicious of moves to build the arena.

Acting through Champion and backed by some Native Advisory Board members, Mameyiguda expressed the fears of twenty-six dance leaders that "they will be like race horses in the race course who run and break their legs but [are] not paid anything for their trouble."[28] Notwithstanding official assurances of the noncommercial nature of the proposed scheme, the *amagoso* threatened to withdraw from *ingoma* dancing unless they were "advised as to how much money [they] will be paid for such services rendered."[29] Although the arena failed to materialize, a committee composed only of whites was eventually able to disperse Mameyiguda's doubts and to stage the first "Natal Native Dancing Championships" in June-July 1939 in which more than fifty teams participated free of change

One of the most readily observable results of the restructuring of *ingoma* was the emergence of a completely new type of "traditional" dance regalia. Prior to the Dancing Championships most dance troupes in Durban had preferred vividly colored cloth skirts and a cape-like shoulder covering over a pair of long trousers, vests, and car-tire sandals. When the white organizers of the spectacle suggested that more "traditional"-look-

FIGURE 11. Mameyiguda and his dance troupe, ca. 1933 (EMI Archives)

ing regalia be worn to enhance the visual impact of the dancing with tourists, most teams readily adopted a completely different outfit of animal skins, sticks, and shields that now forms the standard *ingoma* "uniform" (Thomas 1988:198f.).

At a less conspicious level the domestication of *ingoma* and its incorporation into the Dancing Championships also implied a shift of the site of conflict among dance troupes to more "official" terrain thereby changing both the symbolic manifestation of ritualized conflict and the type of opposing factions involved. As Harold Thomas argues, by 1940 a deep rift had evolved between more factory-based *ingoma* troupes and those composed mainly of domestic workers.[30] The former had a distinct advantage over the latter, because their employers provided regalia and, more significantly, as residents of the same compound they had more opportunity for regular practice. As a result of this, the factory-based troupes won all the prizes at the 1939, 1940, and 1941 Dancing Championships, a fact which greatly angered the troupes comprised of domestic workers. And to add insult to injury, from 1950 the Bantu Administration Department insisted on the latter teams being formed into five composite troupes that would match in size and hence in spectacle the five participating factory-based troupes.

If official complacency did much to reinforce internal antagonisms within Durban's *ingoma* scene, some dance leaders developed their own tactics of maintaining their teams' *esprit de corps*. The career of July M. illustrates this quite clearly. July had been a senior member of Mameyiguda's troupe before he succeeded him as chairman of the Amagoso Committee in 1949. But July was an "independent thinker" (Thomas 1988:157); he frequently clashed with the municipal authorities on matters such as the maintenance of the dancing grounds and admission fees, and at one point even increased the latter unilaterally. But as an acknowledged spokesman of the domestic-worker faction, July resented the official preference given to the factory teams and on occasion delayed the payment of prize money to these troupes.

Evidently, for all the NAD's skillful maneuvering, the domestication of *ingoma* was also made possible by the rivalry between dance teams. The opposition between dance groups was one of the main sources of the *ingoma* aesthetic, and over the years some of the more apt dance leaders had been successfully manipulating official control mechanisms in order to strengthen their own positions. Similarly, the commercial exploitation of dance competitions in part agreed with the traditional ethos and aesthetic norms of preindustrial Zulu performance whereby individual social status was enhanced through the demonstration of competence in performance. Thus in forging a new urban dance culture migrant workers in Durban were never simply the victims of the "system"; the domestication of *ingoma* required consent and at the very least had to be part of a process of negotiation.

Postlude: "Self-Disciplined Citizens"   The debate over the content and role of "traditional" dancing in South African society continued until the late 1940s. Thus it is perfectly in the logic of the linkages between South African political history and the ideological discourse about urban popular culture that when the Nationalist government came to power in 1948 and announced its program of apartheid, the National Education Department launched a debate on "The Preservation of African Music and Dancing" in the pages of its *Native Teachers' Journal*. Traditional dancing, some teachers argued, was a "retrograde step in the onward march of the Native people," while others deplored the "laxity in the matter of sex" in *ingoma* songs. Apart from the editor himself, only a minority of teachers were more in favor of the project of incorporating *ingoma* and other dances into school curricula, suggesting that only the tunes should be taught and used "in gardening as practice for road digging and mining." The department, for its part, formulated the need for an "adaptation of African dancing to conform with the ideals of Christian civilization." With the view to "produce citizens who are socially adaptable, self-disciplined, physically fit and well-developed," department officials such as musicologist Percival Kirby encouraged the "less suggestive Native dances."[31]

It was clearly these socially adaptable and self-disciplined citizens that had long been the dream of South African capital, and thus the idea to use *ingoma* dancing as a form of social control won an increasingly larger following. From the time of the Second World War numerous mines on the Witwatersrand as well as the larger Durban companies such as Huletts S. A. Refineries, Dunlop, Lever Brothers, John Orrs, and the S. A. Railways supported *ingoma* dance teams.[32] The Chamber of Mines currently even maintains a 2,500 seat dance arena at its Gold Mine Museum in Johannesburg that is being advertised as follows: "Everyone is hot-footing it to the African Tribal Dancing these days! A 2,500 seat arena is the happy stamping ground on Sundays for jubilant African mineworkers."[33]

But the resurgence of "tribal dancing" in the service of officially decreed social peace is not the last chapter in the tale about *ingoma*, "tradition," and popular performance in South Africa. On May Day 1985, in Durban's Kingsmead Stadium where sometimes *ingoma* dancers entertain tourists, an *ingoma* team trained by an official of the independent black trade union COSATU danced to the thundering applause of thousands of workers.

Five　　　　　　　"An African Star": Reuben

T. Caluza and Early Popular

Music in South Africa

When it comes to black popular musical traditions, South African musicology has never made for a pretty picture. One representative product of South African musicological endeavor, the *South African Music Encyclopedia*, while offering detailed information on a plethora of white musicians, sweeps over the creative work of generations of black musicians in a rubric as obscure as "Bantu Music" and in a dozen or so entries on classical composers. One South African musicologist, writing about Durban in the same compendium, has the following to say about Durban's black musical history: "There had been Zulu choirs since the late nineteenth century and some had been on overseas tours, but very little individual talent emerged" (Jackson 1979:436).

If this rather somber picture is now receiving some radical revision as researchers retrieve the work and lives of such remarkable individual talents as John Bhengu (Phuz'shukela), Mameyiguda Zungu, Enoch Mzobe, and Edwin Mkhize, one composer more than any other needs to be looked at from a fresh perspective. Reuben Tholakele Caluza was arguably one of the most colorful and popular musicians of the 1910s and 1920s, but with the exception of David Coplan's *In Township Tonight!* he never received more than some polite and perfunctory treatment in encyclopedias, journals, and academic theses (e.g., de Beer 1967). A thorough examination of his life and work therefore still needs to be attempted. But to do this we first have to familiarize ourselves with the history of Natal in the late nineteenth century and with some South African geography.

"A Very Small Village
of Christians":
Caluza's Family and
Birthplace Siyamu

"The road out of Pietermaritzburg goes past
Machibise and through Malinyane; then one
follows this route to Edendale, heading for the
Umsunduze River; Siyamu is in this vicinity."
This is how, in his novel *Indlela Yababi* (The Way
of the Wicked), the poet and journalist Rolfes R. R. Dhlomo describes
Siyamu, home to some of South Africa's most remarkable musicians and
poets of the earlier decades of this century. It is into this "very small village of Christians" (Dhlomo 1947:1) that Reuben Tholakele Caluza was
born on November 14, 1895, the only child of Mordecai Caluza and his
wife, Mejile née Nxele.

Almost half a century earlier, in 1847, the Presbyterian missionary
James Allison had led some four hundred and fifty people whom he had
converted in Swaziland to Edendale. Among his first converts was Reuben Caluza's great-grandfather Reuben Inhlela "Tuyana" Caluza. His
exact date of birth and birthplace are unknown, but since he was born of
Hlubi stock among the Tlokwa under their chief Sekonyela, his ancestors
must have been among those displaced by Shaka's military expansion,
seeking refuge in an area of what is now the Orange Free State. It is here,
in the 1830s, that the Rev. Allison converted Reuben Tuyana and took
him and several other families to Swaziland and finally to Edendale.

Reuben Tuyana and his wife Susan had two sons: Isaac Silevana,
born in 1840 in Lesotho, and John Masibekela Mlungunyama, born soon
after the arrival of Allison's congregation in Edendale. Isaac, who later
became a leader in the Zulu Congregational Church, had two sons:
Joshua and Mjeli. They ran Caluza Brothers, a bicycle shop in downtown
Pietermaritzburg, but not much else is known about that branch of the
Caluza family. As for John Masibekela, he and his wife Sarah, née Zondi,
occupied a farm called Samvula or Falkland. Like most of the land at
Edendale occupied by Africans, the farm was purchased from a white
farmer and was valued at more than £300. John and Sarah had twelve
children, two of whom died as infants. The lives and careers of some of
the remaining offspring, however, give us an idea of the intellectual and
emotional climate in which the young Reuben Tholakele grew up.[1]

Only Mordecai Caluza, the oldest son of John and Sarah and Reuben Tholakele's father, remained in Siyamu. He worked on his father's
farm and taught in the local mission school, while his wife Mejile Nxele
spent a good deal of the week in Pietermaritzburg as a domestic worker.
Although most of Mordecai's siblings never completely cut their ties with

Genealogy of the Caluza family

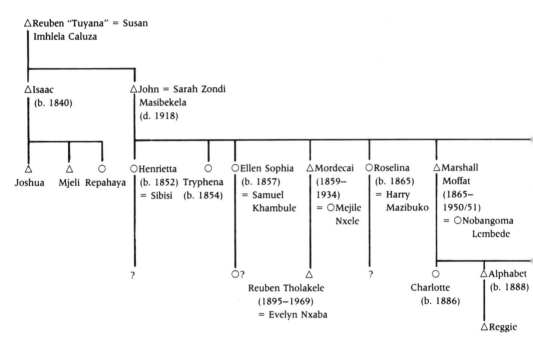

their rural home, some came to occupy the sparse top positions in the urban social fabric that were available to blacks at the time. Michael Caluza, for instance, first worked as a teacher in the Pietermaritzburg Presbyterian Church before he moved to Johannesburg in 1907. Here he was eventually ordained a minister of the Ethiopian church in 1918 under its head H. R. Ngcayiya. His older brother Marshall Moffat first worked on his father's farm before he, too, moved to Johannesburg in 1898. Here he first worked as a colportage wagon driver for the British and Foreign Bible Society. At some time before the Anglo-Boer War he joined the Plymouth Brethren, however, only to form his own small "Ethiopian-type" church, the Christian Brethren Meeting, in 1912. For a living, Moffat ran the Caluza Printing Press, a moderately successful enterprise with a monthly average turnover of £12. In 1930 he lost his church building and lodgings in the city and moved to Eastern Native Township where he seems to have intensified his clergical work within

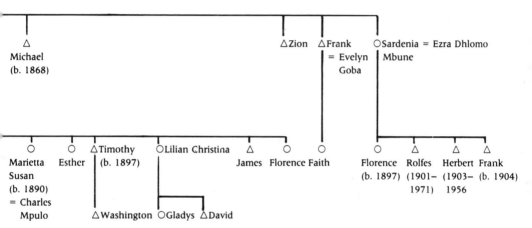

the ANC as leader of the United National Church of Africa in 1937. He died in Johannesburg in 1950 or 1951.

Most of John and Sarah Caluza's daughters did what was expected from girls brought up in the sociocultural climate of a place like Edendale: they married young men from one of the respected and prosperous farming families at Siyamu. Ellen Sophia, for example, married into the Khambule family, and although not much is known about her husband Samuel's property, the Khambules, along with the Msimangs, belonged to Natal's wealthiest African landowners. The marriage of Sardinia Mbune to Ezra Dhlomo proved to be a particularly productive one, if not in number of offspring but in their accomplishments: of the five children, two sons, Rolfes Robert Reginald (1901–71) and Herbert Isaac Ernest (1903–56), became important poets and cultural leaders.

Teaching, farming, and preaching—these then were the main pursuits of a family of proud men and women, whose thinking revolved around two core concepts of mid-Victorian ideology: "progress" and "improvement." There was hardly a black community in Natal that could be seen to embody these values in a more perfect way than Edendale. English visitors to Edendale felt that the village was "a piece of Yorkshire" (Statham 1881:182), and, indeed, English values saturated its everyday practices "to the extent that they would become common sense for the people under its sway" (Magubane 1979:55f.). Music was not only one of the main focal points of socialization and leisure-time activities in Edendale; it was a worldview. Choral music, in particular, contained "an assurance of civilized advancement,"[2] and the extent to which Edendale residents were devoted to musical performance as an expression of "civilized advancement" can be gauged from one of the most memorable cultural and political events in the annals of the community.

Inspired by Orpheus McAdoo's troupe of Jubilee Singers that had visited Pietermaritzburg in 1891 and its African counterpart, the South African Choir, Saul Msane and a group of fourteen Edendale residents billed themselves as the "Zulu Choir" (see fig. 12) and traveled under white management to London in April 1892. The tour turned sour when the managers requested the group to pose as "Zulu warriors" and to per-

FIGURE 12. The Zulu Choir in Edendale, ca. 1892.
Back row, 6th from left: Saul Msane.

form in traditional garb at the London Aquarium in a show advertised as "From the Wilds to Westminster." Through their mouthpiece *Inkanyiso Yase Natal,* mission-educated Africans alleged that by acceding to these requests the choir was misrepresenting the aspirations of black Christians and "showing the English public how like savage heathen they can become, and how unlike civilized men and Christians."[3] Accompanied by a great deal of controversy and legal complications, Saul Msane and four singers eventually left the troupe and returned to South Africa, performing in Natal as the "Zulu Christian Choir."[4]

Caluza's Early Years Such conflicts were symptomatic of a community whose members were continually caught between two worlds—traditional Zulu and colonial society—neither of which was prepared to accept them fully. Thus despite the overwhelming sense of self-confidence that permeated Reuben's childhood, this ambiguity was to shape profoundly the destiny of Siyamu in the 1890s. In addition, Reuben's childhood began to be overshadowed by events of much grander dimensions. The rinderpest of 1896–97 and the traumatic effects of the Bambatha rebellion of 1906—Reuben was only eleven years old—transformed social relations in Siyamu as well as the consciousness of its inhabitants. They sounded the death knell of the old generation of Natal's black landowners and rang in a new dawn for what Caluza's cousin Herbert Dhlomo later called the "generation of huts and slums."[5]

The careers of the more prominent members of the Caluza family are deeply marked by the transition between these two eras. Thus, Moffat and his son Alphabet were exempted from native law, a privilege which the colonial administration granted to a minority of landowning literate blacks, and so were the younger brother Frank and his wife Evelyn (née Goba), a graduate of the Inanda Seminary. (Frank and Evelyn's only daughter, Faith, presently lives in Imbali township near Edendale, an accomplished singer and pianist in her own right, and as Tholakele's closest relation she is the most important surviving source of information on the composer's life.) In 1913, however, when the Native Lands Act was passed, Reuben's great-uncle Isaac had to realize that Natal was indeed "no longer a black man's country" when he unsuccessfully applied for permission to purchase land.[6] Isaac Caluza was the first but not the last of the Caluzas to lose confidence in black advance under white rule: Frank became an active leader in the Durban branch of the ANC, Michael joined the African Methodist Episcopal church (AME), while Alphabet became an ardent propagandist of the Industrial and Commercial Workers' Union

(Bradford 1987:96). None of these organizations seriously challenged the foundations of the existing social order, but they provided a forum in which black political perspectives could develop. This intellectual environment and the transition from the roots in an independent peasant community of *amakholwa* to the experience of increasing rural impoverishment and political regimentation form the background to Reuben Caluza's early years between 1895 and 1912.

Reuben received his primary education at the Presbyterian church school in Pietermaritzburg, and it is here that he first began to show signs of an unusual musical prowess. Music had always occupied a special place in the social life of the Caluzas. Reuben's grandfather John, for example, had even acquired the unusual skills of conducting the church choir as well as reading and writing staff notation. Both of Reuben's uncles Moffat and Zion played the organ, that "icon of respectability" for the educated Christian elite, to use an expression by Jim Campbell, which adorned most parlors in Edendale. Mordecai Caluza was not only fond of music, but also quick to realize his son's talents. He bought a portable organ for Reuben, and although Reuben did not receive formal tuition, he was soon considered one of the finest keyboard players in Natal.[7] Whether Reuben already played the cornet, baritone horn, and other brass instruments in which he later became keenly interested remains uncertain.[8] But what seems clear is the fact that the young Reuben was an excellent vocalist and versatile instrumentalist with a keen sense for experimentation.

Despite the ubiquitous organs, brass instruments, and church hymns, Reuben's Edendale home was not completely closed off musically from more traditional Zulu performance practices. Thus the folk songs and dance songs of the late nineteenth century formed an integral part of Reuben's musical socialization—as did more Westernized performance genres. Popular dances such as *umqumqumbelo* were regular activities of Edendale youth, and Caluza soon earned a reputation as a skilled *isicathulo* dancer.[9] Whether at this time the *isicathulo* performed at the missions was distinct from the one popular on the Durban docks is relatively insignificant in view of the fact that, unlike previous composers, Caluza's musical education spanned the whole spectrum of black performance culture regardless of class or regional origin. "He valued," recalls Ohlange choir member Selina Khuzwayo, "every music that was done by anybody."

Reuben's musical socialization, however, took a sudden turn when he entered the Ohlange Institute as a boarder in 1908 or 1909. The

Ohlange Institute had been one of Natal's most active centers of middle-class musical life (chapter 3). But it was the arrival of the thirteen-year-old Caluza, in particular, that seemed to spark the formation of a number of highly appraised ensembles. By 1910 Caluza had organized the boys' choir, the Royal Singers, that competed successfully in and around Durban, and formed his own male quartet that consisted at one point of Samuel Makhanya, D. Opperman, Moses Nkukhu, and Caluza himself. In 1911 he also led a drum-and-fife ensemble that was raising funds for the school.[10]

"Sweet and Patriotic Songs": Ragtime and African Nationalism   Caluza had not quite completed his studies at Ohlange when the black peasantry was shaken to the roots by one of the harshest pieces of legislation in South African history. The Native Lands Act of 1913 robbed masses of African landowners and squatters of their rural base of subsistence, but it also sparked off black opposition to the act which soon culminated in the foundation of the South African Native National Congress in 1912. During the first decades of its existence the SANNC, later to be named the African National Congress (ANC), remained a conservative, middle-class association of people of rank whose cultural activities reflected the ideological straitjackets of Durban's minute black elite. Music, too, had been an important component of early nationalist discourse since the early 1870s. In Durban the young ANC formed a music committee consisting of John Dube, W. J. Makhanya, A. J. Mthethwa, Henry S. Nkwanyana, Charles Cele, and S. Khumalo, which organized a series of fund-raising concerts before it eventually sank into anonymity.[11]

Unlike some of the younger musicians such as William Mseleku, Caluza was not a politically minded man. He never joined the ANC and did not perceive the articulation of popular protest as a form of organized political response. But as a "very moralistic" man and person of conservative instinct, he was sensitive to any injustice.[12] It was this blend of moderate nationalism with a moral, Christian viewpoint that became the main spiritual source of his songs.

Caluza composed his first published song, "Silusapho Lwase Afrika" (We Are the Children of Africa) (HMV GU 11), at the age of seventeen.[13]

> *Silusapho lwase Afrika.*
> *Sikhalela izwe lakhithi.*
> *Zulu nomXhosa noMsuthu hlanganani sikala ngeLand Act.*

> We are the children of Africa.
> We are crying for our land.
> Zulus, Xhosas, Sothos unite over the Lands Act issue. . . .

"Silusapho Lwase Afrika" was adopted as the official anthem of the
SANNC in 1913 and was followed in quick succession by a set of further
songs promoting the Congress and calling for national unity: "Vulindhlela Mtaka Dube" (Pave the Way, Dube) (HMV GU 5), "Bashuka
Ndabazini" (What Is Congress Saying?) (HMV GU 42), and "Yekan' Umona Nenzondo" (Don't Be Jealous) (HMV GU 3). In terms of musical
genre and political imagery, these songs are best understood as anthems,
or in Benedict Anderson's apt phrase, as the "echoed physical realization
of the imagined community" (Anderson 1983:132). In terms of technique, they are indebted to the older generation of choir composers such
as John K. Bokwe and Enoch Sontonga. The latter is remembered as the
composer of the national anthem "Nkosi Sikelel iAfrika," a hymn-like
tune composed in 1903. According to Sontonga's biographer Mweli
Skota, the song so moved John Dube that he asked for permission to use it
for his Ohlange choirs. Over the years the song became popular and
eventually replaced Caluza's "Silusapho" as official anthem of the ANC in
1919 (Skota n.d.:78; Walshe 1971:204).

Caluza's early nationalist songs are a good example of the futility of
bringing plain structural approaches to bear upon analyses of popular
black music in South Africa. An etic analysis of the surface structure in
these compositions would indeed bring to light only a limited number of
technical resources. Additional insight, however, from an historical and
anthropological investigation into black South African cultural dynamics
shows that in a country where the appropriation of elements of the
hegemonic culture by a subordinate class of blacks was received with
panic by the dominant white society, black achievement to a large extent
had to be couched in defensive, assimilationist language. Barred from
being different and at the same time being suspected of wanting to be
"black Englishmen," black South African cultural innovators were indeed negotiating a difficult path that rarely met with approval from their
white mentors. Thus Percival Kirby and other South African musicologists claims that Bokwe's, Sontonga's, and Caluza's compositions
were "without a trace of the devices used by European composers to mitigate the 'squareness' of the design or to inject vitality into the melody or
character into the harmony" (Kirby 1979:94). Such harsh criticism was
of course motivated by racial prejudice and misinterpreted the composers' intentions. Such compositions, as John Blacking noted, are not

examples of "'black Englishmen' applauding the music of the dominant culture" (Blacking 1969:48). Nor are they simply the products of untalented, minor composers with a poor grounding in formal Western music education. As Blacking observed, the appropriation of the triads and cadences of European hymn tunes "expressed the new relationships and values of urban groups, who expected fuller participation in the social and political life of the community into which they had been drawn economically" (Blacking 1980a:198).

But the use of such fundamental techniques of Western composition was by no means unambiguous. For the musical idiom that signaled black nationalist aspirations also served to express loyalty toward the British. Thus "Bayete" (Hail, Your Majesty) (HMV GU 12), composed in honor of the Prince of Wales's visit to South Africa in 1925, combines a triadic melodic structure with lyrics that a reviewer called "loyal to the core":[14]

> *Bayete nkosi.*
> *Mtwana sakubona.*
> *Z'yaku bingelel' ingane zako!*
> *Bayete nkosi.*
>
> We salute your majesty.
> Your children are saluting you.
> Rule us, your children!
> Salute, your majesty!

In 1915 Caluza completed his studies and joined the staff at Ohlange at an annual salary of £40. Within a short time he took over the leadership of the Ohlange Choir from Lingard D. Bopela, a future ICU activist, and within two years transformed the choir into one of the country's ablest performing groups. The history of the Ohlange Choir began in 1908 when John Dube tried to alleviate the strained financial situation of his college by taking a brass band on fund-raising concert tours. The idea proved successful, and from at least 1912 the choir undertook similar tours of the major Natal towns as well as Johannesburg. By 1917 these tours had become annual events and included Reef compounds and mining centers.[15]

Countrywide tours by a black performance group were an unusual, high-profile, and almost political enterprise that ran numerous risks. Curfew regulations restricting concerts and passes that were required of all blacks traveling outside Natal were but some of the obstacles. In view of official suspicions of any traveling, organized group of blacks, Dube's applications for passes were accompanied by promises to "avoid centres where there is rebellion." Such assurances, however, rarely appeased the white farmers in the interior, nor could they prevent outbursts of rowdyism. For example, at Loskop, Boer farmers were stirred up by fears that the choir's visit "was aiming at causing friction between blacks and whites," and they promptly called in the police. On another occasion, the virulent racism of Boer farmers and opposition to the choir almost cost Caluza's life. On the Reef, concerts took place under the auspices of Witwatersrand Native Labour Association *indunas,* but rarely went undisrupted by drunk migrant laborers.[16] Choir member Selina Khuzwayo recalls:

> We started from Durban, did all the locations in Durban, there were not many then, . . . and from there we came to Pietermaritzburg. In Pietermaritzburg we used to do Indian halls, colored halls, last the city hall. From the city hall we traveled in our own train that was arranged by the Principal John Dube, then traveled the whole of Natal. We started from Mooi River, from Mooi River went to Estcourt, from Estcourt we went to Ladysmith, from Ladysmith went to Dannhauser, from Dannhauser went to Vryheid, now Zululand way. From Vryheid, I still remember, then we started now to Johannesburg. In Johannesburg we started in Germiston, Jeppe, from Jeppe then went to all these compounds. . . . When we finished the compounds, then of course we were invited by the churches now. . . . Finished that, we got into our train, back home. That's how John Dube and Caluza raised funds for that Ohlange Training College.[17]

But the tours not only helped to keep the Ohlange Institute financially afloat, they also provided cultural models able to satisfy the needs of the entire spectrum of black society by expressing an overarching black identity. Unlike mission-type concerts of *imusic,* Caluza's shows attracted audiences made up of "all classes, from everywhere."[18] Over the years the concerts developed into one of the earliest-known forms of variety show for blacks that combined brass band performances, *imusic,* sketches, dress competitions, and more unusual attractions such as ballroom dancing, film shows, traditional drum-and-reed-flute ensembles, *isicathulo,* and back-to-back dances.[19] The highlight of all Ohlange concerts, however, was "ragtime" songs. As one *Ilanga* critic remarked: "The Ohlange Choir is a choir that satisfies everybody, because it can sing ragtime music [*iRagtime*], classical music as well as other types of music admired by black audiences."[20]

IRagtime was the third category besides *isiZulu* and *imusic* recognized by Zulu-speaking urban performers and audiences. The emphasis on ragtime in the repertoire of the Ohlange Choir illustrates the continuity of urban musical traditions based on the Afro-American, minstrel, and vaudeville models favored by John Dube and the older generation of urbanized mission graduates. Minstrel performances had been popularized by Dube's Inanda Native Singers as early as 1904, and bone playing and cork-burnt faces were standard musical fare at Ohlange (chapter 3). As a pupil, Caluza had even formed his own fully fledged blackface minstrel troupe called "Coons" that had regular appearances at Durban's New Location hall. Octogenarian Eva Mbambo, a member of the Ohlange Choir from 1921 to 1924, recalled that bone playing even featured in Caluza's shows as late as the 1920s.[21]

But what Durban audiences during the First World War and in later years perceived as ragtime was not based on the developed artistic piano compositions of Scott Joplin. Caluza only came to know Joplin's compositions during his studies in the United States,[22] and until the late 1920s, therefore, the only sources for South African "ragtime" were the minstrel tunes, sheet music, and gramophone records of music hall songs of British provenance. These were readily available in Durban's music shops and were eagerly absorbed by black performers. Thus the Ohlange Choir was perfectly in tune with the most recent trends when it performed Tin Pan Alley composer Paul Wenrich's "Moonlight Bay" in Durban's New Location Hall in 1916. J. Gumede's Georgedale Choir even took things somewhat further and presented "Ragtime Crazy" in the sanctified environment of the Methodist Church in Grey Street.[23]

If "political" songs such as "Silusapho" solemnly underscored black demands for freedom and justice, "ragtime" songs such as "Moonlight Bay" with their syncopated melodies were potentially more congruous with Zulu speech patterns. The distortion of normal speech rhythm and prosody in Xhosa and Zulu had been tolerated in most nineteenth-century choir music (*makwaya*) of the mission-educated elite. For these converts had accepted the supposed superiority of the symbols of Western civilization such as four-part choral hymnody over autochthonous forms of cultural expression such as Zulu prosody. In vernacular compositions by elite composers until at least the publication of John Dube's collection *Amagama Abantu* in 1911, the integrity of Zulu speech modes was secondary to Western sound structure. Although black audiences had long discovered the natural relationship between "ragtime" songs and some of their own dance songs, the problem with American and British syncopated music lay in the disparity between a seemingly African, lively rhythmic texture and English lyrics that could hardly capture the black experience in modern South Africa. And thus as late as 1915 one *Ilanga* correspondent could still complain about the lack of "people who are really gifted in composing Zulu songs."[24]

But 1915 was also the year when Caluza completed his studies at Ohlange, and when the Ohlange concert tours and "ragtime" performances began to develop into a regular feature in Durban's musical calendar. As a result of the growing interest in syncopated music, from around 1915 Caluza composed a number of songs exploiting the harmonic and rhythmic precepts of British musical hall songs. The most famous of these was "Ixeghwana or Ricksha Song" (Old Man or Ricksha Song) (HMV GU 5) composed in 1917 (see example 2).

EXAMPLE 2. R. T. Caluza, "Ixeghwana."

Ngabon' ixegwana
limbet' ingubo
limhlophe lithe qwa
ikhanda kanye nezinyawo.
Irishalam lifak' izimpondo
ligcobe nezitho
lifana no ricksha bakithi.

. . .
O ricksha nkosi, baas, miss,
mina tata wena round the town.

I saw an old gray-bearded man,
who had covered himself with a blanket,
and his feet were white, too.
My ricksha with big horns
and white legs,
jumping around and looking for passengers.
. . .
"Oh ricksha Sir, boss, miss.
I you take [in *fanakalo*] round the town."

Ricksha pullers had long been one of the strongest and most militant sectors of Durban's black working class, with their own distinctive dress and street cries. Thus it was small wonder that songs from the milieu of the ricksha pullers had always been a component of Durban's black popular culture. Performances of "Ixeghwana" brought out the ricksha pullers in full force, and during one of the strikes of Durban's ricksha men Caluza's composition even surfaced as a protest song. In a sense, as P. Kirby pointed out, the words of "Ixeghwana" with their inkling of *fanakalo* mine pidgin words could indeed be seen as "a criticism of the European attitude to the African" (Kirby 1979:90). But such criticism of white racism was by far less relevant to Caluza's audiences than may appear at first sight. Two things made Caluza's "Ixeghwana" so popular among all strata of Durban's black population. First, the song formulated a critique of those members of the black community who had sacrificed their cultural roots for the benefit of only a fleeting acceptance in white society, and who by speaking *fanakalo*, that supreme form of canonized racial stereotypes, had accepted the ultimate form of white racism, the contempt for the most sacred of all Zulu traditions—the language. Second, "Ixeghwana" was the first composition by a black South African composer that merged topical lyrics in the vernacular with "ragtime," the most polished form of musical entertainment of the time. It was these qualities that were to earn Caluza the "admiration of all Blacks"[25] and a modern English *izibongo* (praise poem) entitled an "An African Star":

Midst Afric's host of sons and daughters,
A nation full of power and honour.
Whose darkness, light has sworn to conquer,
There lives a son whose colour and talent
Set Afric's great and true distinction.

Afric's traditions, and modes of old,
Her cries, and passion, her appeal for light,
In strains of sweet, patriotic songs,
Shall now and ever live.

Of whom do Afric's old and young pride?
The name CALUZA "The African Star."
His love for man, his BANTU airs,
LOVE, FAME, and PRIDE for him have found.

For those of Afric's host whose eyes have seen
His mode of tread on AFRICAN STAGE,
Have had his name translated.
HONOUR! LONG LIFE! PEACE! to the African
Star.[26]

The reception of Caluza's music, as mirrored in poems such as "An African Star," demonstrates how "ragtime" songs blended with the cultural symbols fostered within the emerging black nationalist movements in South Africa. Rather than thought of as derogatory and racially biased, syncopated music was seen by many South African blacks as an expression of racial pride. Through the Ohlange Choir and its "ragtime" performances, wrote R. R. R. Dhlomo, "many have felt proud of being black: many have shed tears because of patriotic resurgence."[27] In his later recordings of the more solemn "Vulindhlela Mtaka Dube," for example, Caluza even introduces the song with a lively "ragtime" piano solo, thereby demonstrating the compatibility of the hymnodic, nationalist idiom with *iRagtime.*

White South African audiences were wary of the nationalist connotations underlying black interpretations of these songs, despite the facts that syncopated music was rooted in nineteenth-century minstrelsy and that the popularity of "ragtime" songs transcended racial barriers. Not surprisingly, then, plans by Littin A. J. Mthethwa's Zulu Union Choir, a thoroughly Western-trained choir with an exclusively Western classical repertoire, to stage a concert of "ragtime" songs in the Durban Town Hall in 1917 met with no small degree of opposition. Mthethwa was a gardener and ANC veteran in Durban and with his family had formed the Zulu Union Choir in 1914 to raise money for the war fund (Samuelson 1929:208–12). But for the choir's manager, former Secretary of Native Affairs R. C. Samuelson, the choir was first and foremost an attempt "to counteract the innumerable tendencies to bring collisions between the White peoples of this Country and the Natives" and "to make the Natives see that we are truly their Friends."[28] The conservative Dube realised the black nationalist underpinnings of "ragtime," and advised Mthethwa's choristers that they should "forget about rhythmic dance and ragtime songs and sing pure music [*imusic*] only."[29]

"It's Like That in Town": Caluza's Songs in Popular Performance after the First World War

If "ragtime" songs, in the minds of black people, expressed nationalist sentiments and antiwhite opposition, Caluza's compositions were also marked by a profound ambivalence toward the value systems and cultural formations of black urban society. In quick succession over a period of ten years until the mid-1920s, Caluza composed a series of songs that reflected the precarious situation of Durban's black intelligentsia caught between a self-conscious urbanism and rural nostalgia, and hemmed in between white hegemony and black popular opposition. One of the earliest of the songs in this mold, possibly even predating "Ixeghwana," is "Ingoduso" (Fiancée) (HMV GU 1), composed ca. 1915:

Sikhelel' umtaka Baba
abambopha len'eGoli.
Wa esibiza ngokuthi unguMqafiqafi.
Waboshwa zimbangi zaseRautini.
Zamfakel' utshwal' endlini
yake zase ziyakombisela abaseshi nonongqayi.
Bamfikel' ebusuku umtakababa bamshaya negezinduku,
bati hamba mfana uyisigebengu uthengisa ngotshwala.
Washiya ingoduso.
ingoduso igoyil' ekhaya.
Way' eqonde umsebenzi.
Waqal' ukukhumbula ingoduso yakhe kanye nabuko.
Lapho bemthata bemqondisa endlini emnyama
yase Marshall Square,
zamubamba ngebhantshana zambopha.
Washiya ingoduso
igoyil' ekhaya.
Nankoke umvuzo
wokukhohlwa yingodus' ekhaya.

We yearn for our brother
who was arrested in Johannesburg.
He called himself a clever man.
He was arrested because of jealousy of rival groups in Johannesburg.
They put liquor in his room and called the police.

They got to his house at night and beat him up,
and drove away saying he is a bandit who sells liquor.
He left his fiancée,
he left his fiancée sad at home.
He meant to work for her.
He started thinking about his fiancée and his home.
When they arrested him and took him to jail
at Marshall Square,
he was handcuffed by the detectives.
He left his fiancée
sad at home.
That is the price
of forgetting your fiancée at home.[30]

"Ingoduso" was followed by "Intandane" (Orphan) (ca. 1917) (HMV GU 73), "Kwati Belele" (While They Were Sleeping) (ca. 1918) (HMV GU 23), and "Umtaka Baba" (My Brother) (ca. 1918) (HMV GU 69), songs that explore the complex network of cultural intergroup relations and the diversity of social characters produced in the expanding urban context. Thus "UBhatata" (Sweet Potatoes) (HMV GU 61), composed before 1924, pokes fun at a young rural *lobola-* (bride-price) paying suitor who is so shocked by the white bed sheets in the home of his *amakholwa* future parents-in-law that he prefers to sleep under the bed:

Insizw' etize yasel' intombi.
Yasi vaka shel'ekweni layo.
Yafi k'ekwe ni bay'nik' umbhede.
Nokudhlaya kudhlaka.
Yabon' amashidi ayemhlop' eteqwa.
Ya yiqa l'ukubon' umbhed' omhlophe qwa.
yangena ngaphansi kamatlansi.
Eb'suku yavuka yantshontsh' ubhatata.
. . .

A young man paid *lobola* for a woman.
He paid his in-laws a visit.
They gave him food and a bed.
He did not eat much.
He saw the white bedsheets.
He had never seen a bed with white sheets before,
and so he slept under the mattress.
He woke up at night and stole a sweet potato.
. . .

Clearly, the laughter that was provoked by the young man's confusion about the subtleties of middle-class forms of social conduct served to distance urban Africans from their rural counterparts. At the same time, urbane demeanor and dapper dress were interpreted as deformations of "Christian" codes of behavior and translated into images that rural Africans could understand. Thus in "UBunghca" (AmaOxford Bags) (HMV GU 1), possibly Caluza's most popular song, the fashionable piece of clothing is likened to the red-billed hornbill (*ngomkholwane*) (see example 3).

EXAMPLE 3. R. T. Caluza, "UBunghca" (AmaOxford Bags).

Nxa nivakashela eThekwini,
niyozibon' intomb' eziphambili,
zingena ziphum' emawotela.
Nezintomb' eziphambili.
Niyobon' izinsizwa eziphambili.
Zingen' ewotela lika T.D.
zithi woza la wetha, kukhona kudla kuni?
Akubalek' uwetha ukudl' okukhona.
Zithi leth' isitshulu leth' ilayisi.
Letha noloz'bhifu nom' inyama yesiklabhu.
Zizangez' gubhu imsiko yase-Merika.
Abanye fak' isitali, behamba bebhungca
zabeqhenya beti njengomkholwane, bhungca ngesitaliyana.
Manje beza ngamaOxford bags,
bafake kanye nama double breast coat,
bafak' izigqok' eyizimbenge

zamakawa z'yakind' intombi,
amasilik' avuzayo, namabhantsh' akhindiwe.
Kukhon' izintomb' eziphambili
kukhon' ez' fana no dadenje.
Nezinsizw' ezingasay' emakhaya.
Imihuqa nemigovu.
Zibanjiwe banjiw' eSamseni.
Iyabagwinya iMayville.
Bayakhala bayalamb' omam' ekhaya.
Yek' usizi olukululwe zinsizwa.
Kunjani na eGoli?
Zinjani na siqat' eGoli?
Babanjelw' isiqata nesigomfana.
Yiwo lo umvuzo wokubhunguka.

When visiting Durban,
you will see beautiful girls,
entering hotels.
Elegant ladies.
You will also see elegant young men.
They enter T. D.'s hotel
and call the waiter, and ask him: "What kind of food do you
     have?"
Or they ask the waiter to bring the menu.
Then they will say: "Bring stew and rice."
"Bring roast beef or mutton."
They are dressed in American style.
Some will come dressed in Italian style, with trousers,
the legs tied like a red-billed hornbill, as in Italian trousers.
Some come with their Oxford Bags
and wear a *double-breasted coat,*
big brimmed hats,
short ladies dresses,
expensive silks, short coats.
There are also fashionable girls,
and also ones just like you and me.
And young men who no more go back to their homes.
Old crooks and hobos.
They are trapped in Samseni.
Mayville is the only place for them.
Their women at home are crying and suffering.
It is sad, gentlemen.
How is Johannesburg?
How is the liquor in Johannesburg?

They are being arrested for concoctions brewed in their
    homes.
That is the price of forgetting one's relations.[31]

In "Abaqhafi" (HMV GU 44), according to Absalom Vilakazi, Caluza describes the young migrant and "his absolute lack of respect for
old traditions" (Vilakazi 1965:76), whereas "Ematawini or Excuse Me
Please" (In Town) (HMV GU 43) reflects the amazement new arrivals in
Durban might have felt at the complexities of town life and the adroitness
of the "Excuse-me-people," the slick and well-adapted urban dwellers:

Nisibona silapha nje nasiphum'ekhaya.
Sigudl'ulwandle sabon' izimoba
nemishini yoku gay' ushukela
nabant' abatheng' ithiligi.
Sadlula lapho kesafik' eThekwini
nisaka ngwa' zintombi kanye nezinsizwa
zasehlaze nyuka emgwaqweni.
Zihamba ziqenya zingen' impahla.
Abanye bey' olwandle abanye kwaMadala.
Zabethi Excuse me please gidedele.
Me want some cup-a-tea, because me hungly.
Insizwa zifake izigqoko,
nentombi zihambis' okwamada ngez' cathulo.
Abany' ubonenj' ukutina bo besikholo.
Kunjal' wematawini.
Kukhon' inhlobo izinhlobo zabantu.
Ababin' abahle
abaziqenya yo kanye nabatobile.
Kukhon' abaqhafi nabalungile.
    . . .

As you see us here we are from home.
Along the coast we saw sugarcane fields
and a sugar mill,
and people who buy treacle for their beer.
We went to Durban
and we got attracted to young women and men
marching up and down the streets.
They are proud of their clothes.
Some of them were going to the beach and to Madala.
They say: "*Excuse me please*, can I please pass?
Me want some cup-a-tea, because me hungly."
Young men were wearing hats,

and young women were walking like ducks.
You could see that some of them were students.
It is like that in town.
There are all kinds of people.
Ugly ones
and beautiful ones, proud and simple people.
And some are embarrassing.
And you also find gangsters.
. . .

Songs such as these provided Durban's urban blacks with models for self-parody that minimized the trauma of rural economic and cultural decline. At the same time these compositions satirized the overassimilationist tendencies within the upper reaches of Durban's *amakholwa* as are evident, for instance, in the malaprop English spoken by them ("because me hungly"). While the mimicry of black ignorance by blacks may have been snobbish, it was certainly not racist. However, as the word "hungly" suggests, black parodies of blacks imitating whites may on occasion have borne a superficial resemblance to white racist mockery of "black Englishmen." For "hungly" stemmed in fact from the ostensible vocabulary of the "Chinaman," another victim of white South African racial venom and an established figure of the white minstrel stage and its "coon" songs that black minstrels in the United States never adopted specifically. Furthermore, South African black English does not generally substitute *r* by *l*. A closer look therefore at the sources of such images in Caluza's songs has much to tell us about the processes that might have led to such stereotyping.

Caluza's own recording of the song with his Double Quartette of 1930 (HMV GU 43) clearly reveals that "hungry" is being sung, and it thus stands to reason that the "hungly" in the Lovedale Tonic Sol-fa score stemmed more from the imagination of the composer than from real performance practice. Such discrepancies between printed score and practical performance were of course characteristic of all vital popular performance, and distinctions in the printed text were generally subject to constant practical revision. Yet in such crucial matters as racial stereotypes, such fine lines as between "hungry" and "hungly" were always present to black performers.

At the same time Caluza was sensitive to the deteriorating middle-class position in the urban economy. A song such as "Idiphu eThekwini" (The Dipping in Durban) (HMV GU 41) illustrates this quite vividly. In November 1923 the Durban city fathers had introduced a new dispensation that provided for the compulsory medical examination of all black workseekers and for a procedure referred to as "dipping." The process whereby male workers were "deverminized" in tanks was met with bitter and fierce popular resistance and was later abandoned. But *idiphu*, as the practice was known to Zulu-speaking Durbanites, nevertheless became the target of extensive comment in popular songs such as Caluza's "Idiphu eThekwini", that was sung by critics from across the entire spectrum of black society:

> *Zithini lapha ngediphu eThekwini?*
> *Babalekelani abantu eThekwini?*
> *Webakithi abamnyama bame njalo nje.*
> *Sikhulumele wena Mafukuzela!*
>
> . . .
>
> *Siyanibonga Mathibela noBlose ngokusizana noMafukuzela.*

> What are you people saying about the dipping in Durban?
> What is chasing people away from Durban?
> You fellow countrymen, long live the black nation.
> Talk on our behalf, Mafukuzela! [John Dube]
>
> . . .
>
> We thank you, Mr. Mathibela and Mr. Bulose for cooperating
> with Mafukuzela.

On a similar level, Caluza's song "Sixotshwa Emsebenzini" (We Are Being Expelled from Work) (HMV GU 23), composed in 1924, criticizes the Industrial Conciliation Act that threatened to push black artisans, shop assistants, nurses, and other black professionals into the army of jobless and underpaid laborers:

> *Kuvel' indaba enkulu bakithi ivelelethin' abamnyama.*
> *Abamhlophe bas'kiph' emsebenzini.*
> *Manje sebefak' abakubo.*
> *Kukade sibakonzile sibasebenzela kahle.*
> *Kepe namhla abamnyama baxosh' emsebenzini,*
> *baxotshiwe eThekwini baxotshiwe eGoli.*
> *Abaningi bayazula ngokuswela umsebenzi.*
> *Kepa ke sitheliswa imali abasikiph' emsebenzini.*
> *Bazosibopha nxa ingeko.*
> *Sizoshonaphi bakithi?*

> A serious problem is facing the black nation.
> Whites are expelling us from work.
> They only employ whites.

We have been working for them for many years, without any
  problems.
But now blacks are excluded from work
in Durban and in Johannesburg.
Most are idling, because they have nothing to do.
But we have to pay rent.
We are going to be arrested without money.
What are we going to do, people?

The brunt of "dipping," job reservation, and other restrictive measures
that made the lives of black Durbanites miserable was clearly borne by the
majority of urban poor. It was small wonder therefore that songs such as
these met with no small degree of appreciation among Durban's laborers.
At the same time, however, songs such as "Idiphu" and "Sixotshwa" afforded the black intelligentsia with a platform from which to proclaim
their leadership role.

On the other hand, the identificatory "we" in these compositions
did not generally imply approval of working-class cultural forms of organization and recreation. A series of songs that Caluza wrote about alcohol
demonstrates this quite clearly. The consumption of alcohol, as Paul la
Hausse has shown, played a crucial role in the formation of working-class
cultures in Durban. But local black leaders suspected alcohol as a challenge to one of the central tenets of their ideological hegemony. As the
1920s drew to a close, municipally produced beer increasingly came to be
resented by African working-class women as emasculating and as a
threat to independent beer brewing and frail family budgets (la Hausse
1984). But apart from the boycott of beer halls, the growing opposition to
Durban's municipal beer monopoly, known as the "Durban system," also
generated various forms of popular struggle including songs. Unfortunately, most of the presumably traditional tunes remain unrecorded.
What did survive were at least four compositions that Caluza wrote about
young migrants in Johannesburg who are led astray by the excessive consumption of *isikilimikwik'* (Kill-Me-Quick) and illicit liquor brewing. The
songs are "Ingoduso," "Umtaka Baba" and "Kwati Belele." The fourth
song, "Kwa Madala" (At Madala) (HMV GU 62), is a song about Durban
and is more ambiguous in its admiration of urban life and the role of beer
halls than "Ematawini":

. . .

Sidlul' eThekwini kwaMadala.
Lakugewa la kwaMadala.
Abanye bathengela n'uswidi kwaMadala.

Ilapho kuhlangane lwako na kwaMadala.
Sihlule lapho sayesafika eMatsheni.
Sathu kungena sabon' umsebenziwa bantu.
Kuthengis' ukudlane emphahl' ezigqokw' abantu.
Kukhona ne nkantini la kuthengis' utshwala.
Ilapho kuphelela kon' imali yensizwa.
. . .

We were at Madala in Durban.
It is always busy at Madala.
You see people buying sweets at Madala.
People meet there at Madala.
From there we moved on to Matsheni.
We were surprised when we saw the good work.
People sell food and clothes.
There is also a canteen where they sell beer.
Men spend all their money there.
. . .

"The Natural Dignity of Zulu Primitive Life" Traditionalism and Ethnic Consciousness in Caluza's Songs

Caluza's ambivalent position vis-à-vis the lifestyle that was evolving in Durban was that of a man deeply committed to the country. But Caluza's rural orientation, and that of many of his contemporaries, was a janus-faced ideology that could be read and instrumentalized for quite diverse interests. In the eyes of D. M. Malcolm, Chief Inspector of Native Education in Natal and a lifelong supporter of the composer, Caluza's songs involved images of rural harmony; they expressed the "Zulu regrets for the passing of their own social courtesies" and the "natural dignity of Zulu primitive life" (Caluza [1928]). Clearly, in the face of growing urban unrest, whites perceived new forms of urban black culture as a potential threat to their hegemony, and the white ideologues of segregation therefore advertised the virtues of the precolonial social order. "Natural dignity," in the parlance of the masters, meant nothing else but submissiveness of the servants.

At another level, in the hands of Natal's black leaders, the symbols of the past were used to legitimize and mystify their class position. As Shula Marks has shown, Natal's larger black landowners—Caluza's intellectual foster fathers—gave priority to development schemes in rural reserves over national issues such as the removal of the African franchise in the Cape. Within this strategy the Zulu monarchy and its symbols could be used to play a "self-consciously modernizing role" (Marks

1986:70; 1989). Thus, for all the superficial signals of Zulu ethnic consciousness, compositions such as "Elamakosi" (For the Kings) (HMV GU 43) expressed the continuity of precolonial political leadership and the cohesion and intact social relations of the precolonial order as models of a "modern" Zulu nation:

> *Izizwe ezimnyama zikhalul' izwe lazo.*
> *Ilizwe la okoko esese mukwa lona,*
> *elabuswa oTshaka, be noDingane,*
> *be noCetshwayo, kuze kufike kuDinizulu,*
> *kufike kuSolomoni,*
> *oyinkosi yamaZulu oyingugu lamaZulu.*
> *Kwang' inkosi ngabanaye imvikile ezingozini.*
> *Elalibuswa oMshweshwe oyinkosi yab'e Suthu,*
> *kanye naye uSobhuza oyinkosi yamaSwazi*
> *babebusa ngo buqawe babethand' izizwe zonke.*
> *Balibusa lab'e Suthu kanye nalo lamaSwazi.*
> *Elabuswa oHinsa na oNgqika,*
> *oDlambe, kuyo fika kuGcaleka*
> *kufike kuDalinjebo.*
> *Balibusa lamaXhosa kanye nalo lamaMfengu.*

The black people cry for their land.
Our forefathers' land which was taken away from us,
and which belonged to Shaka, Dingaan,
Cetshwayo, Dinizulu,
and Solomon,
king and hero of the Zulu.
May the Lord be with you.
It was Moshoeshoe, king of the Sotho,
and Sobhuza, king of the Swazi,
who were brave and loved their entire people.
They ruled the Sotho and the Swazi.
The land was ruled by Hinsa, Ngqika,
Dlambe, Gcaleka,
and Dalingebo.
They ruled the Xhosa and Fingo.

Clearly, in Caluza's mind there was no contradiction between loyalty to the hereditary leaders of the Zulu, the continuity and legitimacy of traditional customs in a modern industrial state, and the search for a secure position *as middle class* in that society. A striking illustration of this is the seeming incompatibility of the "loyalist" lyrics with a Western sound structure in a song such as "Sikulekel' uSolomon" (We are praying for Solomon) (HMV GU 61), composed ca. 1915 (see example 4).

Example 4. R. T. Caluza, "Sikulekel' uSolomon."

Sikulekel' uSolomoni, inkosi yethu Mazulu.
Kwang' inkosi nga naye
abuse ngoku thula.
Apheph' ezingozini
acume abe nodumo.
Wafela ePitoli umtwana kaCetshwayo.
Washiy' abantu bake kanye nezintandane.
. . .

We are praying for Solomon, king of us Zulus.
May the Lord be with him,
and may he rule the land in peace.
May he prosper,
be safe and famous.
He died in Pretoria, Cetshwayo's son.
He left his people behind as orphans.
. . .

What at first sight might appear a mere formal inconsistency is in fact the result of a conscious effort to merge the textual and musical metaphors of a "Zulu Christian" nationalism. Conversely, the occasional chromaticism in Caluza's melodies which some musicologists consider to be an unusual feature of African music is in fact a deliberate reminiscence of traditional Nguni tonality.

Caluza's role as a "modern Zulu composer" would appear to make him a classical example of what students of popular culture have frequently described as "cultural brokers." In David Coplan's terms, for instance, black South African musicians must be seen as "leaders in the adoption and creation of innovations" who "mediate between cultures in contact" (Coplan 1985:237). But as such "agents of active change" who diminish the "distance between musical genres at the community core and those near the boundaries," as Philip Bohlman describes the brokerage role of popular musicians (Bohlman 1988:102), musicians in modern South African society do not play the role of quasi-autonomous mediators. For all the autonomy that has been accorded in this book to processes of artistic creation, composers such as Caluza were nevertheless responsive to the cultural choices that were constantly being negotiated in the formation of modern South African society. Therefore the innovations that resulted from Caluza's modernizing role in the creation of a popular performance medium must also be accounted for in wider sociocultural terms. It is to these changes and the context in which they evolved that we must now direct ourselves.

"Novel Situations":
Stage Performance
during the 1920s

Until 1930 concerts (*ikhonsati*) and competitions had not only been the sole form of musical entertainment available to mission-educated blacks, but also the most important and popular form of African social gathering. The structure of *ikhonsati* events had significance beyond middle-class views of organized leisure time and later influenced working-class formats of performance such as *isicathamiya* competitions (chapter 6). Early church and school choirs had put a great deal of their creative energies into providing exact copies of English turn-of-the-century musical events, including such subtleties as *ankori* (encores).[32] But by the turn of the century, and under the distrustful eyes of missionaries, mission choirs began transforming the structure of concerts into "a form of combined auctioneering and gambling."[33] Herbert Dhlomo has provided us with a vivid description of these highwater marks of cultural activity:

> There was no formal programme. The programme was spontaneous, dictated by circumstance, and rich in novelty. The stage choir would open the performance . . . by singing two or three songs. Immediately after, the chairman would get down to business and ask the audience to "buy" what choir (or favourite song) they liked. The people were also free to buy off the choir, soloist and song they did not like. . . . As

would be expected, this procedure led to all kinds of novel situations. For the sake of revenue the promoters encouraged it in every way possible.[34]

Such "novel situations" provided ample opportunities for the elaboration of aesthetic values and the intense interaction between performers and audience that had traditionally characterized African performance. But above all, "novelty" created a sense of a community bound by the consciousness of being in the vanguard of cultural modernization. As a result, elite newspapers such as John Dube's *Ilanga* frequently carried reports of concerts and competitions such as the following description of a "bidding" scene in 1917:

> Messrs. William Gumede and Z. L. S. Made from Ladysmith argued about which choir should sing. Gumede said that the Ohlange Choir should sing, whereas the other wanted the boot dance [*isicathulo*] by Skuni Jojilanga. The whole concert stopped because of the two gentlemen who eventually engaged themselves in a kind of "bidding." The money started from 1s. and Mr. Gumede failed to go beyond £1.0.6. Mr. Made's "bidding" went up to £1.4.0 and the other one surrendered. Mr. Made's home team mates took him to the stage on their shoulders, followed by a great applause from the audience. Then Skuni Jojilanga went up the stage with his choir and sang nicely. When T. D. finished announcing the money paid by the two, he had already lost his voice.[35]

It was the "novel situations" and the reaction against slavish imitations of Western stage practices that became a fertile ground for some of Caluza's most radical and lasting innovations. For Caluza not only composed "sweet, patriotic" songs, he also revolutionized the entire concert and stage practice of Natal's black middle class in at least four spheres. First and foremost among these was the introduction of *ukureka* (ragging), the step movements of "ragtime." The combination of music and dance movements had been one of the sore spots in nineteenth-century mission culture. Restrictions on dancing had produced the interpretive song-cum-movement genre called action song. Black urban audiences, in particular, were tiring of performance modes as taught in rural missions, and as one observer noted in 1917,

> have a totally negative attitude toward college and school choirs. They maintain that college and school choirs do not know music. These urban people have been influenced by the fashionable urban choirs and the idea that good music lies in

shouting, noise, as well as body movements (actions), even when singing songs like 'Ponder My Words, O Lord.'[36]

At the outset of Caluza's career, such restrained forms of stage movement had already become accepted as a tolerable solution to the problem of how to merge Western music with African concepts of the unity of movement and sound. But when Caluza introduced straightforward "ragtime" steps into what used to be plain "stand still" concerts, the effect was nothing short of sensational.

But more than the "beautiful movements of the waists of the singers" that "added to the beauty of the music,"[37] it was the second innovation, the careful orchestration of synchronized movement, that impressed the audience. A complete professional, Caluza insisted on strict rehearsal discipline of his performers, and imbued them with a stronger sense of accuracy than had traditionally been the case. As Selina Khuzwayo explained:

> He would come and tell you: "Look here, don't move your chin this way, because you spoil the whole setup." You know, if it was left hand, we had to play left hand, all of us played left hand. If it was right hand, all of us played with the right hand, if it was the right foot, all of us with the right foot. It was that order with Caluza.[38]

The third innovation was Caluza's stage costumes and the "dramatization" of his songs that he developed from about 1918, and that established his fame as the country's leading entertainer. The beginning of this development coincided with his registering at Mariannhill, St. Francis College, for further studies,[39] and it may well have been during this period that he began experimenting with more elaborate forms of stage performance in songs such as "Isangoma" (Witch Doctor) (HMV GU 73), composed in 1919–20. It is arguable to what extent Caluza was influenced by the one-acters and skits Mariannhill missionary Bernhard Huss and his students were staging in Durban and Mariannhill (chapter 3). Be this as it may, to Mariannhill graduate and Hiver Hyvas veteran amateur performer R. T. Mazibuko, who attended early Caluza concerts, Caluza appeared as

> a person who has been given a peculiar gift of observation. And after he has observed a thing, he started to build it into a story which he transformed into music. Mostly the actions which were performed by his choir were the most entertaining of them all, when they could imitate ricksha pullers, when they could imitate the witch doctors, when they could imitate

how the Zulu girls in the olden days used to do the girls'
dance. . . . It was not only the harmony of the music, it was
also the actions that accompanied his music.[40]

Drama and storytelling have long been recognized as important elements of Zulu oral literature even though praise poetry accounts for some
of the more weighty examples of the splendor of Zulu verbal arts. Researchers have found much evidence of a remarkable persistence of
traditional Zulu poetry in modern forms, and claims that most modern
Zulu poetry, in one way or another, is based on older models of panegyric
do not seem wholly unfounded (Finnegan 1970:121, 145–46; Gunner
1986, 1988). In Caluza's songs, however, there is little confirmation of
such assumptions. Rather it can be argued that the literary pendant of the
"novel situations" in Caluza's shows was a kind of linguistic and poetic
repertoire whose continuity with the tradition was disrupted. There are
hardly any references in Caluza's songs to the format and imagery of traditional praise poetry, nor does the Zulu of these songs bear any resemblance to the kind of "deep" Zulu in evidence in more rural genres such as
amahubo, ukubhina, isigekle, umakhweyana bow songs, and other songs.[41]
In fact, none of the traditional reference points are present here that the
enthusiastic author of "An African Star" described as "Afric's traditions,
and modes of old." Rather the narrative element in these songs and the
use of a certain everyday Zulu that was and continues to be spoken in
urban areas, as well as the frequent use of Zuluized English terms, make
Caluza's songs into a new literary genre altogether, in both poetic technique and content.

Fourth and last, the desire to liven up the austere and stifled atmosphere of "stand still" concerts through "novel situations" inevitably
contributed to a variety of comical elements. These had of course been a
mainstay of American and British minstrelsy as well as of the turn-of-the-
century European variety stage. "Comic" and "laughing" songs were staple items in black mission and school concerts, and as late as 1920, the
solidly middle-class group the African Male Voice Choir could present the
"laughable sketch" "De Skeleton in De Office."[42] But apart from these imported forms, Zulu-speaking performers drew on their own vigorous
traditions of comic mime and humor. Much research still needs to be
done on what appears to be one of the most salient components of traditional Zulu folklore, but in the urban context both Western and African
traditions of humor had long merged to produce such genres as *ukukomika,* a migrant dance form that fused parody of white military drill with
ingoma choreography (chapter 4).

These and other traditions of comedy had been available to Caluza from his youth, but in addition to being a "loveable and charming" person, Caluza possessed another indispensable quality for a professional stage entertainer: an unusually developed sense of humor. "He could laugh, that man," Faith Caluza recalled. As early as 1916 Caluza had gained a reputation as the Harry Lauder of Natal. Records by the Scottish comedian and music hall star Lauder were popular in Durban, and soon after Lauder's tour of South Africa in 1920, Caluza specialized in an adaptation of the burlesque "The Man They Left Behind," one of Lauder's earliest hits on the variety stage in London.[43]

The combination of action, stage costumes, Zulu lyrics, instrumental accompaniment, synchronized "ragtime" movements, and humor in Caluza's performances together provided for the foundations of a genuinely modern and African musical variety show. Caluza's shows influenced working-class performers such as early *isicathamiya* choirs as well as the first, top vaudeville groups such as the African Own Entertainers.

R. T. Caluza in London and the United States, 1930–1935
In 1928 Caluza decided to publish a collection of his songs. The book, entitled *Amagama Ohlanga Lakwazulu* (The Zulu Songs of Ohlange —see fig. 13), sold out within a few weeks, and by August 1929 Lovedale Press, hoping for a "very profitable investment," was considering a second edition. After due consultation with the London Society of Authors of which Caluza had become the first African member, the composer agreed to have the songs published as single leaflets with a royalty of 25 percent. Caluza's correspondence with his publishers shows him as a shrewd businessman, a talent which he was to demonstrate again later in his life when he opened a number of trading stores.[44] By 1936 seventeen songs had been published, but only 5,000 copies had been sold—973 copies alone of "Ama-Oxford Bags." No doubt this was a result of the waning interest in Caluza's songs, and not surprisingly, by 1940 the royalty due to the composer had only accrued to just under £100.

Slightly more profitable was the recording of his compositions. The rise of the South African recording industry from modest beginnings in 1908 to the foundation of Eric Gallo's company in 1926 and the opening of South Africa's first recording studio in 1932 must be connected with the names of two black musicians: Griffith Motsieloa and Reuben Caluza. Motsieloa was an experienced cultural organizer and widely traveled man of the world, who held a degree in elocution and enjoyed a renown

"Amagama Ohlanga Lakwazulu"

By R. T. CALUZA.

FIGURE 13. The cover of R. T. Caluza's *Amagama Ohlanga Lakwazulu,* 1928.

as "London's favorite Bantu actor." No sooner did Caluza sign a contract with His Master's Voice than Eric Gallo rushed Motsieloa to London to record a series of items at Finsbury Park together with the medical student Ignatius Monare. Although Motsieloa reached London ten days before Caluza, he had forgotten his music in South Africa. His wife Emily posted the sheets to London and soon after, both companies, Gallo and HMV, started a series of recording sessions that were to alter the course of popular music history in South Africa.

Caluza's group included his wife Evelyn, Beatrice Sinaye Khuzwayo, Thembani Ngcobo, Nimrod Makhanya, Gule, Meinod Dlamini, Irene Msane, Alexander Hlubi, and A. Ndimande. With the exception of the teachers Evelyn Caluza, Gule, Ndimande, and Dlamini, all the singers were pupils from the Ohlange Institute and the nearby Inanda Seminary. In little over a month, from September to October 1930, Caluza and his musicians recorded 150 songs (see fig. 14). Forty-four of these were Caluza's own compositions, while the rest were Zulu, Basotho, and Xhosa folk songs, hymns, sketches, nursery rhymes, and folk tales. Some of the records proved exceedingly popular with black South Africa record buyers. Thus up to March 1935, HMV had sold 86,436 copies of the 366

FIGURE 14. Caluza's Double Quartet, recording at the HMV studios in London, 1930. From left: Alexander Hlubi, Irene Msane, Thembani Ngcobo, Gule, Mrs. A. Ndimande, Nimrod Makhanya, Sinaye Khuzwayo, Mrs. E. Caluza, M. Dlamini, R. T. Caluza. (Ilanga Lase Natal, November 21, 1930)

titles in its African catalog, but of these more than 18,800, that is, 21 percent, were Caluza's songs. HMV GU 1 with "Ingoduso" and "AmaOxford Bags" sold 3,800 copies, while sales of the popular folk song "Ngi sebenzel' u-My Love" (HMV GU 8) reached a phenomenal 6,656 copies (Phillips 1938:299).

Caluza's recordings proved so popular indeed that few leading choirs and vocal ensembles of the time could afford not to incorporate them into their repertoire. The Humming Bees Quartet even recorded "Umtshado" (The Wedding), composed for Caluza's marriage to Evelyn Nxaba in 1924, and "Influenza 1918" for Columbia (Columbia GR 43), while the Wilberforce Institute Singers and St. Peters Hostel Choir recorded "Sanibona" (Greetings) and "Ixeghwana," respectively (Columbia GR 13). Somewhat lesser groups such as the Wonderful Three and W. P. Zikali and Radebe's Trio put classics like "Isangoma," "Kwati Belele," "Ixegwana," and "Umtakati" on record (Columbia AE 2, AE 4).

Meanwhile the South African black press and some black papers in the United States such as DuBois's *The Crisis* applauded Caluza's recordings as a breakthrough that made African music respectable at home and in the international entertainment arena (Wesley 1931). At home in South Africa, the advent of modern recording technology and large-scale record production for the African consumer were hailed as unmistakable proofs of the continuing integration of blacks into modern society and hence progress. The gramophone, wrote elite critic and Columbia talent scout Mark Radebe, would give "lastingness to the untrained Bantu voice," and preserve Africans' "most treasured cultural inheritance."[45]

Certainly, the sales figures of Caluza's records were extraordinarily high for the embryonic African record market in South Africa. But they did not quite translate into commensurate earnings for the composer and his musicians. By 1931 Caluza had received fifty dollars in royalties on five of the HMV records with his own compositions, and was expecting to receive at least a further $300 on the remaining songs. Whether these payments ever came forth must remain doubtful, as Caluza continued to depend on additional sources of income such as eight acres of sugarcane that netted $300 in 1931. Griffith Motsieloa, for his part, seems to have fared slightly better as an employee of Gallo's with a salary of £3.3.0 per week.[46] In general, however, such contracts set unfortunate precedents for the kind of exploitative practices that have plagued black musicians until today and that led to an early awareness of the need for strong musicians' unions.[47]

The HMV recordings of 1930 were not only a turning point in the history of South Africa's black performing arts and entertainment industry, they also marked a watershed in Caluza's life and professional career. For the composer had not fully completed his contract with His Master's Voice when he was awarded a scholarship to study music at the Hampton Institute in Virginia. Since the 1890s McAdoo's *alma mater* had supported a number of South African students, including the Ohlange graduate Madikane Cele (chapter 3). As early as 1920 Caluza had tried to accompany Cele on his second visit to Hampton, but the plan failed possibly due to the difficulties of obtaining a passport. However, in 1930, with the backing of John Dube's friends Bernhard Huss, C. T. Loram, and the lawyer Louis Stoiber, Caluza obtained a scholarship from the Phelps-Stokes Commission and enrolled at Hampton for a B.S. degree.[48]

Apart from the routine course work in general music, Hampton offered the advantage of providing a congenial environment for the serious encounter with genuine Afro-American music. The head of the music department at Hampton was Nathaniel Dett, one of the principal promoters of the revival of Afro-American sacred musical traditions. Obviously, spirituals had not been entirely unknown at Ohlange; John Dube must have heard them during his studies at Oberlin College in the mid-1880s, and D. H. Opperman, one of Caluza's teachers at Ohlange and a very active musical amateur, was an AME member and thus probably familiar with the slave songs.[49] But it was Dett and other prominent black musicians like Paul Robeson and Roland Hayes, whom Caluza met, who deepened his appreciation of the Afro-American heritage.

For a musician steeped in the traditions of Nguni vocal polyphony, a comparison of Zulu music and Negro spirituals must have been a particularly attractive project. Thus Caluza not only embarked on a comparative study of Zulu folk music and Negro spirituals, he also spent time investigating the tonal structures of traditional Zulu music. These studies led him to determine the role of semitones as a function of speech modes, an idea which musicologist David Rycroft was to elaborate on more than forty years later (Caluza 1931; Rycroft 1971:218). But with the prevailing naive eurocentrism of the time, Caluza also concluded that the "Zulus are not careful about authentic and plagal cadence" and that "instead of singing the notes as they should be sung, they approach them with a slur" (Caluza 1931:153).

Caluza soon formed an "African Quartette" with fellow students from Sierra Leone and Liberia. The quartet toured the New England states extensively in 1931, performing Caluza's arrangements of Zulu songs such as "Litshe li ka Ntunjambili" as well as Negro spirituals. Later, together with Hampton's celebrated Hampton Quartette, the group was honored to appear before President Roosevelt.[50]

At the same time, Caluza's interest in the "social courtesies" of his people received further impetus through the growing anthropological interest in African art, music, and culture. Thus he served as adviser to Franz Boas at Columbia University and recorded a number of folk tales for Boas's assistant Jules Henry. In London he assisted James Stuart in talks about Zulu music and made phonograph recordings for the linguist A. Tucker at the School of Oriental and African Studies.[51] He was also invited to publish three folk songs in Nancy Cunard's famous anthology *Negro* (Cunard 1934). But it was black Americans, in particular, who after a wave of "back to Africa" movements had developed a special interest in African history and culture. As a result of this interest, Caluza supplied Hampton with some seventy pieces of Zulu material culture. By 1934 he was reportedly collecting material for a book on Zulu folklore.[52]

In short, "America had opened his eyes not only in matters musical, but also ethnographic."[53] In an article for Hampton's in-house journal *Southern Workman* Caluza deplored the fact that "the Zulus are in a transitory stage and the tendency among some of them is to belittle all their customs and folk songs." A dedicated man interested in traditional music would "lead to fame a body of men whose unspoiled and unselfish love for musical expression will bring an inspiring and uplifting message to the world" (Caluza 1931:154).

In May 1934 Caluza graduated from Hampton. It was felt that he had a talent for composition and "with the proper direction" would "make quite a little contribution to the African music"—a strange assessment to make of a mature man, whose best and most popular compositions were written between the age of seventeen and twenty-five. In fact, little evidence has survived to prove a traceable impact of the formal training he had received at Hampton on his later work. Significantly, the "Rondo for Orchestra" and the string quartet "Reminiscences of Africa" which he submitted in his final year in 1934 were based on themes from his earlier compositions, but unfortunately the scores of neither work have survived. In 1935 Caluza enrolled at Columbia University with scholarships from private sponsors and the Carnegie Corporation. After a year, and in line with middle-class views of the Afro-American heritage, Caluza submitted another string quartet on "Go Down Moses" for his M.A. and graduated in June 1935, aged 40.

"A New Confidence":
Caluza the Folklorist
and Educator

In 1936 Caluza returned to South Africa to assume the leadership of the newly formed School of Music at Adams College in Amanzimtoti, near Durban. Herbert Dhlomo and the cream of South Africa's black society organized lavish receptions in Pietermaritzburg and Johannesburg to celebrate the "brilliant career of a Zulu musician," and the mayor of Pietermaritzburg honored "the son of Pietermaritzburg who has achieved so much and has brought credit to the city and Bantu."[54] But the city that celebrated its greatest musician and composer in 1936 was no longer the one that Caluza had left in 1930. The country had seen the passage of piece upon piece of segregationist legislation, and in 1935, finally, the Hertzog government had abolished the Cape franchise. The economic depression had severely hit the black population, and with the Native Lands Amendment Act of 1936 the political and administrative protostructures of today's "homelands" had been put in place. Caluza's Edendale had exploded into a commuter suburb of some 5,000 inhabitants whose sanitary conditions, in the words of one official report of 1938, were "deplorable in the extreme."[55]

It is within this context that Caluza's work at the School of Music at Adams College between 1936 and 1946, and, indeed, the last three decades of his life, must be seen (see figs. 15 and 16). Adams College was a private college under the tutelage of the American Board of Missions. Founded as a mission in 1835, the school was directed by the liberal senator Edgar Brookes. Plans for a school of music had been mooted by Brookes and Ngazana Luthuli since at least 1934. Funding of almost £600 for the project was secured from a wealthy Honolulu couple, members of the American Congregationalists, and by 1939 construction of a new school building was completed.[56]

FIGURE 15. The School of Music at Adams College, 1936. (Harvard University)

In supporting the idea of a school of music Brookes argued that music was "a sphere in which the Bantu incontestably hold their own and a new confidence will be the inevitable result of achievement in it." Apart from general music education the school would "record, develop, and adapt Bantu folk music." This argument was essentially derived from the ongoing debate in liberal circles about the effects of the large-scale social dislocation of blacks on liberal reform projects. The late 1920s and early 1930s had seen a systematic attempt by an expanding South African school of anthropology to grasp the conflicting and often violent forms of "culture contact" in terms of the continuity and stability of African social institutions in the urban context, and the continuing links of African city dwellers with their rural background. As a result, South African anthropologists emphasized the differences between Western, urban "civilization" and African society and increasingly stressed the functionality, and indeed legitimacy, of traditional cultural practices in the adaptive process. African cultural practices were no longer inherently inferior to European "civilization," but simply different from it.

This perspective contributed to a substantial growth of musicological studies of indigenous traditions that eventually culminated in the publication of Percival Kirby's *The Musical Instruments of the Native Races of South Africa* in 1934. At one time a music inspector in the Natal Education Department, Kirby had earlier suggested that "the musical training of the Native will have to proceed along European lines."[57] By the late 1930s, however, he argued for "the deliberate recognition of indigenous music by all educationists" (Kirby 1949:621). Kirby's views were seconded by Hugh Tracey who was then responsible for the embryonic South African Broadcasting Corporation in Durban. As members of the music advisory committee at Adams, Tracey and Kirby gave talks on traditional African music and greatly influenced thinking on music education. Tracey went as far as to assert that

> however beautiful and useful European music is to Europeans it can have very little importance to Africans. . . . The African who manages to learn to play the piano and becomes conversant with the whole European repertoire has achieved only an imitative faculty.[58]

On a parallel platform, white liberal cultural initiatives helped black cultural leaders form the Zulu Society in 1937, an organization aimed at the diffusion of popular discontent through a focus on Zulu cultural traditions and "proper" Zulu morals. In its cultural nationalism, as Shula Marks points out, the Zulu Society was marked by an ambiguity that characterizes most Third World nationalist movements. The new elites had to mobilize their societies in terms of the traditions and in a language that the rural masses could understand. Socioeconomic advance and incorporation into industrial society had to be propagated in the name of tradition (Marks 1989). But many of the traditions invoked were in fact "invented traditions" (Hobsbawm and Ranger 1983) constructed around the disparate remnants of a shattered rural order. Thus most of the folk songs on Caluza's HMV recordings were anything but relics of an unbroken tradition emanating from an archaic past. Many were creations of urban intellectual elites and as such not part of the collective musical heritage. Lindi Msane, for instance, one of the choristers in Caluza's Double Quartette and later a Pitch Black Follies full-time professional, had to learn most of these songs and dances from scratch.[59]

Whereas, as we have seen, Caluza's Zulu nationalism of the 1920s was composed of quite diverse and partly conflicting ideological strands, it was replaced by a more unambiguously defined brand of backward-looking nationalism in the mid-1930s. Thus when Caluza assumed his new functions in 1936 and set out to remodel the syllabus along the lines of Hampton, two black folk traditions—traditional Zulu music and Negro spirituals—were to become key themes. Although Caluza opposed Tracey's overprotective and potentially segregationist views,[60] he drafted a detailed proposal for research on traditional music which clearly bears the mark of Hugh Tracey's ideas on fieldwork. The composer probably never obtained financial assistance for his project, a fact which nonetheless could not prevent him from offering courses in "Bantu Music" and fieldwork in traditional music.[61] In addition, broadcasts of traditional Zulu music involved Caluza's choral groups, Mseleku's Royal Amanzimtoti Entertainers, as well as rural ensembles recruited by the Zulu Society. In the minds of white critics, these broadcasts elevated Zulu music to status "as a work of art rather than an ethnological curiosity."[62]

Kirby's, Tracey's, and Caluza's educational efforts eventually laid the foundations of early apartheid educational policies of the late 1940s that used culture and performance as a vehicle to produce the ideal subjects of white *baaskaap:* citizens, as the *Native Teachers' Journal* put it, "who are socially adaptable, self-disciplined, physically fit and well-developed."[63] Ultimately, the concern for self-discipline and social adaptability, that is, availability as a cheap and disposable labor force, also conditioned the use of spirituals in black cultural and educational politics. In Natal American missionary institutions such as Adams College and Inanda Seminary had always acquainted their students with Ameri-

Figure 16. R. T. Caluza (middle, front row) at the African Authors Conference, 1936. (*Bantu World,* December 26, 1939)

can, and to an extent Afro-American, culture. Negro spirituals, therefore, had long been an integral part of school concerts, Selby Ngcobo, Hilda Matthews, Faith Caluza, and others being among those who presented longtime favorites such as "Were You There" and "Steal Away." But not all components of Afro-American culture were greeted with like benevolence. Contributors to Adams's journal *Iso Lomuzi* complained about a kind of music "in the dormitories and round about the school campus during recreation periods" which showed that "good music even in our school is not free from the strong competition of its rival, namely jazz music."[64] White liberals and black leaders viewed jazz—even of the diluted kind that was available in South Africa—as a corruption of a vaguely defined and poorly understood authentic African music and as insufficient equipment for young Africans "for their social entertainment and their moral services."[65] "Moral services" was a formula that was popular with white liberals and black elite leaders to describe the black acceptance of white hegemony and a subordinate role of the black masses in shaping the world for themselves. Along with censored film shows, debating circles, and soccer games, the singing of spirituals was seen as an important agent for "moralizing the leisure time" of blacks.

It is within this logic that Caluza saw Negro spirituals as "a valuable link between the negro race in the old and the new worlds."[66] And no sooner did he commence work at Adams than he requested permission from Hampton's President Arthur Howe to transcribe Dett's *Hampton Book of Spirituals* into Tonic Sol-fa. The book never materialized, but around that time Rev. Alexander Sandilands had already started collecting material for a Tonic Sol-fa collection of spirituals. However, the work was not to be published until 1951, as *A Hundred and Twenty Negro Spirituals*.[67]

At this same time Caluza trained a choir and a Male Voice Quintette to perform the "sorrow songs" on a more regular basis. The Quintette consisted at various stages of its history of musicians such as Simon Ngubane, Sihauli Dube, and Waterston Bokwe and gave concerts of Negro spirituals like "I Want to Be a Christian" as well as minstrel tunes such as Stephen Foster's "Massa's in de Cold Ground."[68] The concurrent revival of spirituals and minstrel songs was by no means coincidental. No less a person than Caluza had demonstrated the affinity of spirituals and minstrel music that existed in the minds of black South Africans as early as 1930. With his Double Quartette he recorded "AmaNigel Coons" (HMV GU 40), a peculiar reinterpretation of the well-known spiritual "Good News, the Chariot's Coming":

> *Oh, AmaNigel Coons,*
> *I don't want to leave you behind.*
> *Look out for the Nigel Coons,*
> *they come from Winterton.*
> *They've come for to entertain,*
> *I don't want to leave you behind.*
>
> . . .
>
> *O, umqombothi,*
> *I don't want to leave you behind.*
> *O, madoda, isimangaliso,*
> *I don't want to leave you behind.*
>
> Oh, liquor,
> *I don't want to leave you behind.*
> Oh, men, African beer,
> *I don't want to leave you behind.*

Like blacks in the United States, black South Africans thought that Foster's songs "retain all the characteristics of American Negro folk music,"[69] and Foster songs eventually circulated in sheets and records in the vernacular. The Wilberforce Institute Singers recorded a Xhosa version of "Susannah" (Columbia OE 9), while Durban-born and -bred comedian Ndaba Majola put a Zulu adaptation of "Good Old Jeff" on disk (Columbia AE 76).

Conclusion: The Last Years   Despite Caluza's seemingly indefatigable energies as an organizer, educator, and folklorist, he composed fewer and fewer songs, and in the end it seemed that "it was no longer the same thing."[70] Among the songs that were composed during his term at Adams are "Nyikithi," "Pick-up Van," "Umaconsana," "Inanda Seminary," and a "Carpenter's Song." Only the first song, "Nyikithi," based on a traditional work song, remains popular today.

But what are the reasons for Caluza's decline as a composer? By the early 1930s his older compositions had become firmly established as standard concert items and set pieces at competitions and *eisteddfodau.* But at the same time there emerged in Johannesburg, Durban, Port Elizabeth, in fact, every major urban center in the country, an entirely new and much more comprehensive subculture whose one and only point of reference was America. The stars of this sophisticated world of dance halls and movies were Shirley Temple, Fred Astaire, and Fats Waller. Younger musicians, many of them mission graduates who still acknowledged and indeed were brought up under Caluza's "ragtime" influence, emulated the American models and joined the new South African jazz bands. Some attempted to broaden their popularity with older listeners by adapting older material. John Mavimbela and his Johannesburg-based Rhythm Kings reflected the transition quite vividly: they performed a "jazz" arrangement of "Ematawini," "Influenza," "Insizwa Ezimbili," and "Umantindane" on a live broadcast in 1935.[71] Another elite band of the time, the Jazz Revellers, teamed up with the Albert St. Mixed Quintette in a recording of Caluza's "Izintsizwa Ezimbili" and "Woza Mfowetu" (Columbia AE 8). In the final analysis, however, such refurbishing of Caluza's songs could be no more than a superficial adaptation; in substance, with regard to style, images, and lyrics, Caluza's songs were the popular music of the immediate postwar era and the 1920s.

In addition to declining popularity, from the late 1930s Caluza was also bowing to pressure from his wife Evelyn to expand his commercial operations. Born of the wealthy Nxaba family of Groutville, Evelyn Kastinah was used to "a life in luxury,"[72] and pressed Caluza to open four stores in Pietermaritzburg, Bulwer, and Kwa-Dlangezwa. In 1947 Caluza retired from his teaching duties at Adams and withdrew from active musical life. Caluza may have been persuaded to agree to a part-time teaching position in the Education Department of the University of Zululand, which opened in 1962, because of its proximity to his Kwa-Dlangezwa store. However, ill health and an amputated leg forced him to resign after a few years. Reuben Tholakele Caluza died on March 5 1969, in Kwa-Dlangezwa.[73]

Caluza's native village Siyamu, the "very small village of Christians," is now called Kwa-Caluza and forms part of a vast periurban commuter slum servicing the white industry and homes of Pietermaritzburg. The once-peaceful peasant communities of Edendale have

FIGURE 17. R. T. Caluza shortly before his death in 1968. (University of South Africa, Documentation Centre for African Studies, Champion Collection)

become torn by crime and bloody fraticidal strife. These divisions may perhaps not be the same that have chronically beset the early black nationalist movement, but they are certainly as fatal as the disunity among the country's oppressed that Caluza bewailed in his "Yekan' Umona Nenzondo" (Don't be Jealous):

> . . .
>
> *Ikhon' int' ebulal' isizwe sakith' esimnyama.*
> *Izwe lakithi liyafa labulawa amagqubu libulawa na umona.*
>
> Something is killing the black nation.
> Our nation is dying because of grudges and jealousy.

Nevertheless, popular culture, songs, dances, poetry, and theater continue to thrive amid this world of grudges and jealousy. To South Africa's hardened youth—abandoned, as the poet Wally Serote says, to a merciless future, engaging in the *toyi-toyi* and brandishing pictures of Ghaddafi on top of burning barricades—the music of Caluza has no meaning. But in order to be truly meaningful, the reconstruction of South African society will still have to meet the challenge embodied in the histories, works, and visions of people such as Reuben T. Caluza, the "African Star."

Six

"Singing Brings Joy to the Distressed": The Early Social History of Zulu Migrant Workers' Choral Music

One of the central issues in studies of the cultural processes surrounding labor migration in Latin America and Africa in recent years concerns the role of music, dance, and theater as vehicles of the adaptation of rural populations to the urban environment. As James Koetting, for instance, argues in the course of a study on the music of Kasena migrants in Accra, Ghana, traditional Kasena music helps to "prevent social breakdown on the one hand and social integration on the other" (Koetting 1975:31; also Coplan 1985:233–34; Hampton 1977). Methodologically the idea of performance as a mechanism of adaptation rests on two related sets of assumptions: first, a "dual" economy and a corresponding social and cultural divide between town and countryside; and second, on the historical and stylistic evolution of performance categories within the broader process of the formation of class-based urban cultures in modern Third World societies.

This chapter looks at the early history of a genre of Zulu male choral music in South Africa called *isicathamiya* and its relationship with labor migration. More recently, one representative example of the *isicathamiya* style reached the top notches of the international pop charts as a result of the appearance of the Durban-based *isicathamiya* choir Ladysmith Black Mambazo on Paul Simon's Grammy Award–winning album "Graceland." Among the most vital contexts of present-day *isicathamiya* are competitions that are being held every weekend in a number of location halls, hostels, and similar venues in Johannesburg, Durban, and other urban centers. Under a set of strict rules and adjudicated by white judges, up to thirty choirs compete for cash prizes in events that usually last from Saturday night to Sunday morning.

The roots of *isicathamiya* reach well back to the turn of the twentieth century and have primarily been associated with Zulu-speaking migrants. Together with other forms of expressive culture among South African migrants such as Sotho miners' *sefela* songs and Zulu migrants' *ingoma* dance styles, Zulu male choral singing has been closely linked with half a century of industrialization and urbanization in the most advanced political economy of the African continent, and as such it constitutes one of the most compelling and complex statements about the experience of millions of black migrants in South Africa.[1]

What is being discussed here through an examination of the history of *isicathamiya* until the 1950s is, in the first instance, the by-now-familiar argument that the evolution of a style such as *isicathamiya* is not simply a case of the modernization of a once-rural genre through the effects of labor migration. Certain forms of migrant culture and migrant consciousness such as *isicathamiya* represent more than a historical phase, more than a passing moment in the inevitable transition of rural cultures toward the formation of urban working-class musical cultures. More specifically, it appears that the development and function of *isicathamiya* cannot be understood solely in terms of a rural-traditional performance style being used as a mechanism of urban adaptation. The participation of migrant workers in *isicathamiya* performance rather than soccer, disco dancing, and other such solidly urban cultural activities and the choices different groups of migrant performers make about dress, dance, and vocal style in *isicathamiya* do not allow us to determine criteria of successful urban adaptation, to "tell the migrant worker who is urbanizing from the one who is not" (Coplan 1982a:114). As ethnomusicologists increasingly come to agree on the nonisomorphic relationship between song structure and social structure, performers' and audiences' aesthetic choices can no longer serve as indicators of class position, nor can the stylistic development of genres based on such choices be accounted for in terms of urban adaptation alone (Waterman 1986:25, 28).

The autonomy of forms of expressive culture, the nonreducibility of consciousness to relations of material production, and the linkages between social structure and migrant performance therefore have to be seen primarily as a problem of symbolic mediation, of social action as communicative practice (Comaroff 1985:5). *Silapha nje siphuma ekhaya*, "As we are here, we come from home"—statements such as these are recurrent in *isicathamiya* songs and seem to delineate the fundamental experience of migrant workers.[2] "Here" and "home" are key notions in a "poetic mode of representation" of two worlds whose realities differ radically from each other (Comaroff and Comaroff 1987:193). The "here" (*lapha*) is the amorphous present, the town, the factories, oppression, insecurity, crime, and loneliness. "Home" (*khaya*) is the distant and idealized past, the family, order, affection, and security. But these images are not absolute dichotomies (Uzzell 1979). At one level, that of poetic discourse and song lyrics, black migrants have constructed a model of society that makes sense of the jarring contrasts in no better terms such as the dichotomous "here" and "home." At another level, however, such as patterns of musical sound, kinetic patterns, and dress, much less rigid conceptual models of this society begin to appear. Ultimately, a picture of a tradition emerges which is characterized by a deep-reaching articulation of urban and rural cultural elements. This entails the simultaneous existence of very different orders of meaning and of communicative channels that are not necessarily expressions of one view of the world alone. Zulu-speaking migrant performers do not perceive themselves as puppets entangled in the strings of a "dual" economy of some sort. Nor do they portray themselves as wanting to assimilate completely to the urban lifestyle. Rather than a strategy of urban adaptation, the osmosis in migrant performance genres such as *isicathamiya* is a result of the increasing articulation of South African black migrants' heterogeneous worlds (Comaroff 1985:153–56; Comaroff and Comaroff 1987).

Given this strangely oscillating experience, migrant performers' *isicathamiya* songs, lyrics, and choreography, like the expressive symbols of migrants elsewhere, are potent resources for action aiming at the definition of social space and at a secure location within these multiple, contradicting worlds (Turino 1988:130). They enable people who have been decentered to reconstruct their universe in terms which they can control. By creating multilevel symbols in which to reflect upon the experience of migration, *isicathamiya* performers are part of the very reconstruction of the migrants' world.

"Coons" and School Choirs: The "Prehistory" of Isicathamiya

The "prehistory" of *isicathamiya* starts in the second half of the nineteenth century, or as one correspondent to the Durban Zulu newspaper *Ilanga* established more precisely, it "dates back to 1890."[3] By that time American minstrel shows had become by far the most popular form of stage entertainment in South Africa's expanding urban centers (Cockrell 1987). Despite the crude caricatures of blacks in minstrel shows, the repertoire, performance style, and musical instruments of the minstrel stage were enthusiastically received by the growing black urban population of the late nineteenth century. The deepest impression on black audiences, however, was left by the Minstrel, Vaudeville and Concert Company under the direction of Orpheus McAdoo, who between 1890 and 1898 introduced jubilee songs and the black minstrel repertoire to South Africa. McAdoo's visits became so deeply ingrained in popular consciousness as a turning point in black South African musical history that Thembinkosi Phewa, member of the legendary Evening Birds under Edwin Mkhize, declared: "Our oldest brothers, the first to sing *isicathamiya,* were the Jubilee Brothers. That was in 1891."[4]

By the turn of the century, minstrelsy had reached even remote rural areas with a fairly intact traditional performance culture. Mission school graduates formed minstrel troupes modeled on McAdoo's company or on the numerous white blackface troupes that had established themselves in many South African centers and small towns. But the popularity of minstrelsy and music hall tunes was by no means restricted to the black urban intermediate class of teachers, artisans, and petty traders.

In the mining compounds and barracks of South Africa's industrial heartland, migrant workers were able to watch and appreciate performances by the best vaudeville and "ragtime" troupes of the time, such as Reuben T. Caluza's Ohlange Choir, from as early as the time of the First World War. In and around Johannesburg and in the Transvaal, choir member Selina Khuzwayo recalls, Caluza's show attracted "bigger crowds than anywhere else," while during concerts in rural Edendale "the windows would be blocked up by people from all around."[5] These audiences of farm laborers, miners, and compound residents were impressed by Caluza's skillful combination of dance, action, and Zulu topical lyrics. Above all, the slick entertainment reflected positive, black images of the ideal urbanite, the "coon." In the minds of South African migrant workers, the image of the sophisticated, self-conscious "coon" and its corresponding musical style soon merged into *isikhunzi* (coons), the earliest prototype of *isicathamiya.*[6]

In Johannesburg during the mid-1930s, as Naughty Boys veteran Mbijana Shembe recalls, the *amacoons* used to parade the streets dressed in wide-sleeved shirts, playing military drums with their hands, and performing intricate kicks and steps with their feet.[7] Despite certain overall similarities between coon parades and early *isicathamiya,* the interpretations of what really constitutes *isikhunzi* vary among veteran performers. Most singers, however, agree that it was a genre that was defined less in terms of *what* was sung rather than by the way in which and by whom it was performed. In the first instance, it was a distinctly urban, middle-class style, whose proponents were regarded by working-class audiences and performers such as T. Phewa "as a better group, as a different breed, a class of their own." Early *isicathamiya* protagonists such as Isaac Mandoda Sithole, one-time member of the legendary Evening Birds and Natal Champions, experienced difficulties in singing *isikhunzi*, because "they used to change voices. They sang like school choirs."[8] Second, *isikhunzi* was a low-intensity and low-ranged idiom in four-part harmony. The Zulu term *phansi* (beneath, below) designates both pitch and volume and in a more specific sense was used by informants to refer to the Western way of balancing parts and the Western open voice quality.

Ragtime and Wedding Songs: The "Rural" Sources of *Isicathamiya*   Early migrants who were being confronted with a radically different set of cultural practices in the cities at the turn of the twentieth century transported some of these practices, including *isikhunzi*, back to the countryside. But by the 1920s the social formations in the Natal interior were being shaken to the roots by a turbulent process of social transformation. Massive evictions of African peasants from ancestral land produced the farm labor required by the expanding white farms as well as a steady supply of migrant labor to the industrial centers around Johannesburg and Durban. It is from within the ranks of these dispossessed farm laborers that emerged *ingoma* light dance and songs, the second important source of early *isicathamiya* music.

One of these *ingoma* dances, called *isishameni*, was the creation of Jubele Dubazana, a timber worker in Johannesburg, who combined the upright body posture of the *umqonqo* dance with raised hands and kicking, stamping leg movements. Few elements, if any, of early *isishameni* dancing, such as a stretched-out position of the arms, are preserved in present-day *isicathamiya* choreography. But the significance early *isicathamiya* protagonists attached to dancing and the extent to which these performers remodeled the style, vocabulary, and meaning of farm laborers' *ingoma* dances in the service of a genre in tune with the realities of industrial labor and urban living can best be gauged from the terminological shifts of performance roles and internal group organization in *ingoma* and *isicathamiya* performance. Whereas *ingoma* dancers are organized in *isipani*, oxen plough spans, *isicathamiya* choirs are frequently called a "team" or *ikhlaphu* (club). The names of such clubs further illustrate the transformation of rural forms of youth socialization in age sets toward more urban, Western patterns of association. Thus, early *isicathamiya* groups often used names that were popular with soccer teams. As Tim Couzens suggested, some of these names—such as Shooting Stars—

may have been adopted from stories in mission school readers (Couzens 1983:200f), while names like Crocodiles, Vultures, Firefighters, and Highlanders were equally popular with criminal gangs. In a similar contrast between pastoral and industrial symbolism, *ingoma* dance leaders are known as *ifolosi*, lead oxen (Clegg 1982:13), whereas the lead part in an *isicathamiya* choir is sung by the *khontrola* (controller). Finally, the voice parts are given anglicized names such as *bes* (bass), *thena* (tenor), *altha* (alto), and *soprano* or *fas pathi* (first part).

But modern *isicathamiya* songs are equally indebted to the musical component of *ingoma* dancing. For performers such as Jubele did not content themselves with a new choreography; they also created a new song style in incorporating the more Western, hymn-based wedding songs *izingoma zomtshado* into traditional material (Clegg 1982:11). To *isicathamiya* veteran Paulos Msimanga "*ingoma* and wedding songs are closely related and have tremendously influenced *isicathamiya.*"[9] Traditionally, wedding songs such as *inkondlo* had been sung by mixed groups in polyphony, a fact which favored the transition to four-part structures. But with increased missionization in the countryside, traditional wedding songs presumably became the first Zulu repertoire to be Westernized both in musical substance and in choreography.

Despite the affinity between wedding songs, *ingoma* dance songs,

FIGURE 18. A rural wedding in Natal, ca. 1900. (Mariannhill Archive)

and early *isicathamiya* styles, performers stress the conscious display of Western, "civilized" techniques implied in the use of four-part harmony. "In wedding songs there is no control," Durban Crocodiles veteran Job Kheswa points out. "A person sings whichever voice part he likes. But in *isicathamiya* you must be cautious and not produce a dischord."[10]

In actual fact, neither wedding songs nor the connected choreography were anything but rural. As early as the 1920s wedding songs were commonly choreographed in imitation of the urban "ragtime" movements popularized by Caluza and his Ohlange Choir. Around 1925, near Pomeroy in the remote Msinga area and one of the most important regions of origin of the leading *isicathamiya* choirs of the 1930s and 1940s, Gilbert Coka, a thoroughly city-bred teacher, attended a female initiation ceremony and was pleased by the simultaneous performance of an "old Zulu dance of hand clapping" and a "Europeanized ragtime march" (Coka 1936:286f). By the early 1930s in one of the remotest parts of Natal these ragtime-like dances had first become known as *umgandyana* and later as *stishi* (stitches). The movement patterns of this "ragtime"-derived dance consisted of shuffling double steps, the dancers wearing tapping shoes that produced a clicking sound.[11]

In the context of modern *isicathamiya* competitions choirs have preserved a form of dancing known as *ukureka* (ragging or ragtime). It consists of slow steps that are danced as the choir enters the hall from the door in files of two. The accompanying songs are called *amakhoti* (chords) and according to veteran singer Paulos Msimanga are "borrowed from wedding songs." As a result of the musical affinity between "chords" and wedding songs, the corresponding dance movements "have got a similar effect of *ukureka*,"[12] the "ragtime" steps of wedding songs. By at least the 1930s traditional wedding songs, one of the stylistic sources of *isicathamiya*, became also known as *boloha* or *umbholoho*, a term the older generation of listeners still prefers to *isicathamiya*. Doke and Vilakazi found the term to be etymologically related to Xhosa or Afrikaans for "polka" and defined it as a "dance with boots on (as on farms on festive occasions, Nigger minstrels, etc.)" and as a "rough concert or night carnival party" (Doke and Vilakazi 1948:43).

By the late 1920s the history of *isicathamiya* had completed its formative stage. What seems to emerge as the logical result of the "prehistory" of *isicathamiya* is the fact that it can by no means simply be construed as a case of transformation of a "traditional," rural performance tradition through rural-urban migration. Not only had the changed social relations in the countryside long produced cultural formations that contained strong admixtures of urban cultural practices, but the agents of these transformations were often the same within one generation. At the very least, both in the compounds and in the rural "reserves" the migrant laborer who admired Caluza's "ragtime" was in close contact with the farm laborer who preferred the virile dance steps of *isishameni*.

Crocodiles and Evening Birds: Early *Isicathamiya* Groups — It is in this situation of rural-urban cross-fertilization during the 1920s that the first fully fledged choirs were formed. But the reconstruction of the chronology of early *isicathamiya* choirs is complicated by both contradictory oral evidence and the fact that many choirs frequently only recorded ten or more years after their formation. However, irrespective of these uncertainties of research in South African black musical traditions, the choir that can be established with some degree of certainty as one of the oldest *isicathamiya* groups is the Crocodiles. Founded in 1914 in Botha's Hill near Durban by Lutheran preacher and land-owning farmer Mzobe and members of his family, the Crocodiles initially confined their activities to rural wedding ceremonies in Umbumbulu and Inanda on the outskirts of Durban, performing *izingoma zomtshado* and folk songs. But when Isaac Mzobe assumed leadership of the group in 1920–21, the Crocodiles increasingly found themselves competing against the second-most-important *isicathamiya* group of the time, the Durban Evening Birds. Edwin "Siqokoma" Mkhize, a Dundee-born man, had formed the Evening Birds in the early 1920s and had forged them into a formidable group that was based at the Msizini (Somtseu) barracks. The choir dominated Durban's *isicathamiya* scene until well into the 1940s but only recorded four songs for Columbia (YE 42–43, 49, 51).[13]

A fourth group that must be added to the list of pioneers, one whose history remains somewhat elusive, was called Amanzimtoti. Crocodiles veteran Enoch Mzobe maintains that Amanzimtoti was led by Caluza, after he had assumed the leadership of the new School of Music at Adams College in 1936. An alternative view is held by Ngweto Zondo of the Johannesburg-based Crocodiles Singers which was founded in 1938 and is not to be confused with the Durban group of that name. In Zondo's view, Amanzimtoti was a Johannesburg group, an assumption that is lent some credibility by the fact that in the early 1940s the Better label issued at least one recording of a typical male choir called the Amanzimtoti Male Voice Choir (Better XU 41). Either way, both musicians agree that "singing really comes from these groups like Amanzimtoti. All these choirs that mushroomed were taking it up from these people, Amanzimtoti in Natal. . . . Amanzimtoti was singing *isikhunzi*."[14] In the same period, another part of Natal, between Vryheid and Swaziland, became a second important center of *isicathamiya* music with choirs such as the Vryheid-based Boiling Waters under "Khabanyawo," Van Voice, and a group called Germans.

The repertoire of these early groups consisted indiscriminately of anything from traditional and modernized *izingoma zomtshado* wedding songs and hymns, to folk tunes and material of the *isikhunzi* category. By the late 1920s and early 1930s, performance genres were anything but separate categories reserved for specific class uses. Zulu-speaking, urban mission-educated musicians performed Western music and ragtime in the style of Caluza known as *imusic* and *iRagtime,* at the same time maintaining a strong interest in *isiZulu,* a category that comprised traditional material arranged for choir. Conversely, some working-class performers such as Amanzimtoti occasionally sang *imusic* and *isikhunzi* tunes.

A fascinating example of the blurred and partially overlapping contours of elite performance repertoires and early *isicathamiya* is offered by "Jim Takata Kanjani," a folk tune that was extremely popular during the 1930s. It was a standard item in the repertoire of Petros Qwabe, a comedian and member of the elite vaudeville troupe Pitch Black Follies.[15] At the same time, the tune was recorded in 1932 by both the Bantu Glee Singers (HMV GU 137, reissued on Rounder 5025, A1) and Dhlomo's Double Quartette (Gallo GE 102). The Bantu Glee Singers were a solidly middle-class vaudeville troupe formed around 1931 by Nimrod Makhanya. The Transvaal-born Makhanya had been a member of Caluza's Double Quartette when it traveled to London in 1930 to record for His Master's Voice. Back in South Africa, Makhanya devoted his attention to a wide range of popular traditions, including Zulu sketches, folk songs, and *ingoma* dance song. Dhlomo's Double Quartette, by contrast, was a far more short-lived enterprise initiated by dramatist-novelist Herbert Dhlomo. In any case, such recordings sold well throughout South Africa, and both versions of "Jim Takata Kanjani" must have been widely popular among migrant workers. They were cited by Ngweto Zondo's Crocodiles as one of the oldest *isikhunzi* tunes in their repertoire.[16]

Apart from records, live performances by tap dance troupes also provided object lessons for migrant performers. On some occasions, both repertoires shared the concert platform, as for example in 1938, when the

Darktown Strutters, the leading vaudeville group of the period, competed against the Crocodiles in Durban's Natal Workers' Club.

Imbube: The Career of Solomon Linda   Both Johannesburg and Durban had witnessed periods of explosive urban growth immediately after the First World War that did much to sharpen the class contours of their black population. However, it was not until the consolidation and expansion of the country's manufacturing industry in the mid-1930s that working-class formation reached a stage where it produced the cultural forms, the dance clubs, trade unions, sports organizations, and musical performance practices that form the bedrock of present-day working-class culture in South Africa. It is against this background that the emergence of *imbube*, the first genuine *isicathamiya* style, and the career of its pioneer, Solomon Linda, have to be seen.

Solomon Popoli Linda was born in 1909 in the vicinity of Pomeroy, in the heart of Msinga, one of the most poverty-stricken rural areas of Natal. But Msinga was also a wellspring of Zulu migrants' musical creativity and the home of such dances as *umzansi*. Solomon spent most of his youth at his grandmother's home in Makhasane, attending Gordon Memorial School and herding cattle. After a series of short periods of employment in Johannesburg, his "home boys" Boy Sibiya and Gideon Mkhize agreed to employ him at their Mayi Mayi Furniture Shop in Small Street in 1931. Throughout this period Linda sang in a choir called Evening Birds led by his uncles Solomon and Amon Madondo. But the group folded in 1933, and Linda found employment at the Carlton Hotel. Subsequently, he formed a new group that was to become one of the most successful and most innovatory *isicathamiya* groups of all time. The new Evening Birds consisted of Linda as soprano, Gilbert Madondo, alto, Boy Sibiya, tenor, and Gideon Mkhize, Samuel Mlangeni, and Owen Sikhakhane, basses—all Linda's home boys from Pomeroy (see fig. 19).

Despite the sophisticated urban appearance of choirs as "clubs," the network of home boys remained an important rural-oriented foundation for the emergent cultural formations of migrants. Home boy networks that are based on common regional origin and kinship ties among migrants have been among the earliest and most enduring organizational patterns devised by workers throughout Africa in an attempt to minimize the effects of proletarianization and to provide some measure of stability in an uncertain environment (Epstein 1958; Harries-Jones 1969). Sever-

FIGURE 19. Solomon Linda and the Evening Birds, ca. 1941. From left: Solomon
Linda, Gilbert Madondo, Boy Sibiya, Gideon Mkhize, Samuel Mlangeni, Owen Sikhakhane.

al studies of South African labor migration have pointed to the importance of such networks among South African migrants (Beinart 1987;
McNamara 1980). Among the organizations that duplicate the structures
of home boy–based associations such as savings clubs, burial societies,
soccer clubs, and *ingoma* dance teams are *isicathamiya* choirs.

Initially the Evening Birds performed at weddings for ten shillings,
but they eventually became involved in the expanding network of choir
competitions and concerts on the Reef that was concentrated in hostels,
location halls, and compounds. Hostels, in particular, were alive with
creativity. In Johannesburg, Linda and his home boys might have so-
cialized with fellow workers at the Wemmer Barracks and in the
Municipal Men's Hostel in Wolhuter Street. Both hostels were well
known for their male choirs, while the latter was described by *Umteteli*
journalist Walter Nhlapo as "an arsenal of song and song-birds" where
"on any night, on the corridor, stairs, rooms, bathroom, kitchen you meet
and hear good, bad and indifferent renderings."[17]

In 1939 Linda decided to take a job offer as packer at Gallo's newly opened record-pressing plant in Roodepoort. His choir soon attracted the attention of Gallo's talent scout Griffith Motsieloa, and before long one of Linda's songs, "Mbube" (Lion) (Gallo GE 829, reissued on Rounder 5025, A5), topped the list of the country's best-selling recordings for the African listenership. Like most early *isicathamiya* tunes, "Mbube" was based on a wedding song which Linda and his friends had picked up from young girls in Msinga and whose words commemorated the killing of a lion cub by the young Solomon and his herdsboy friends.

While neither the words of "Mbube" nor its anchorage in a wedding song were particularly original, in the view of Evening Birds member Gilbert Madondo, it was Linda's performance style in conjunction with a number of other innovations that revolutionized migrant workers' choral performance styles. First, the Evening Birds were the first migrant-worker choir to depart from the *isikhunzi* principle of one singer per voice part and to augment the bass section by two singers.[18] While this alteration modernized early *isicathamiya* performance, in substance the strengthening of the bass section meant a return to traditional choral practices of ceremonial performance genres. Be this as it may, as a result of Linda's "invention," early *isicathamiya* groups rarely numbered more than six to eight singers, and when larger groups became fashionable in the 1950s, the principle of proportional preponderance of bass voices remained untouched:

> If the choir has eight members, the distribution of voices would be: first part (leader), one voice; second part (alto), one voice; third part (tenor), one voice; and fourth part (bass), five voices. If there are ten or more members, the next to be reinforced would be the third part, or tenor, for example: first part, one voice; second part, one voice; third part, two voices, and fourth part, six or more voices." (Sithole 1979:277f)

Concurrently with the reorientation toward traditional performance practices, Linda codified the harmonic texture of *imbube* music by using a simple $I = IV = I\overset{6}{4} = V^7$ pattern for all his songs. Almost as a counterweight to the traditional emphasis on bass parts, this basic chord sequence linked early *isicathamiya* music to the more Westernized genres popular among the upper strata of South Africa's urban black society, because it formed one of the lowest common denominators of all early urban African music regardless of class origin and specific ideological functions.

In 1938, in addition to his musical innovations, Linda became the first *isicathamiya* performer to introduce group uniforms and striped suits,

signaling urban sophistication at a time when Durban choirs still preferred the more old-fashioned baggy trousers called "Oxford Bags"
immortalized in Caluza's song "UBunghca" (HMV GU 1). Elegant dress
remains one of the main attractions of a successful *isicathamiya* performance, and at least since the early 1960s many weekend competitions
have combined both choral music and "swanking" shows.

To interpret Linda's innovations, however, as indications of a clear
shift toward an adaptation to urban values and life-style is to misunder-
stand the "space" in which migrants such as Linda's Evening Birds
developed and pursued strategies of survival that made use of the best of
both worlds, the urban and the rural. Striped suits, Western chord structures, and lyrics such as those of Linda's "Savumelana" (We Agree) are
certainly expressions of migrants' desire to become "modern":

> *Hhayi amadevana asemzini esibiza ngabafokazana*
> *Sizowashaya lamadevana asemzini uma esibiza ngabafokazana*
>
> We do not want young men from our in-laws to call us
>   peasants.
> We will beat them, if they call us peasants.
>   (GB 1049 "Savumelana" (We Agree))

At the same time, this antirural stance does not contradict a more
critical perspective on urban ways as in the words of the following two
compositions by Linda that describe the bitter experiences of a Durban
migrant:

> *Ngihambile eThekwini.*
> *Abafana badlala ngami.*
> *Izingane we mama zidlala ngami.*
>
> I have left Durban.
> I was cheated by young boys.
> Oh mother, I was cheated by young girls.
>   (GB 829, "Ngihambile" (I Have Left))

> *Sahamba sahamba safika eThekwini*
> *basitshintshela ngemali eluhlaza.*
>
> We went to Durban and we were robbed of our money.
> They took our money and gave us ordinary paper in ex-
>   change.
>   (GE 874, "Hamba phepha lami" (My Money Is Gone))

Likewise the following song (GB 800, "Masakane" (Let Us Be
United!)) does not so much articulate a critique of urban immoral behav-

ior as it reflects how older migrants perceived the threat through the growing independence of young men and women to the moral foundations of the homestead economy as the backbone of migrants' reproduction.

> *Izintombi nezintsizwa xwayani amashende.*
> *Nanto usizi oluvela emashendeni.*
> . . .

> Men and women should avoid having extramarital affairs.
> These affairs bring misery to the families.
> . . .

"Gambling" and "Bombing": *Isicathamiya* Performance during the 1940s

Throughout the 1930s and 1940s until their demise in 1948, Linda's group maintained a leading position among South Africa's *isicathamiya* choirs that was fiercely contested by other prominent choirs in Johannesburg and Durban: the Crocodiles Singers under Isaac Mzobe and the Evening Birds under Edwin "Siqokoma" Mkhize, in particular. The latter group had already been in existence since at least 1932, and as we have seen assumed a leading role in Durban's *isicathamiya* scene. In later years Mkhize also directed the Dundee Wandering Singers, one of the most active recording *isicathamiya* choirs of the 1950s.

Choir competitions had long been an established forum for the performance of school and mission choirs. But when early *isicathamiya* choirs began to compete against each other, they merged the aesthetic of the concert stage with the more rural format of *ingoma* dance competitions that had evolved in response to intensified struggles over land and job opportunities. Linked to middle-class notions of competitive concerts as the ideal format for musical performance is the idea that competitions are organized around set pieces which all choirs have to perform. This explains why some of the popular tunes of the time were recorded by most *isicathamiya* choirs and all classes of performers in general. Apart from the famous "Jim Takata Kanjani," another song, "Igama La Le Ntombi" (This Lady Is Now Famous), was a favorite of *isicathamiya* audiences and admirers of vaudeville alike. Consequently, the song was recorded by both Linda's Evening Birds (Gallo GE 145) and the Darktown Strutters (Columbia YE 15).

In the case of Mkhize's Evening Birds and Solomon Linda's group, competition was further enhanced and exploited by the record industry. As Solomon Linda's widow recalls, on record Mkhize's voice was difficult to distinguish from Linda's, a fact which led to frequent disputes among *isicathamiya* groups about the identity of the Johannesburg and the Durban Evening Birds.[19] This and the fact that both choirs were called Evening Birds might have induced some producers to swiftly rename Mkhize's group Singing Birds for a series of records on the Bantu Batho (BB 503) and Columbia labels (YE 42–43).

Somewhat less popular than the two Evening Birds groups and the Crocodiles were the C to C (Cape to Cairo) Choir, Johannes Duma's Morning Stars from Estcourt (see fig. 20), the Orlando Naughty Boys, and Mkatshwa's Alexandrians.[20] The last group also affiliated with the Industrial and Commercial Workers Union (ICU) in Johannesburg and recorded extensively during the late 1930s and early 1940s (ILAM 735–36S: Gallo GE 143, 145, 185). The linkages between *isicathamiya* perfor-

Figure 20. The Morning Stars, ca. 1941.

mance and political and union militancy illustrate an important aspect of early working-class consciousness. Contrary to the assumption that *isicathamiya* is one of the prime musical examples of an co-opted working-class consciousness, protest against oppression and exploitation has always been one of its main components (Andersson 1981:127f; Hamm 1989:300). Until the late 1940s politically motivated *imbube* songs such as the Dundee Wandering Singers' "Poll Tax" or Linda's "Yethul' Isigqoko" (Take Off Your Hat) (Gallo GE 887) were even aired from the Durban studios of what later became the South African Broadcasting Corporation (SABC).

Furthermore, choirs such as Mkatshwa's ICU group and Linda's Evening Birds illustrate the fusion of two quite diverse sets of ideologies in emergent migrant culture. In the early 1930s, when Mkatshwa's choir was presumably formed, the ICU had been reduced from a mass organization with a predominantly rural following of farm laborers to a middle-class organization based on nationalist rhetoric. Choirs like the Alexandrians and the Evening Birds bridged these two class-based forms of ideological discourse in performing the rural songs of the migrants as well as nationalist hymns propagating ICU and ANC slogans. One of the offspring of this peculiar aesthetic marriage is "Mayibuye IAfrika" (Come Back Africa) by the Evening Birds (Gallo GB 3040). The tune is traditional, but it was arranged by Gallo talent scout and journalist on the Chamber of Mines–funded black weekly *Umteteli wa Bantu,* Walter Nhlapo. Likewise, in the late 1930s Mkatshwa's choir teamed up with the popular dance band Merry Blackbirds for a series of Gallo records (ILAM 735–736s, GE 143, 145, 185).

David Coplan is correct of course that such musical enterprises across class barriers were designed to broaden the constituencies of a somewhat-isolated middle-class leadership (Coplan 1985:134). At the same time, they represent a musically ill-informed attempt by the expanding record industry to deepen its hold on a highly fragmented market. Lindi Msane, for example, exstar of the elite vaudeville troupe Pitch Black Follies, recalls not without some contempt that concerts by the Follies were sponsored by Gallo and therefore had to feature renderings of Linda's "Mbube" in order to boost the company's sales figures.[21] But for all the marketing strategies and commercial categorizations of listeners' tastes, audiences elaborated their own criteria for what was popular. Sometime in the late 1940s the highly polished vocal quartet Manhattan Brothers had to experience that an audience accustomed to *imbube* was perfectly familiar with American swing. Manhattan Brothers member Dambuza Mdledle recalled that during a competition against the Dundee Wandering Singers and Natal Evening Birds at Johannesburg's Bantu Sports, the Manhattan Brothers felt

> that we had to teach the gospel of jazz to an audience that was still new to it. For it seemed that everybody looked down on us and did not like our music. . . . Our pianist took his seat and played the introduction to "Walking My Baby Back Home." To our surprise, the audience picked up the tune and joined in the singing.[22]

If Linda's Evening Birds were generally regarded as the most advanced *isicathamiya* group in terms of musical structure, Isaac Mzobe's Crocodiles have to be credited with the introduction of fast synchronized tap dancing called *istep*. Whereas the Evening Birds preferred slow "step by step movement, first backwards, then forwards," the Crocodiles, according to Gilbert Madondo, usually won the favor of Johannesburg audiences by the display of fast, fidgeting footwork. Previous styles had been characterized by stiff, immobile body postures, but dancing by early *imbube* groups featured intricate footwork contrasting with a straight, uninvolved torso. Samson Ntombela recalls that in early *imbube* dancing, dancers "were told to fidget with their feet, but the body had to be straight and uninvolved. And people would turn slowly."[23] The contrast between the virile, fighting movements of *ingoma* and the subtle, almost silent footwork of *isicathamiya* signifies the transition from the pastoral symbolism of "bullness" in *ingoma* to slick city behavior, and has been aptly described by South African ethnomusicologist Elkin Sithole. The steps in *isicathamiya*

> have to be gentle, as if stepping on eggs or tiptoeing on forbidden ground. . . . in *cothoza mfana* an upright posture is desired. Legs are stretched or kicked out as gently as possible. Even if the halls are uncemented, there is little or no dust at the end of the dance. (Sithole 1979:279)

Yet, if elaborate movement was admired by urban audiences as a skillful adaptation of the models suggested by local tap dance troupes and American movie stars, other predominantly Natal-based *isicathamiya* groups drew on older models of the ideal African inspired by rural missions. It is these models and their origin in the Natal midlands that gave rise to *isikhwela Jo*.

If we are to believe the Warden (Orange Free State)–born Mbijana Shembe, who joined the Johannesburg-based Naughty Boys in 1937, *isikhwela Jo* was introduced to Johannesburg by Mkhize's Durban Evening Birds. Other veteran performers such as Thembinkosi Phewa maintain that *isikhwela Jo* was pioneered by the Natal group Shooting Stars. Originally from northern Natal, recalls Phewa, "these singers were used to church singing. They came down to Durban and brought in the influence of the higher tones that they were introducing into male-only singing."[24] Although only recorded in the mid-1940s, the high-pitched, yelling choral sound pioneered by the Shooting Stars in songs such as "Yek'Emarabini" (HMV JP 23, reissued on Rounder 5025, A8) had already become known as *isikhwela Jo* in Durban in the late 1930s. Johannesburg audiences first became acquainted with the style under the name *isikambula* (Gambling).

Isikhwela Jo is best translated as "attack, Jo!" and refers to the cues given by the lead singer to the choir before they burst out into the high-pitched yells that are the hallmark of this style. Much of the aesthetic appeal of *isikhwela Jo* is grounded in the ability to beat competing choirs in terms of volume rather than poetic imagination or structural ingenuity. During the war audiences compared the choral yells with exploding bombs and renamed the style *'mbombing* (Bombing).[25] While choral *fortissimo* yells and high falsetto are not entirely unknown in traditional vocal music, especially in regimental war songs, in *isikhwela Jo* the high-pitched sounds more likely represented a far-less-masculine attempt at substituting the female parts of Western hymnody with male-falsetto singing. As Thembinkosi Phewa explained:

> We first heard of [Western] music at school and were encouraged by teachers to sing church hymns. . . . By singing in church we got to know that there is soprano, alto, tenor, and bass, and not singing in unison as the *ingoma* dancers do. . . . After we left school, we continued to sing. We just wanted to show that the males could do it alone without females.[26]

That migrant workers accustomed to male-only performance genres should have drawn on middle-class aesthetic metaphors of urban status is hardly surprising, since the rural mission choirs were the most readily available symbols of successful urban adaptation and upward social mobility. The identification with middle-class urban behavior was not restricted to four-part harmony, but even reinvigorated older forms of stage behavior predating Caluza's "ragtime" and action songs. *Isikhwela Jo* performers banished all dancing from competitions because church choirs, according to Natal Champions veteran Isaac Sithole, "don't move when they sing. Girls stand in front and boys at the back. So we also stood like that, 6 or 8 boys."[27]

Imbube and *isikhwela Jo* remained the dominant styles throughout the 1940s and 1950s, but like Caluza's "ragtime," Kumalo's classical songs, and other types of mission- or school-oriented choral music in the 1930s—and for reasons that can only be discussed in the context of postwar socioeconomic developments in South Africa—*isicathamiya* performance generated little stylistic innovation until the early 1970s.

Conclusion   The early history of Zulu-speaking migrants' *isicathamiya* choral music clearly illustrates that the trajectories of migrant performance are less likely to be governed by processes or urban adaptation, but have to be understood as a cultural strategy corresponding with the articulation of a rural, domestic mode of production and urban wage labor. Although some of the characteristic stylistic features in *isicathamiya* performance were derived from models that were considered by audiences and performers as quintessentially rural, their ultimate origins rested in the urban context. As an example of this, performers pointed to *ukureka* "ragtime" movements and songs or *izingoma zomtshado* wedding songs when they wished to talk about the "rural" sources of their modern and "civilized" repertoire. Similarly, distinctions between class backgrounds of *isicathamiya* substyles were blurred by the operation of techniques of cross-connotation. The multilayered nature of *isicathamiya* performance, the presence of diverse and sometimes heterogeneous symbolic levels through the use of several communicative channels such as dress, choreography, melodic and harmonic structure, and principles of internal group structure enabled migrants to metaphorically define a space in which their survival could best be organized. The definition of this space and its defense depended on principles of social orientation that were not solely grounded in models of either successful urbanization or exclusively rural rootedness.

Seven   Conclusion: South African

Black Music and the Wider

African Field

The evolution of black musical performance in South Africa during the early decades of the twentieth century provides a fascinating illustration of a number of themes in popular performance studies in Africa. Although the time for large cross-cultural comparisons of performance in modern Africa may not yet have come, sufficient material has emerged from the West African coast and East Africa to enable us to concentrate on some of the fundamental aspects of modern performance in Africa prior to the Second World War. Such comparison is facilitated by the fact that despite the great diversity of musical styles and cultural contexts in Africa and irrespective of the unevenness of regional sociopolitical development, the advent of the European colonial powers during the latter half of the nineteenth century brought large stretches of the African continent under the sway of two or three homogeneous metropolitan cultures. Thus while the emerging popular musics of South Africa, Nigeria, Sierra Leone, and Kenya may have little in common structurally, European and particularly British domination makes for a number of broader patterns in the linkages between popular performance culture and social transformation over large areas of the continent.

The southernmost tip of the African continent was not the first part to come into contact with European commerce, technology, and political power, but because of the discovery of vast mineral deposits—diamonds and gold—during the 1870s and 1880s, southern Africa soon saw the rise of an industrial giant that by the end of the century was producing no less than 25 percent of the world's gold. But what cultural transformations came to pass under the eyes of this giant soon outstripped everything that had hitherto appeared in African cultural and social history. In a sense, the cultural shifts black people in South Africa witnessed and helped to bring about during the earlier decades of the twentieth century were to be repeated by Africans elsewhere in Africa much later and at a much slower pace.

The early phases of popular musical history everywhere in Africa are primarily the product of the continent's increasing integration into the world economic and political order since the late nineteenth century (Coplan 1981:446). This wider process and its concomitant social transformations—urbanization, industrialization, colonization—were instigated by a number of social agents whose interaction resulted in the social, political, and cultural metamorphoses that affected all African societies profoundly.

Among the most potent agents of African cultural change were European missions. Early black South African music, in Durban as much as in other centers, is inconceivable without the deep effect English and American missionization had on traditional Nguni musical concepts and practices. Elsewhere in Africa, but particularly on the West African coast, European Christian missionization and local indigenous traditions blended to form some of the most creative syncretic performance styles in Africa today.

But the late nineteenth century also saw the rudiments of Afro-American missionization and its ideological influence upon emerging African Christian cultures. Like Orpheus McAdoo in South Africa, other black Americans in British Africa had much influence on the development of modern popular performance idioms. Apart from the earlier Afro-American settlements in Liberia, black American missionaries in Ghana and Nigeria spread Negro spirituals and Afro-American folk songs deep in the West African coastal hinterland. In Sierra Leone the "Creole Shout" developed as a re-Africanized, Christian adaptation of Afro-American ring shouts (Coplan 1981:447).

An equally powerful influence on emerging popular performance genres throughout Africa were the musical practices of colonial military institutions. African military corps not only trained Africans to play brass instruments and Western military drums, they also provided alternative models of social organization and identity in view of declining chiefly authority. Young urbanizing Africans readily absorbed these patterns and molded them into highly popular performance categories such as the unique East and Central African *beni* dance (Kubik 1982:48–50, 192–203; Ranger 1975).

Military service and particularly African involvement on the European theater of war during the First World War brought thousands of

Africans from South Africa and other African countries in touch with a great variety of performance traditions from the West, particularly from the United States. Thus one of the most pervasive external factors of musical change in most British colonies was the popular music that had evolved in the United States from the mid-nineteenth century. Through its various offshoots and subsequent derivatives such as ragtime, vaudeville, and music hall ballads, American popular music left its imprint on virtually every kind of modern African performance. Visiting and local blackface minstrel troupes in South Africa were of course the earliest and most numerous representatives of American popular entertainment. But both white and black entertainers toured Ghana, such as the Afro-American vaudeville duo Glass and Grant in the early 1920s. These comedians influenced Ghanaian performers Williams and Marbel as well as the Sierra Leonese Collingwood-Williams and Nichols. In Ghana the concert party, a West African adaptation of the minstrel show, not only featured step dancing, but also stage figures such as Kofi Sharp and Tommy Fire, the Ghanaian equivalents of the Zip Coon and Jim Crow (Collins 1987:181).

Internal and in particular interethnic cultural contact through labor migration to mines, plantations, and cities was probably the single-most-effective mechanism of African cultural dynamics. The evidence from South African migrants' performance genres as well as other African traditions created by migrants suggests that labor migration across large areas yielded similar musical results. *Gombe,* for instance, was an occupational song form which blacksmiths and carpenters from coastal Ghana had brought back from other parts of the West African coast where they had come into contact with sailors and soldiers of other ethnic groups. As a distinctly interethnic genre, *gombe* music in turn became one of the indigenous, "traditional" sources of Ghanaian highlife (Collins 1987; Hampton 1977). The same holds true of some Sotho concertina styles that influenced Zulu concertina playing and likewise evolved into post–Second World War popular band styles such as *mbaqanga.* Interestingly, like some musical traditions among migrant miners from Northern Ghana (Saighoe 1984), *isicathamiya* music itself was never the product of such interethnic culture contact. Nor did an oral poetic genre such as Sotho miners' *sefela* seem to have absorbed foreign influences beyond an overall style of delivery based on the principle of rising attack and falling release that is common throughout sub-Saharan Africa (Coplan 1988: 355). Yet these "songs of the inveterate travellers" crucially flourish in the ethnically mixed environment of mine compounds, where interethnic contact made for the transformation of the Zulu *indlamu* dance into the Sotho competitive genre *indlamo.*

The single-most-important factor, however, in the history of African popular performance was the intense interaction between the nascent music industry and growing numbers of musicians who were turning to alternative models of performance other than those prescribed by rural tradition. In South Africa this was a process that had been initiated as early as the 1920s, while the large-scale production of records in other African countries did not set in before the end of the Second World War. Either way, by the 1920s and 1930s in South Africa and in some of the more advanced colonial economies such as Nigeria and Kenya, the music of the cities and gramophones had become a dominant factor in their musical history. In fact, migration and infrastructural development had opened traditional community and cultural boundaries to outside influence and homogenized cultural practices to an extent unknown in precolonial intercultural exchange. With the onset of colonization rural traditions were drawn into the orbit of European music technology (musical instruments and gramophones) which had long established itself in the coastal urban centers of West and East Africa. Thus as much as the development of early blues in the United States was never simply a matter of continuity, but of the interaction of rural Afro-American traditions and commercial vaudeville (Oliver 1984), the flux of African migrants to the cities was rarely only a case of musical change through one-directional rural-urban migration. What filtered into the cities in many cases had been the result of the massive impact of gramophone records and new entertainment genres on rural traditions. In remote areas of Angola, for example, as Gerhard Kubik has shown, by the mid-1960s rural "traditions" were thriving that were in fact the product of early contact with South African popular music through labor migration (Kubik 1991). Likewise, the later history of popular Ghanaian music has been described as a re-Africanization through the growing incorporation of earlier, rural traditions. But these "traditions" were in themselves based on earlier imported and Westernized stylistic genres such as *gombe* (Collins 1987). In South Africa, finally, as the early history of *isicathamiya* demonstrates, the penetration of the countryside by the commercial recording industry renders rigid distinctions between rural and urban musical cultures meaningless.

Anthropologists of modern African cultures seem to have agreed on the fact that practically nowhere in Africa can the evolution of popular art forms be accounted for in strict class terms (Barber 1987:23). Evidence from African cities lends support to the hypothesis that performance practices rarely conform to social boundaries. Christopher Waterman's study of Nigerian *juju* music, for instance, shows that although a high degree of social differentiation in early colonial Lagos was mirrored in a complex network of performance genres, the boundaries between these genres, patrons, and social events were permeable. Thus early *juju* not only satisfied traditional Yoruba as well as Christian values, *juju* performances also catered to members of the Victorian urban elite and rural migrants. By blending components of the musical traditions of each of these heterogeneous social and cultural groups, *juju* musicians were able to create and consolidate stable networks of patronage in a time of severe economic depression and general insecurity in the cities (Waterman 1990).

Similarly, the development of Swahili *tarabu* was not only a question of Zanzibari royal support and the assimilation of classical Arabic music by the educated urban elites of Dar Es Salaam and Mombasa. Rural traditions from the East African coast and Arabic folk traditions from the Arabian peninsula mingled to produce a distinct Swahili popular performance style that appealed to all classes of the urban agglomerations of the Kenyan and Tanzanian coast (Graebner 1991).

This book has been concerned with the fact that due to the fragmented and ambiguous nature of class formation in early twentieth-century South African society, the concept of homogeneous class cultures is inappropriate. In Durban, for instance, black residents may have perceived class-based distinctions in their performance activities, but the analysis of recorded material reveals that virtually all sectors of the city's black population drew on the same stock of musical techniques and practices. Future research will have to show how the growing class differentiation in South African society, the development of popular music after 1945, and the growth of black resistance to political and cultural domination intertwined and gave rise to distinct, socially differentiated popular styles in the 1950s and 1960s.

The most useful insight then to be gained for the ethnomusicologist and social historian from the South African evidence is the need to situate the development and ideology of modern performance styles within a network of fluctuating group relations. The chapters in this book, each from a different angle, have demonstrated that inasmuch as an individual's consciousness, experiences, traditions, value systems, and ideas do not derive automatically from his or her "objective" position in the process of material production, South African black performance culture cannot be based on the notion of organic and homogeneous class cultures. Rather, the myriad performance genres grow out of the constant mobilization, manipulation, and appropriation of the most diverse symbols and cultural resources by different social actors (Coplan 1986:32f.). In this view, performance cultures are processes of active structuralization of social relations rather than institutions annexed to social classes.

Despite the ubiquity of urbanization in South Africa and the modernization of the South African countryside, calling into question the validity of the concept of untouched rural musical traditions (Bohlman 1988:126), the music of the preindustrial past remained an important influence on the evolution of modern popular performance in South Africa as much as in other African urban regions. While this must in part be attributed to the persistence of deep-structural features beyond the normative mechanisms of aesthetic control, tradition and its progressive redefinition by various social actors served as a powerful focus of social and political alignment. In fact, most of the conflicts that arose over the trajectories of black popular performance in South Africa before the Second World War were fought over the role and legitimacy of tradition, but rarely on the question of modernization as such.

Of particular interest in the South African context was the tendency among nation builders, community leaders, and ethnic authorities to invoke images of traditional social and cultural cohesion when they wished to mobilize the "masses." The earlier history of black popular culture in South Africa offers a wealth of examples of how black nationalism and ethnic alliances were frequently constructed and contested in the sphere of popular performance. Perhaps one of the most intriguing illustrations of the ways in which black South Africans manufactured a musical tradition virtually from a vacuum may be the Negro spirituals introduced to South Africa by Orpheus McAdoo's Virginia Jubilee Singers. Recognizing certain surface similarities between spirituals and traditional music of southeastern Bantu-speaking peoples with regard to polyphonic texture, black Christians in adopting spirituals—and not without meeting with some opposition from white mission-educated intellectuals—simply thought to reappropriate something that was originally theirs. At the same time of course the Africanness of the "sorrow songs" was seen to be fully compatible with black aspirations for civilized status.

Similar processes have also been and are presently at work in most other African countries. What seems to emerge as one of the most central aspects of traditional performance in a modern context is the fact that in most African countries questions of tradition, heritage, and cultural identity become enmeshed, and in actual cultural and political practice most often inextricably so, with notions of ethnicity, community, and national development. Traditional culture and performance, in the overwhelming consensus of opinion, are necessary correlates of social development and "modernization." Tradition and community are thus the two most crucial axes in the social grid system around which popular African cultural symbols and practices crystallize. African popular arts do not become detribalized and "modern" simply because it is particularly in the multiethnic, fluid, and rapidly changing African urban landscape that they grow. Quite to the contrary, the more recent "re-Africanization" of popular performance is perhaps one of the most striking developments in African music after 1945. Paradoxically, it is through a process of "secondary acculturation" that this takes place. Thus John Collins observed that in West African popular music "to copy today's Western pop style is to turn toward the African roots of this music"—or as Nigeria's Fela Anikulapo-Kuti phrased it: "I had been using jazz to play African music, when really I should be using African music to play jazz. So it was America that brought me back to myself" (Collins 1977:60).

Some gaps remain. The research on *isicathamiya*, for instance, must be broadened so as to determine the extent to which shifts in the composition of audio, choreographic, and other components of such group performances allow for insights into the patterns of group alignments among migrant workers over a longer period of time. Similarly, the transformation of early Zulu acoustic solo guitar music to modern *mbaqanga* music through the changes introduced by Phuz'shukela in the early 1950s needs to be explored in terms of migrants' changing perceptions of ethnic boundaries and shifting emphasis on traditional cultural loyalties. Other researchers might even want to cast their net wider by relating the early development of guitar and concertina *maskanda* traditions to the "ethnic fusion" rock created by Juluka in the late 1970s. In either case, the vitality and resurgence of ethnicity as a central factor in South African politics as well as black oppositional culture, music, and dance must remain an important focus of black performance studies.

As the precise nature and dynamics of the relationship between class and cultures, town and countryside, popular and traditional are coming to be charted, studies of black popular performance in South Africa will not only advance ethnomusicology as a whole. Such studies are also providing a crucial corrective to rigid, economistic views of South African society that can only assign a secondary role to nonmaterial, "subjective" forces such as consciousness, culture, and the arts in shaping and changing society. But it is in the sphere of popular performance that the winds of change often blow much earlier and harder than elsewhere. It is through the prism of black popular performance that the contours of a humane and habitable South Africa become more clearly visible. The creative and spiritual foundations of this new society were laid during the earlier decades of this century in the songs and dances, plays and vaudeville revues of "African stars" such as Reuben Caluza, Enoch Mzobe, William Mseleku, Solomon Linda, Mameyiguda Zungu, and many others whose stories remain yet to be written.

Notes

Preface 1. See, for example, Kavanagh 1985, Naledi/Medu 1985, Sole 1984 and 1985, and various issues of *Critical Arts,* in particular 2, no. 1 (1981), 3, no. 1 (1983), and 4, no. 3 (1987). For a critique of this debate from a musicological point of view, see Erlmann 1985b, and the studies by Sitas, particularly Sitas 1987.

Chapter One 1. See also Wright 1986.
2. See also Coplan 1985:147–49.
3. *Umteteli wa Bantu,* October 29, 1932.
4. For a similar constructivist argument about "black" and "Afro-American" music see Tagg 1989.
5. See also the discussion of "popular," "black," and other cognate terms in South African theater in Coplan 1987b:5–8.
6. See, for instance, in this regard Peter Manuel's discussion of popular music and what he calls the "lumpen proletariat" (Manuel 1988:18–19) as well as his comments on Adorno's critique of popular music (1988:10).

Chapter Two 1. Report of Trooper L'Estrange relative to his arrest of Mr. R. A. Collins of the McAdoo Minstrels. Natal Archives, Minister of Defence, Minute Papers, vol. 26, LW 1624/98.
2. *Times of Natal,* March 30, 1898.
3. Information obtained from an interview McAdoo granted to the *Uitenhage Times,* reprinted in *Graaff-Reinet Advertiser,* September 22, 1890.
4. *Southern Workman,* April 1882, p. 43.
5. Doug Seroff, personal communication, July 18, 1987. The details surrounding McAdoo's career between the time he left Hampton Institute and his involvement with Loudin's troupe remain unclear. While most of the information in this paragraph is based on material kept in the archives of Hampton University, other evidence contradicts some of these data. For instance, in an interview with the *Friend of the Free State,* August 25, 1891, McAdoo gave 1880 as the date when he joined Loudin's troupe. Although McAdoo's role in the Hampton male quartet is an established fact, the dates of his quartet activities are uncertain. A photograph in the archives of Hampton University, dated "1881 to '83," shows McAdoo as a member of a quartet consisting of McAdoo, Evans, Daggs, and Hamilton. According to information supplied by D. Seroff, the quartet came to supplant a larger mixed student choir in 1887, by which time McAdoo was already on tour with Loudin.

6. The literature on the Fisk group is extensive, but of doubtful scholarly merit. For a useful summary see Hamm 1983.

7. Information supplied by Doug Seroff in a letter to the author, July 3, 1986.

8. *The Freeman,* May 3, 1890. I am indebted to Doug Seroff for this and all following references from nineteenth-century Afro-American newspapers. A short biographical sketch of Mattie Allen appeared in *Journal of Negro History* 22 (January 1937): 131.

9. McAdoo to Armstrong, London, 1890, Hampton University Archives.

10. *Cleveland Gazette,* October 31, 1891.

11. *Southern Workman,* November 1890, p. 120.

12. *Cape Argus,* July 8, 1890.

13. *Cape Argus,* July 1, 1890.

14. The literature on the minstrel theater is extensive, but for the best discussion to date see Toll 1974.

15. *Cape Argus,* August 21, 1862.

16. *Natal Mercury,* October 7, 1865. I am indebted to Dale Cockrell for this and the following quotes from the *Natal Mercury.*

17. *Cape Argus,* August 21, 1862.

18. In South Africa, the term "coloured" is the official category of "racial" classification for persons of mixed "European" and African origin and their descendants. As such it is rejected by most of those to whom it is applied, and is therefore used here in quotation marks.

19. Green 1951:193; *Cape Mercantile Advertiser,* September 20, 1869; Bouws 1946:105.

20. *Natal Mercury,* March 7, 1871.

21. *Natal Mercury,* December 28, 1880.

22. *Natal Mercury,* April 27, 1889.

23. *Transvaal Advertiser,* February 2, 1891.

24. *Cape Argus,* July 1, 1890.

25. Orpheus McAdoo had made the acquaintance of the Lochs when "Lord Loch had been Mayor of Melbourne, Australia and in that capacity had received and feted Loudin's Fisk Jubilee Singers on several occasions during 1886–1889. The Jubilee Singers participated in several charitable activities sponsored by Lady Loch at that time and established a special relationship with the Lady and her husband" (D. Seroff, personal communication, July 3, 1986). For McAdoo, the Lochs were his most important contacts in South Africa, as he wrote to General Armstrong in a letter published in *Southern Workman,* November 1890, p. 120. See also Legassick 1980.

26. *Worcester Advocate,* March 27, 1897.

27. *The Friend of the Free State,* August 18, 1891.

28. *Kaffrarian Watchman,* October 15, 1890.

29. *Daily Independent,* August 11, 1890.

30. *Kaffrarian Watchman,* October 17, 1890.

31. *Grahamstown Journal,* April 10, 1897.

32. *The Press, Weekly Edition,* September 25, 1897.

33. *Diamond Fields Advertiser,* August 8, 1896, November 30, 1896, and May 11, 1897.

34. *Cape Times,* June 28, 1897.

35. *The Freeman,* April 12, 1897.

36. *Cape Argus,* January 21, 1898.

37. *Cape Times,* January 20, 1898.

38. *Cape Argus,* June 15, 1898.

39. *Queenstown Free Press,* May 1, 1896.

40. *The Freeman,* October 26, 1895.

41. Other illustrious black American visitors of the time were AME Bishop Levi J. Coppin, whose *Observations of Persons and Things in South Africa* (n.d.) is an important document on the early history of the AME Church in South Africa, and F. Z. S. Peregrino, editor of the *South African Spectator* and author of, among other works, *Life Among the Native and Coloured Miners of the Transvaal* (1910). On Peregrino, see also Saunders 1978.

42. *The Freeman,* January 4, 1899.

43. *Southern Workman,* October 19, 1890, p. 104.

44. *Transvaal Advertiser,* February 9, 1891.

45. *Transvaal Mining Argus,* no date, quoted in *Port Elizabeth Telegraph,* February 3, 1891; Landdros to Staats Secretaris, January 3, 1891, Transvaal Archives, SS vol. 2650, r98/91. I am indebted to Renata Robertson for a translation from the original Dutch.

46. Transvaal Archives, Landdros Pretoria, H. Siviele Hof van Landdros, vol. 276b, H. S. Pollington v. O. M. McAdoo.

47. *Cape Argus,* October 8, 1896.

48. Orpheus McAdoo to Paul Kruger, November 25, 1890, Transvaal Archives R 16459/90.

49. General Joubert to Paul Kruger, July 9, 1890, Transvaal Archives R 1410/91.

50. Hollis to Armstrong, August 5, 1890, quoted in *Southern Workman,* November 1890, p. 110.

51. U.S. Department of State, Consular Agent in Johannesburg to U.S. Consul General, Colonel J. G. Stowe, April 9, 1898. Transvaal Archives, microfilm A 686/337–38.

52. Harry Dean and James Brown to Secretary of State, Johannesburg, August 28, 1903, quoted from Keto 1972:388.

53. *Kaffrarian Watchman,* no date, quoted from *Southern Workman,* January 20, 1891.

54. Plaatje later fondly remembered seeing the Jubilee Singers as a young man. See *Negro World,* February 12, 1921. I am grateful to Brian Willan for this reference.

55. *Diamond Fields Advertiser,* August 15, 1890.

56. *Leselinyana,* October 1, 1890. I am indebted to Naphtalie Morie, Morija, for a translation of this text as well as of all following quotes from this newspaper.

57. Ibid.

58. *Imvo Zabantsundu,* October 16, 1890. Other articles appeared in *Imvo Zabantsundu,* April 30, 1896, and March 10, 1897.

59. *Inkanyiso Yase Natal,* November 22, 1895.

60. *South African Citizen,* December 1, 1897. See also "Gemel," "Coloured Newspapers that I have known," *Cape Standard,* March 29, 1938. I am indebted to Tim Couzens for bringing this article to my attention.

61. McAdoo to Armstrong, no date, quoted in *Southern Workman,* November 1890, p. 120; and Eugene McAdoo to the editor, no date, quoted in *Southern Workman,* January 1894, p. 15.

62. *Southern Workman,* February 1891, p. 146.

63. McAdoo to Armstrong, no date, quoted in *Southern Workman,* November 1890, p. 120.

64. *Leselinyana,* January 15, 1891. A detailed report on Mbongwe's death also appeared in *Inkanyiso,* October 1, 1891.

65. William W. Stofile to Armstrong, November 3, 1890, quoted in *Southern Workman,* February 1891, p. 146.

66. K. Charles Kumkani and Samuel Cakata to Armstrong, October 31, 1890, quoted ibid.

67. *Southern Workman,* February 1891, p. 146.

68. Bud-M'Belle to Armstrong, September 16, 1890, Hampton University Archives.

69. Ngcayiya, a future head of the Ethiopian church and later the African Methodist Episcopal Church in South Africa, had already seen the Jubilee Singers during their visit to Burgersdorp November 1–3, 1890. Ngcayiya was then a teacher at the local Wesleyan Mission School, and McAdoo's visit must have inspired him to try his hand at a choir along the lines of McAdoo's troupe. On November 3, he organized a "musical evening," highly applauded by the local press: "The gift of song and the sense of harmony seem natural to the coloured race, and nothing but efficient training is wanting to enable our native talent to compare favourably with their American cousins, the Jubilee Singers." *Burgersdorp Gazette,* November 6, 1890. For Will Thompson see *Diamond Fields Advertiser,* March 13 and May 11, 1897.

70. *Diamond Fields Advertiser,* September 13, 1890.

71. Interview with Kate Makhanya (Manye), conducted by Margret McCord, now Mrs. Nixon, in Durban in the early 1960s. I am indebted to Mrs. Nixon for providing me with a transcript of this interview.

72. I am currently preparing a manuscript on the history of the "South African Choir" entitled "Heartless Swindle—The South African Choir in England and the United States, 1890–1894."

73. See, for instance, Lea 1925, Thompson and Wilson 1971, and Odendaal 1984. For a contrary view see Campbell 1987.

74. *Voice of Missions,* June 1, 1898.

75. *Voice of Missions,* June 1896.

76. *Leselinyana,* October 1, 1890.

77. *The Freeman,* October 26, 1895.

78. *Natal Mercury,* April 5, 1898.

79. *South African Citizen,* May 4, 1898.

80. *The Freeman,* October 6, 1900. Nothing much is known about the further fate of the "Coloured Minstrel Company." Only Will Thompson resurfaces, first in June 1898 as pianist of the Balmoral Minstrels (*Diamond Fields Advertiser,* June 25, 1898), and then in October 1898, as a member of the American Salesman Variety Company (*Diamond Fields Advertiser,* October 1, 1898), both resident companies in Kimberley. Thompson's involvement with the American Salesman Variety Company contradicts the somewhat mysterious notice in *The Freeman* of December 24, 1898, in which Jose Jalvan announces Thompson's death in Cape Town in August 1898.

81. *Umteteli wa Bantu,* November 7, 1925, May 4, 1929, October 6, 1923, and June 21, 1930; *Ilanga,* November 2, 1923, and December 28, 1923; *Workers' Herald,* March 18, 1927.

82. See NTS 1423, 12/214; *South African Christian Recorder,* August 15, 1925; *Umteteli wa Bantu,* April 16, 1927.

83. *Umteteli wa Bantu,* November 3, 1934. At one point, Herman Gow was also directing the Harmony Kings, a quartet about which little else than the mere

fact of its existence is known. See *Umteteli wa Bantu,* January 8, 1938. For a tribute to A. S. Vil-Nkomo, see *Umteteli wa Bantu,* October 1, 1938.

84. *Umteteli wa Bantu,* January 12, 1935, and September 11, 1937.

Chapter Three   1. See Coplan 1985. Other major cities whose "white" popular musical activities have been investigated include Cape Town (Bouws 1966) and Pietermaritzburg (van der Spuy 1975); and scores of M.A. and Ph.D. graduates in musicology have poured much ink over the "musical life" of the white communities in such unlikely places as Bloemfontein and Kimberley. However, black urban traditions such as Cape Town's "Coon Carnival" remain sorely neglected (see Pinnock 1987).

2. *Natal Witness,* March 27, 1863.

3. *Ilanga,* May 28, 1904, and June 24, 1910.

4. Tonic Sol-fa is a form of musical notation devised by John Curwen in the mid-nineteenth century that uses a combination of letters and other symbols to indicate pitch and rhythm.

5. *Ilanga,* February 3, 1905, September 22, 1905, and August 24, 1906.

6. *Ilanga,* May 17, 1912, and January 21, 1916.

7. *Ilanga,* June 3, 1904, May 18, 1909, March 11, 1910, July 5, 1912, and May 1, 1914.

8. *Ilanga,* March 11, 1910, June 21, 1911, December 24, 1915, and January 5, 1917.

9. *Ilanga,* November 12, 1915.

10. Solomon Plaatje also mentions that "Tipperary" was popular among South African blacks (Plaatje 1982:19).

11. Interview with R. T. Mazibuko.

12. Interview with R. T. Mazibuko.

13. *Ilanga,* June 3, 1904; Oliver 1984:108.

14. Schimlek 1949:42; interview with R. T. Mazibuko.

15. *Ilanga,* January 9, 1920. B. Vilakazi, on the other hand, claims that it was the Mariannhill plays that furthered the development of popular Zulu music. See B. Vilakazi 1942:273 and also *Ilanga,* November 14, 1919. Some of the one-act skits were published in the January and April 1921 issues of the *Native Teachers' Journal.*

16. In the South African context "location" refers to segregated residential areas for blacks.

17. *Ilanga,* March 21, 1919.

18. *Zonk* August 1951:28.

19. For the recordings see HMV GU 76–79, 86–89, 94–96, 102–5, 110–13, 116, 118–21, 126–29, and 134–45.

20. Adapted from Tracey 1948:82, 112.

21. Adapted from Tracey 1948:14, 92.

22. *Ilanga,* June 23, 1922.

23. For a fuller discussion of the performance component in Isaiah Shembe's Nazareth Church, see Mthethwa n.d., and Larlham 1985.

24. Tracey 1948:35, 97.

25. 1930–32 Native Economic Commission, Evidence 6268. Quoted in Marks 1989:221.

26. *Ilanga,* November 22, 1912, November 12, 1915, and December 24, 1915.

27. See the program in the archives of Hampton University, and Curtis

1920:57–58. For a photograph of "The African Chief in Royal Attire" from the show see *Southern Workman,* June 1913.

28. These cylinders are kept at the Archives of Traditional Music, Indiana University. The Summary Report accompanying the cylinders mentions ca. 1918 as the year of their recording, but by that time Cele had already left Hampton. On Natalie Curtis see "Natalie Curtis Burlin at the Hampton Institute," *Resound* 1, no. 2 (1982).

29. *Ilanga,* November 12, 1915. As early as 1905, Ohlange teacher Ngazana Luthuli had tried to compile a book of secular songs, but the project evidently never materialized. See ABCFM, South African Mission, Zulu and Rhodesian Branches, 1900–1909, vol. 3, Documents.

30. Zonophone 4243. The British Zonophone company had been producing for the South African market probably as far back as 1900, but by at least 1908 the first recordings of African performers were available. Significantly, they were Sankey and Moody hymns sung in Siswati by a delegation of Swazi chiefs visiting England (Zonophone 4021–23, previously released as G.C. 4-12894–97 and G.C. 2-14145–47, recorded in December 1907). However, the first substantial number of Zulu titles that were advertised in Zonophone's catalog of "Native Records" were Stuart's recordings (4175–85 and 4193–4200). Sibiya's and Ngwane's recordings are Zonophone 4201–13, 4215–19, and 4243–48.

31. Town Clerk Files (henceforth TCF), Native Affairs in the Borough, File 1, 1915–24.

32. Most of the information in this paragraph rests on Clegg 1981a. The decline of concertina music after the 1960s might indicate, among others things, an ideological shift in urban working-class consciousness away from family and rural values.

33. *Ilanga,* June 14, 1909. The earliest-known recordings of concertina music were made by "The Zulu Minstrel" in 1932. See HMV GU 84–85, 93, 101, 117, 124–25, 131–32, and 149–51.

34. In April 1982 I recorded Alson Thombela in Eshowe bowing his *igqongwe* instead of plucking it. Alternatively, the violin also could be seen as an urban extension of the *sikhelekehle* bow. For a recording of the *sikhelekehle,* see B. Mthethwa's and my record *Zulu Songs from South Africa,* Lyrichord LLST 7401, Side B, Track 1.

35. See also J. D. Taylor: Report of Durban and District, 1924–25, p. 6, ABCFM, South Africa Mission, Zulu Branch 1920–29, vol. 2, Reports.

36. *Umteteli wa Bantu,* July 9, 1932.

37. On the Lucky Stars see N. H. Makanya, "Late Isaac Mtetwa (A Tribute)," *Bantu World,* October 23, 1937; and Transvaal Archives, NTS 2714, 241–301. For pictures of the Lucky Stars see Slosberg 1939:194; and *Ilanga,* May 1, 1937. For photographs from the plays see Lloyd 1935:4.

38. *Bantu World,* October 21, 1933.

39. *Ilanga,* January 12, 1917.

40. *Ilanga,* February 16, 1923.

41. *Ilanga,* October 5, 1923, and March 19, 1926. See also Dhlomo's article "Jazzing Craze" in *Ilanga,* August 5, 1927, and "The Dancing Craze among Natives" by M. L. Kumalo in *Ilanga,* November 12, 1926. For a more sympathetic earlier treatment of ragtime, see an article reproduced from the *Negro Year Book* in *Ilanga,* September 3, 1920.

42. TCF, Native Dance Halls and Meetings, 467c, vol. 1, 1931–34, File 1.

43. See also Coplan 1985:96–97.

44. Interview with S. Khuzwayo.

45. Adapted from Tracey 1948:43, 100.

46.*Ilanga,* March 1, 1958. For early recordings of *izidunduma* tunes see *Zindunduma* (Gallo GE 946); *Indunduma* by the Amanzimtoti Players (HMV GU 152); and *Ndunduma* by the Bantu Glee Singers (HMV GU 94), the last two recorded in 1932. For a brief discussion of *indunduma* see Coplan 1985:105.

47. For a useful discussion of *marabi* see Coplan 1985:94–95, 105–9.

48. H. I. E. Dhlomo: "Evolution of Bantu Entertainments," Killie Campbell Africana Library, KCM 8290 Z, MS DHL 1.08, D 58–280.

49. For Durban's dance halls see various documents in TCF, 467C Native Dance Halls and Meetings, 1935; Durban City Council, 63A/467C; TCF, Native Dance Halls and Meetings, 467C, vol. 1, 1931–34, File 1; and TCF, Native Affairs in the Borough, 467, vol. 6, 1931–32, File 2. For the role of homosexuality among migrants see Moodie 1988.

50. Interview with T. Phewa.

51. Ibid.

52. Ibid.

53. Adapted from Tracey 1948:10, 91.

54. *Ilanga,* June 24, 1910. There is a collection of photographs entitled *Bilder aus Südafrika, aufgenommen vom Photographischen Atelier der Trappistenmission. Mariannhill, Natal 1900–1908,* showing a large brass band, in the archives of Mariannhill monastery. Also interview with R. T. Mazibuko.

55. University of Cape Town, Forman Papers, BC 581 C 5.1.20.

56. Huskisson 1969:106–7. During and after the war Masinga also directed the Rhythm Darkies. For four song texts by the group see Tracey 1948:13–14, 35, 48.

57. The information in this paragraph rests on three handbills (*Isaziso*) in the Forman Papers at the University of Cape Town (33L, BC 581 B22.7, 9, and 11). I am indebted to Paul la Hausse for bringing this material to my attention. For a short biographical note on Mogaecho see Mancoe 1934. For the words of an unreleased recording of the Blue Ham Bees see Tracey 1948:58. Gallo test recordings of the Blue Hams that are presently kept at the International Library of African Music are 777–78S, 784S, 786S, 790S, and 947–49S.

58. Interview with T. Phewa.

59. Interview with E. Mzobe.

60. Huskisson 1969:62–64. For some of Kumalo's compositions, published posthumously, see Kumalo 1967.

61. *Ilanga,* June 1, 1934.

62. The information on the Bantu Social Centre was compiled from Durban City Council 315H, Schedules of Attendances at Bantu Social Centre 1934–39, and Minutes of the Executive Meeting, Meeting of September 23, 1935.

63. For a finely etched portrait of these early years of black jazz in South Africa see Ballantine 1991.

64. The figures in this paragraph are based on la Hausse 1984:330, 334; and Phillips 1938:xxxix.

65. See HMV GU 81–83, 90–92, 98–100, 106–8, 114–16, 122–23, 130, 133, 146–48, and 152. Also Interview with E. Mseleku.

66. Interview with E. Mseleku.

67. Interview with R. T. Mazibuko.

68.Mseleku 1936. An even neater meshing of nationalist and Zulu royalist sentiment is evident in G. F. Kumalo's song "IAfrica" (Pietermaritzburg: Shuter and Shooter) of 1937, dedicated to "The Zulu Royal Kraal and to the African National Congress."

Chapter Four   1. Program brochure of Natal Native Dancing Championships, Durban, June 25 and July 2, 9, and 16, 1939. Natal Provincial Archives, Durban Town Clerk Files.

2. Most of this material is found in the Natal Provincial Archives, Durban Town Clerk Files, in particular 467, 1931–34, Files 2, 3, and 6: Native Affairs in the Borough (henceforth NA); 315J, vol. 1, 1938–48: Ingoma Dances and Proposed Native Dance Arena (henceforth ID); and 467, 1935: Native Dance Halls and Meetings 1935 (henceforth ND).

3. This paragraph largely follows Guy 1980 and Clegg 1982.

4. Interview with N. Zondo; Muller and Topp 1985.

5. The information in this paragraph relies heavily on J. Clegg's pioneering studies of *umsanzi* and *isishameni* (1982, 1984).

6. *The Star,* May 17, 1928.

7. Memo by the Director of Native Labour, May 18, 1928, Transvaal Provincial Archives, GNLB, vol. 373, 77/28/48.

8. For a description of the *abaqhafi* and *amagxagxa* see Vilakazi 1965:76–78. For the *amalaita* see van Onselen 1982: 171–201. For the first systematic treatment of *amalaita* in Durban, see la Hausse 1987b.

9. J. M. H. Nyandeni to Advisory Board, Town Council, January 8, 1932, TCF, NA.

10. Chief Mgizo, Evidence to the Native Economic Commission, quoted in Bradford 1987:17.

11. For a detailed discussion of Champion and the ICU see Bradford 1987; la Hausse 1984, 1987a; Marks 1986.

12. A. W. G. Champion to Town Clerk, March 20, 1939, TCF, Ingoma Dances and Proposed Native Dance Arena, 315J, vol. 1, 1938–48.

13. Chief Constable to Town Clerk, October 11, 1934, TCF, NA.

14. J. M. H. Nyandeni to Town Clerk, January 8, 1932, TCF, NA.

15. Report of Native Welfare Officer, June 13, 1934, TCF, NA.

16. Minutes of Native Advisory Board, Meeting of January 17, 1934, TCF, NA.

17. Chief Constable to Town Clerk, October 11, 1934, TCF, NA, 467, vol. 10, 1934, File 6.

18. Minutes of Native Administration Committee, October 15, 1934, TCF, NA, 1934, File 6.

19. Town Clerk to A. W. G. Champion, June 15, 1935, TCF, ND 1935, 467.

20. *Umteteli wa Bantu,* March 2, 1935.

21. *Bantu World,* April 16, 1932.

22. Tracey 1948:19, 94.

23. Adapted from Tracey 1948:33, 97.

24. N. W. O. Shepstone to Town Clerk, June 12, 1935, TCF, 467C.

35. *Ilanga,* May 29, 1931.

26. S. Shepstone to Town Clerk, May 22, 1939, TCF, ID, 315J, vol. 1, 1938–48.

27. See HMV GU 84–85, 93, 97, 101, 109, 117, 124–25, 131–32, and 149–51; and HMV JP 8, 12, 20, 26, and 130.

28. Minutes of the Native Advisory Board, Meeting of March 22, 1939, TCF, ID, 315J, vol. 1, 1938–48.

29. A. W. G. Champion to Town Clerk, March 20, 1939, TCF, ID, 315J, vol. 1, 1938–48.

30. Thomas 1988:156–59. This and the following paragraph are based on Thomas's material.

31. *Native Teachers' Journal,* January and April 1949; Kirby 1949:624.

32. *Dunlop Gazette,* December 1946, p. 18.

33. *The Star, Tonight Supplement,* July 8, 1981, p. 12.

Chapter Five 1. The information in this and the following paragraphs rests on Bryant 1929, two interviews with Faith Caluza, a genealogy of the Caluza family drawn up and kindly given to me by Sheila Meintjes, additional information by Nigel Comley, and the following archival sources: (a) Natal Archives: SNA 1/6/10, Exemption Papers 266/81 Isaac Caluza; SNA 1/1/165, 1893 Exemption from Native Law Marshall Moffat Caluza; Deceased Estates, Death Notice John Caluza, September 25, 1919; CNC 1942/1218/1911; CNC 173/1918; (b) Transvaal Archives: GNLB, vol. 362, File 46/25/30; GNLB, vol. 273, File 169/17/D30; and GNLB, vol. 366, File 60/26/30. For biographies of R. R. R. Dhlomo and H. I. E. Dhlomo see Skikna 1984, and Couzens 1985; for the history of Edendale see S. Meintjes 1983 and 1984.

2. *Ilanga,* June 12, 1911.

3. *Inkanyiso,* March 17, 1892.

4. See Natal Archives, Zulu Choir Papers, SNA; reports in *South Africa,* June 4, 11, 18, and 25, July 2, and October 8 and 22, 1892.

5. *Ilanga,* August 30, 1947.

6. Natal Archives, CNC 66, 426/1912.

7. *Ilanga,* May 17, 1912.

8. Hampton Institute, Secretary for Appointments to Dr. Charles T. Loram, February 15, 1934. Hampton University Archives.

9. *Ilanga,* December 22, 1916.

10. The details about Caluza's early musical experiences are from the following sources: *Ilanga,* March 25 and May 23, 1910, and June 23, 1911; R. R. R. Dhlomo, "The Brilliant Career of a Zulu Musician," *Bantu World,* October 6, 1934; *Inkundla ya Bantu,* December, first fortnight, 1946; Huskisson 1969:23; and Interview with J. Cele.

11. *Ilanga,* August 2, 1912.

12. Interview with F. Caluza.

13. The song was later published as "Si Lu Sapo or I Land Act." Lovedale Sol-fa Leaflets No. 1C.

14. *Ilanga,* September 7, 1928.

15. Natal Archives, CSO 1865, 6884/1908; Dube to Colonial Secretary, December 9, 1908; *Ilanga,* December 21, 1912.

16. *Ilanga,* February 26, 1915, January 9, 1920, January 12, 1923, and January 25, 1924; Natal Archives, CNC 1768/1914; Dube to Chief Native Commissioner, December 7, 1914.

17. Interview with S. Khuzwayo.

18. Ibid.

19. *Ilanga,* December 24 and 31, 1915, and April 5, 1918.

20. *Ilanga,* January 5, 1917.

21. *Ilanga,* November 12, 1915; Interview with E. Mbambo.

22. Interview with F. Caluza.

23. *Ilanga,* December 22, 1916, and January 5, 1917.

24. *Ilanga,* November 12, 1915.

25. *Ilanga,* June 22, and December 14, 1917.

26. *Ilanga,* April 4, 1924.

27. *Ilanga,* October 5, 1923.

28. R. C. Samuelson to Mayor and Town Councillors, November 8, 1923,

TCF, Native Affairs in the Borough, File 1, 1915–24. For a photograph of Mthethwa and the Zulu Union Choir, see Samuelson 1929:117.

29. *Ilanga,* November 23, 1917.

30. Adapted from de Beer 1967.

31. Ibid.

32. *Ipepa Lo Hlanga,* June 26, 1903.

33. F. Bridgman: Annual Report, Durban, 1901–2, p. 2, ABCFM, South African Mission, Zulu and Rhodesia Branches 1900–9, vol. 3, Documents.

34. Herbert I. E. Dhlomo: "Evolution of Bantu Entertainments," Killie Campbell Africana Library, KCM 8290 Z, MS DHL 1.08, D 58/280, p. 2.

35. *Ilanga,* January 12, 1917.

36. *Ilanga,* January 12, 1917.

37. *Ilanga,* January 12, 1917.

38. Interview with S. Khuzwayo.

39. *Ilanga,* May 17, 1918, and January 7, 1921. See also Attendance Register, St. Francis College, Mariannhill.

40. Interview with R. T. Mazibuko.

41. For a good discussion of these repertoires see Joseph 1983, and Rycroft 1975 and 1975/76.

42. *Abantu-Batho,* December 9, 1920.

43. For Lauder and Caluza, see *Ilanga,* December 22, 1916, and December 22, 1922; and Lauder 1928:246.

44. For the entire correspondence see Rhodes University, Cory Library, MS 16,379.

45. *Umteteli wa Bantu,* January 9, 1932.

46. Nxumalo 1949; Interviews with S. Khuzwayo, T. Ngcobo, and I. Msane. Memorandum on Reuben Caluza submitted to the Financial Aid Committee of the Hampton Institute, March 4, 1931, Hampton University Archives. For Motsieloa see Skota 1931:215 and Transvaal Archives, NTS, 2706 15/301. For an obituary of Sinaye Khuzwayo, who died on July 1, 1942, see *Bantu World,* July 23, 1942. For an account of the London journey by Nimrod Makhanya, see *Umteteli,* December 6, 1930.

47. See, for example, "African Artists Get Poor Returns for Records," *Bantu World,* August 5, 1939.

48. For Caluza's application for a passport in 1920 see Transvaal Archives, NTS 2692 (4/301/1) vol. 1, January 1920. I am indebted to Jim Campbell for this reference. Also Huss 1932; *Inkundla ya Bantu,* December, first fortnight, 1946.

49. For a biographical sketch of Opperman, see Skota n.d.:83.

50. For the African Quartette see *Hampton Script,* September 30, 1931, and Program of Student Entertainment, Hampton, April 23, 1931, Hampton University Archives; *Ilanga,* June 2, 1933.

51. The Henry recordings are kept at Indiana University (Pre54-008-F), but the recordings for SOAS seem to be lost. A manuscript of Stuart's talk is in the Stuart Papers, KCM 24084, File 49, Killie Campbell Africana Library.

52. The items are now called the Caluza Collection and permanently housed at the Hampton University Museum. I am grateful to Mrs. Hultgren for directing my attention to this collection. For Boas and Tucker see the file on Caluza in the Hampton University Archives. For Caluza's plans for a book on folklore, see *Ilanga,* April 13, 1934.

53. *Ilanga,* April 13, 1934.

54. *Bantu World,* October 6, 1934; Souvenir Programme, Welcome to R. T. Caluza, Pietermaritzburg, Hampton University Archives; Reception to R. T. Cal-

uza, Esq., Johannesburg, December 10, 1936, South African Institute of Race Relations, AD 843/47.2.3, University of the Witwatersrand.

55. Quoted in Marks 1986:66.

56. For the background to the establishment of the School of Music see ABCFM, South Africa 1935–39, vol. 3, Annual Reports by E. Brookes, Houghton Library, Harvard University.

57. *Native Teachers' Journal,* October 1919.

58. *Iso Lomuzi* 4 (2): 8–9 (November 1935).

59. Interview with I. Msane.

60. Interview with F. Caluza.

61. *Iso Lomuzi* December 1936:9, and December 1938:3; and Transvaal Archives, NTS 9552/184/400.

62. "Marginal Notes. By Wayfarer": clipping from a Durban newspaper, undated, Hampton University Archives.

63. *Native Teachers' Journal,* July 1949. See also Marks 1986.

64. *Iso Lomuzi* September 1932:17–19.

65. *Bantu World,* November 3, 1934.

66. Interview with Caluza in *Bantu World,* March 21, 1936.

67. Sandilands 1951. Sandilands might have discussed his idea with Caluza at an African Authors' Conference convened by the South African Institute of Race Relations director Rheinallt Jones in October 1936. The conference discussed a number of issues relating to literacy, literature, and publications arising from the most recent debate in liberal circles on ethnicity and culture in South Africa. For the conference see Records of the SAIRR, AD 843, B 47.1.2, University of the Witwatersrand. Also *Bantu World,* November 14 and 21, 1936. For Caluza's project, see Caluza to Howe, May 6, 1936, in *Southern Workman,* 1936, p. 326. For Sandilands see Rhodes University, Cory Library MS 16,386.

68. *Ilanga,* November 14, 1936; *Iso Lomuzi* 2 (2): 21 (May 1933), 3 (1): 18 (October 1933), 3 (2): 14 (May 1934), 6 (2): 7 (1937), and 10 (2): 13 (November 1941); and Enoch Chieza, "History of The Adams Quintette," *Iso Lomuzi* 9 (1): (1940).

69. *Iso Lomuzi* 6 (2): 7 (1937).

70. Interview with F. Caluza.

71. *Bantu World,* September 21, 1935.

72. Interview with F. Caluza.

73. *Ilanga,* March 22, 1969.

Chapter Six 1. For *sefela* see Coplan 1986, 1987a, and 1988; and for Zulu migrants' *ingoma* dance styles see Clegg 1982 and 1984, and Thomas 1988. In addition, the role of migrant labor and its cultural correlates in South Africa is reflected in a growing number of studies on such diverse aspects as Tshidi migrants' conceptualizations of work and labor (Comaroff and Comaroff 1987), beer-drinking rituals for returning migrants (McAllister 1981), migrants' homosexual relationships (Moodie 1988), and prostitution among Sotho women in Johannesburg (Bonner 1988). For three earlier studies of *isicathamiya* see Larlham 1981, Rycroft 1957, and Sithole 1979; and for an interview with the leader of Ladysmith Black Mambazo, Joseph Shabalala, see Erlmann 1989. The genre is also briefly discussed by David Coplan in his historical survey of black South African popular performance (1985). As for recordings of *isicathamiya,* some of Ladysmith Black Mambazo's albums have recently become available on the Shanachie label, and a representative cross section of the kind of *isicathamiya* music performed at a number of competitions held in Durban is featured on two albums: *Iscathamiya: Zulu Worker Choirs in South Africa* (Erlmann 1986) and *Mbube! Zulu Men's Singing Competition* (Kivnick 1987). A third album, *Mbube Roots: Zulu Choral Music from South Africa, 1930s–1960s* (Erlmann 1987) is a compilation of vintage recordings documenting the stylistic development of *isicathamiya*.

2. See, for instance, Imfumi Male Voice Choir, SABC Transcription Service, T 5441, B2.

3. *Ilanga*, October 13, 1956.

4. Interview with T. Phewa.

5. Interviews with S. Khuzwayo and W. Msimang.

6. Elkin Sithole, who was an active *isicathamiya* performer in Newcastle during the 1940s, maintains that *isikhunzi* is derived from "grumbling" (1979: 278). Later, in a private communication to me, he suggested that the correct term was *izikunzi* (pl. of *inkunzi*, bull) and signified the deep, bull-like bass parts of *isicathamiya*.

7. Interview with M. Shembe.

8. Interview with I. Sithole.

9. Interview with P. Msimanga.

10. Interview with J. Kheswa.

11. Interview with N. Zondo.

12. Interview with P. Msimanga.

13. Interview with E. Mzobe. For a SABC transcription record of an early Crocodiles tune pressed in 1969, see Rounder Records 5025, Side B, Track 4. As for Mkhize's Evening Birds, both the label and Columbia catalogs incorrectly list Mkhize's choir as Singing Birds. For the words of two of his songs see Tracey 1948:56.

14. Interview with N. Zondo.

15. *Bantu World*, February 12, 1938.

16. Cf. Rounder 5025, A2.

17. *Umteteli wa Bantu*, July 11, 1936; also April 5, 1941.

18. Interview with G. Madondo.

19. Interview with R. Linda.

20. Recordings of the Cape to Cairo Choir are Gallo GE 186–87, ILAM 747–748S, and Bantu Batho BB 521. For recordings by the Morning Stars see Decca D.C. 7, 24–25, 40, and ILAM 898–99S.

21. Interview with I. Msane.

22. *Supplement to the Bantu World*, May 1, 1954.

23. Interview with S. Ntombela.

24. Interview with T. Phewa.

25. An alternative spelling of this term is *ibombing*, but this does not conform with the way most *isicathamiya* veterans pronounce the term.

26. Interview with T. Phewa.

27. Interview with I. Sithole.

References

Alverson, Hoyt. 1978. *Mind in the Heart of Darkness: Value and Self-Identity Among the Tswana of Southern Africa*. New Haven: Yale University Press.

Anderson, Benedict. 1983. *Imagined Communities: Reflections on the Origin and Spread of Nationalism*. London: Verso Editions.

Andersson, Muff. 1981. *Music in the Mix: The Story of South African Popular Music*. Johannesburg: Ravan Press.

Austin, William W. 1975. *"Susanna," "Jeanie," and "The Old Folks at Home": The Songs of Stephen C. Foster from His Time to Ours*. New York-London: Macmillan-Collier Macmillan.

Ballantine, Christopher. 1991. "'Concert and Dance': The Foundations of Black Jazz in South Africa between the Twenties and Early Forties." *Popular Music* 10 (3).

Bame, K. N. 1985. *Come To Laugh: African Traditional Theatre in Ghana*. New York: Lilian Barber Press.

Barber, Karin. 1987. "Popular Arts in Africa." *African Studies Review* 30 (3): 1–78.

Beinart, William. 1987. "Worker Consciousness, Ethnic Particularism and Nationalism: The Experiences of a South African Migrant, 1930–1960." In *The Politics of Race, Class and Nationalism in 20th century South Africa*, ed. Shula Marks and Stanley Trapido, 286–310. London: Longman.

Beinart, William, and Colin Bundy. 1987. *Hidden Struggles in Rural South Africa: Politics and Popular Movements in the Transkei and Eastern Cape, 1890–1930*. Johannesburg: Ravan Press.

Blacking, John. 1969. "The Value of Music in Human Experience." *Yearbook of the International Folk Music Council* 1:33–71.

———. 1971. "Music and the Historical Process in Vendaland." In *Essays on Music and History in Africa*, ed. K. P. Wachsmann, 185–212. Evanston: Northwestern University Press.

———. 1977. "Some Problems of Theory and Method in the Study of Musical Change." *Yearbook of the International Folk Music Council* 9:1–26.

———. 1980a. "Trends in the Black Music of South Africa, 1959–1969." In *Musics of Many Cultures*, ed. E. May, 195–215. Berkeley and Los Angeles: University of California Press.

———. 1980b. "Political and Musical Freedom in the Music of Some Black South

African Churches." In *The Structure of Folk Models*, ed. Ladislav Holy and Milan Stuchlik, 35–62. ASA Monograph no. 20. London: Academic Press.

Bohlman, Philip V. 1988. *The Study of Folk Music in the Modern World*. Bloomington: Indiana University Press.

Bonner, Philip L. 1988. *"Desirable or Undesirable Sotho Women?" Liquor, Prostitution, and the Migration of Sotho Women to the Rand, 1920–1945*. Seminar Paper no. 232. Johannesburg: African Studies Institute.

Bouws, Jan. 1946. *Musiek in Suid-Afrika*. Brugge: Uitgeverij Voorland.

———. 1966. *Die musieklewe van Kaapstad (1800–1950) en sy verhouding tot die musiekkultuur van Wes-Europa*. Amsterdam: A. A. Balkema.

Bozzoli, Belinda. 1983. "History, Experience and Culture." In *Town and Countryside in the Transvaal: Capitalist Penetration and Popular Response*, ed. B. Bozzoli, 1–47. Johannesburg: Ravan Press.

———. 1987. "Class, Community and Ideology in the Evolution of South African Society." In *Class, Community, and Conflict: South African Perspectives*, ed. B. Bozzoli, 1–43. Johannesburg: Ravan Press.

Bradford, Helen. 1983. "Strikes in the Natal Midlands: Landlords, Labour Tenants and the I.C.U.." *Africa Perspective* 22.

———. 1987. *A Taste of Freedom: The ICU in Rural South Africa, 1924–1930*. New Haven: Yale University Press.

Bridgman-Cowles, Amy. 1918. *Annual Report of Umzumbe Station, May 19, 1918*. American Board Commission of Foreign Missions, South Africa Mission, Zulu Branch 1910–1919, vol. 1, Documents. Harvard University.

Bryant, A. T. 1929. *Olden Times in Zululand and Natal*. London: Longmans, Green.

Caluza, Reuben T. [1928]. *Amagama Ohlanga Lakwazulu*. [Phoenix].

———. 1931. "African Music." *Southern Workman*. 60:152–55.

Campbell, Jim. 1987. *Conceiving of the Ethiopian movement*. African Studies Institute Seminar Paper no. 209. Johannesburg: University of the Witwatersrand.

Campschreur, W., and J. Divendal, eds. 1989. *Culture in Another South Africa*. New York: Olive Branch Press.

Cell, John W. 1982. *The Highest Stage of White Supremacy. The Origins of Segregation in South Africa and the American South*. Cambridge: Cambridge University Press.

Chase, Gilbert. 1966. *America's Music: From the Pilgrims to the Present*. New York: McGraw-Hill.

Chernoff, John Miller. 1979. *African Rhythm and African Sensibility: Aesthetics and Social Action in African Musical Idioms*. Chicago: University of Chicago Press.

Clegg, Jonathan. 1981a. *"Ukubuyisa Isidumbu*—'Bringing Back the Body': An Examination into the Ideology of Vengeance in the Msinga and Mpofana Rural Locations, 1882–1944." In *Working Papers in Southern African Studies*, ed. Philip Bonner, vol. 2, 164–98. Johannesburg: Ravan Press.

———. 1981b. "The Music of Zulu Immigrant Workers in Johannesburg—A Focus on Concertina and Guitar." In *Papers Presented at the Symposium on Ethnomusicology*, 2–9. Grahamstown: International Library of African Music.

———. 1982. "Towards an Understanding of African Dance: the Zulu Isishameni

Style." In *Papers Presented at the Second Symposium on Ethnomusicology,* ed. A. Tracey, 8–14. Grahamstown: International Library of African Music.

———. 1984. "An Examination of the Umzansi Dance Style." In *Papers Presented at the Third and Fourth Symposia on Ethnomusicology,* ed. A. Tracey, 64–70. Grahamstown: International Library of African Music.

Cockrell, Dale. 1987. "Of Gospel Hymns, Minstrel Shows, and Jubilee Singers: Toward Some Black South African Musics." *American Music* 5 (4): 417–32.

Coka, Gilbert. 1936. "The Story of Gilbert Coka of the Zulu Tribe of Natal, South Africa, Written By Himself." In *Ten Africans,* ed. Margery Perham, 273–322. London: Faber and Faber.

Collins, John. 1976. "Ghanaian Highlife." *African Arts* 10 (1): 62–68, 100.

———. 1977. "Post-War Popular Band Music in West Africa." *African Arts* 10 (3): 53–60.

———. 1987. "Jazz Feedback to Africa." *American Music* 5 (2): 176–93.

Comaroff, Jean. 1985. *Body of Power, Spirit of Resistance: The Culture and History of a South African People.* Chicago: University of Chicago Press.

Comaroff, John L. and Jean. 1987. "The Madman and the Migrant: Work and Labor in the Historical Consciousness of a South African People." *American Ethnologist* 14 (2): 191–209.

Cooper, Frederick. 1983. *Struggle for the City: Migrant Labour, Capital, and the State in Urban Africa.* Beverly Hills-London-New Delhi: Sage Publications.

Cope, Nicholas L. G. 1985. *The Zulu Royal Family under the South African Government, 1910–1933: Solomon Kadinuzulu, Inkatha and Zulu Nationalism.* Ph.D. diss., University of Natal, Durban.

Coplan, David. 1981. "Popular Music." In *The Cambridge Encyclopedia of Africa,* ed. R. Oliver and M. Crowder, 446–50. Cambridge: Cambridge University Press.

———. 1982a. "The Urbanisation of African Music: Some Theoretical Observations." *Popular Music* 2:113–30.

———. 1982b. "The Emergence of an African Working-Class Culture." *Industrialisation and Social Change in South Africa: African Class-Formation, Culture and Consciousness 1870–1930,* ed. Shula Marks and Richard Rathbone, 358–75. London: Longman.

———. 1985. *In Township Tonight! South Africa's Black City Music and Theatre.* Johannesburg: Ravan Press.

———. 1986. "Performance, Self-Definition, and Social Experience in the Oral Poetry of Sotho Migrant Mineworkers." *African Studies Review* 29 (1): 29–40.

———. 1987a. "Eloquent Knowledge: Lesotho Migrants' Songs and the Anthropology of Experience." *American Ethnologist* 14 (3): 413–33.

———. 1987b. "Dialectics of Tradition in Southern African Black Popular Theatre." *Critical Arts* 4 (3): 5–28.

———. 1988. "Musical Understanding: The Ethnoaesthetics of Migrant Workers' Poetic Song in Lesotho." *Ethnomusicology* 32 (3): 337–68.

Coppin, Levi J. n.d. *Observations of Persons and Things in South Africa.* Philadelphia.

Couzens, Tim. 1982. "Moralizing Leisure Time: The Transatlantic Connection and Black Johannesburg 1918–1936." *Industrialisation and Social Change in*

South Africa: African Class-Formation, Culture and Consciousness, 1870–1930,
ed. S. Marks and R. Rathbone, 314–37. London: Longman.

———. 1983. "An Introduction to the History of Football in South Africa." *Town
and Countryside in the Transvaal,* ed. Belinda Bozzoli, 198–214. Johannesburg: Ravan Press.

———. 1985. *The New African: A Study of the Life and Work of H. I. E. Dhlomo.*
Johannesburg: Ravan Press.

Cunard, Nancy. 1934. *Negro: Anthology made by Nancy Cunard, 1931–1933.* London: Nancy Cunard.

Curtis, Natalie. 1913. "The Negro's Contribution to the Music of America: The
Larger Opportunity for the Colored Man of Today." *Craftsman* 23 (March
15): 661.

———: 1920. *Songs and Tales from the Dark Continent: Recorded from the Singing
and the Sayings of C. Kamba Simango, Ndau Tribe, Portuguese East Africa
and Madikane Cele, Zulu Tribe, Natal, Zululand, South Africa.* New York:
Schirmer.

Dean, Harry. 1929. *The Pedro Gorino: The Adventure of a Negro Sea-Captain in Africa
and on the Seven Seas in His Attempts to Found an Ethiopian Empire.* New York:
Houghton and Mifflin.

De Beer, Zelda. 1967. *Analysis of Choral Works by the Zulu Composer Professor R. T.
Caluza.* B.Mus. thesis, University of Pretoria.

De Waal, E. 1974. "American Black Residents and Visitors in the S.A.R. before
1899." *South African Historical Journal* 6:52–55.

Dhlomo, Rolfes R. R. 1947. *Indlela Yababi.* Pietermaritzburg: Shuter & Shooter.

Doke, Clement M., and Benedict W. Vilakazi. 1948. *Zulu-English Dictionary.*
Johannesburg: University of the Witwatersrand Press.

Dube, John L., and Nokutela Dube. [1911]. *Amagama Abantu: Awe Mishado, Imi-
ququmbelo, Utando, Nawe Mikekelo No Kudhlala.* N.p.

DuBois, William E. B. 1903. *The Souls of Black Folk.*

Edgar, Robert. 1977. *Enoch Mgijima and the Bulhoek Massacre.* Los Angeles: Ph.D.
diss., University of California at Los Angeles.

Epstein, A. L. 1958. *Politics in an Urban African Community.* Manchester: Manchester University Press.

Erlmann, Veit. 1983. "Apartheid, African Nationalism and Culture—The Case of
Traditional African Music in Black Education in South Africa." *Perspectives
in Education* 7 (3): 131–54.

———. 1985a. "Black Political Song in South Africa—Some Research Perspectives." *Popular Music Perspectives* 2:187–209.

———. 1985b. "Review: Fosatu Worker Choirs." *South African Labour Bulletin* 11
(1): 120–22.

———. 1986. *Isicathamiya: Zulu Worker Choirs in South Africa.* 33 1/3 disc. London: Heritage HT 313.

———. 1987. *Mbube Roots: Zulu Choral Music from South Africa, 1930s–1960s.* 33
1/3 disc. Cambridge, Mass.: Rounder 5025.

———. 1989. "A Conversation with Joseph Shabalala of Ladysmith Black Mambazo: Aspects of African Performers' Lifestories." *World of Music* 31 (1): 31–
58.

Feld, Steven, 1984. "Sound Structure as Social Structure." *Ethnomusicology* 28 (3): 383–409.

Finnegan, Ruth. 1970. *Oral Literature in Africa.* Oxford: Oxford University Press.

Further Correspondence Respecting the Affairs of South Africa, August 1878 to February 1879. 1979. London.

Genovese, Eugene. 1976. *Roll, Jordan, Roll: The World the Slaves Made.* New York: Vintage Books.

Gérard, Albert S. 1971. *Four African Literatures.* Berkeley and Los Angeles: University of California Press.

Graebner, Werner. 1991. "Tarabu—Populäre Musik am Indischen Ozean." In *Populäre Musik in Afrika,* ed. Veit Erlmann. Berlin: Staatliche Museen Preußischer Kulturbesitz.

Green, Lawrence. 1951. *Grow Lovely, Growing Old.* Cape Town: Timmins.

Gunner, Elizabeth. 1986. "A Dying Tradition? African Oral Literature in a Contemporary Context." *Social Dynamics* 12 (2): 31–38.

———. 1988. "Power House, Prison House—An Oral Genre and Its Use in Isaiah Shembe's Nazareth Baptist Church." *Journal of Southern African Studies* 14 (2): 204–27.

Guy, Jeff. 1980. "Ecological Factors in the Rise of Shaka and the Zulu Kingdom." In *Economy and Society in Pre-Industrial South Africa,* ed. Shula Marks and Anthony Atmore, 102–19. London: Longman.

Hall, Stuart. 1981. "Notes on Deconstructing 'The Popular.'" In *People's History and Socialist Theory,* ed. Raphael Samuel, 227–40. London: Routledge.

Hamm, Charles. 1983. *Music in the New World.* New York: Norton.

———. 1986. "Rock'n'roll in a Very Strange Society." *Popular Music* 6:159–74.

———. 1988. *Afro-American Music, South Africa, and Apartheid.* New York: Institute for Studies in American Music.

———. 1989. "Graceland Revisited." *Popular Music* 8 (3): 299–304.

Hampton, Barbara. 1977. *The Impact of Labour Migration on Music in Urban Ghana: The Case of Kpehe Gome.* Ph.D. diss., Columbia University.

———. 1980. "A Revised Analytical Approach to Musical Processes in Urban Africa." *African Urban Studies* 6:1–16.

Harries-Jones, P. 1969. "'Home-boy' Ties and Political Organization in a Copperbelt Township." In *Social Networks in Urban Situations,* ed. J. Clyde Mitchell, 297–347. Manchester: Manchester University Press.

Hobsbawm, Eric, and Terence O. Ranger. 1983. *The Invention of Tradition.* Cambridge: Cambridge University Press.

Huskisson, Yvonne. 1968. "The Story of Bantu Music." *Bantu* July.

———. 1969. *The Bantu Composers of Southern Africa.* Johannesburg: South African Broadcasting Corporation.

Huss, Bernard. 1932. "Bantu Music." *The Southern Cross* April 27.

Irvine, Judith T., and David Sapir. 1976. "Musical Style and Social Change among the Kujamaat Diola." *Ethnomusicology* 20 (1): 67–86.

Jackson, George S. 1970. *Music in Durban: An Account of Musical Activities in Durban from 1850 to the Early Years of the Present Century.* Johannesburg: Witwatersrand University Press.

————. 1979. "Durban, Music in." In *South African Music Encyclopedia,* ed. Jacques Malan, vol. 1, 418–41. Cape Town: Oxford University Press.

Joseph, Rosemary. 1983. "Zulu Women's Music." *African Music* 6 (3): 53–89.

Kaemmer, John. 1977. "Changing Music in Contemporary Africa." In *Africa,* ed. P. M. Martin and P. O'Meara, 367–77. Bloomington: Indiana University Press.

Kauffman, Robert. 1972. "Shona Urban Music and the Problem of Acculturation." *Yearbook of the International Folk Music Council* 4:47–56.

————. 1980. "Tradition and Innovation in the Urban Music of Zimbabwe." *African Urban Studies* 6:41–48.

Kavanagh, Robert M. 1985. *Theatre and Cultural Struggle in South Africa.* London: Zed Press.

Keto, Clement T. 1972. "Black Americans and South Africa. 1890–1910." *A Current Bibliography on African Affairs* 5 (series 2): 383–406.

Kirby, Percival R. 1949. "African Music." In *Handbook on Race Relations in South Africa,* ed. E. Hellmann, 619–27. Cape Town: Oxford University Press.

————. 1967. "The Effect of Western Civilization on Bantu Music." In *Western Civilization and the Natives of South Africa,* ed. Isaac Schapera, 131–40. London: Routledge and Kegan Paul.

————. 1968. *The Musical Instruments of the Native Races of South Africa.* Johannesburg: University of Witwatersrand Press.

————. 1979. "The Bantu Composers of South Africa." In *South African Music Encyclopedia,* ed. Jacques Malan, 85–94. Cape Town: Oxford University Press.

Kivnick, Helen. 1987. *Mbube! Zulu Men's Singing Competition.* 33 1/3 disc. Cambridge, Mass.: Rounder 5023.

Koetting, James T. 1975. "The Effects of Urbanization: The Music of the Kasena People of Ghana." *World of Music* 7 (4): 23–31.

————. 1979/80. "The Organisation and Functioning of Migrant Kasena Flute and Drum Ensembles in Nima/Accra." *African Urban Studies* 6:17–30.

————. 1980. *Continuity and Change in Ghanaian Kasena Flute and Drum Ensemble Music: A Comparative Study of the Homeland and Nima/Accra.* Ph.D. diss., University of California at Los Angeles.

Krige, Eileen. 1950. *The Social System of the Zulus.* Pietermaritzburg: Shuter & Shooter.

Kubik, Gerhard. 1981. "Neo-traditional Popular Music in East Africa since 1945." *Popular Music* 1:83–104.

————. 1982. *Ostafrika.* Musikgeschichte in Bildern, Band I: Musikethnologie/Lieferung 10. Leipzig: VEB Deutscher Verlag für Musik.

————. 1988. "Nsenga/Shona Harmonic Patterns and the San Heritage in Southern Africa." *Ethnomusicology* 32 (2): 39–76.

————. 1991. "Muxima Ngola—Veränderungen und Tendenzen in den Musikkulturen Angolas im 20.Jahrhundert." In *Populäre Musik in Afrika,* ed. Veit Erlmann. Berlin: Staatliche Museen Preußischer Kulturbesitz.

Kumalo, Alfred A. 1967. *Izingoma Zika-Kumalo.* Pietermaritzburg: Shuter & Shooter.

la Hausse, Paul. 1984. *The Struggle for the City: Alcohol, the Ematsheni and Popular Culture in Durban, 1902–1936.* M. A. thesis, University of Cape Town.

_____. 1987a. "The Dispersal of the Regiments: African Popular Protest in Durban, 1930." *Journal of Natal and Zulu History* 10:77–102.

_____. 1987b. *'Mayihlome!': Towards an Understanding of Amalaita Gangs in Durban, c.1900–1930*. African Studies Seminar Paper no. 210. Johannesburg: University of the Witwatersrand.

Larlham, Peter. 1981 "Isicathamia Competition in South Africa." *The Drama Review* 25 (1): 108–12.

_____. 1985. *Black Theatre, Dance and Ritual in South Africa*. Ann Arbor: UMI Research Press.

Lauder, Harry. 1928. *Roamin' in the Gloamin.'* London: Hutchinson.

Lea, Rev. Allen. 1926. *The Native Separatist Church Movement in South Africa*. Cape Town: Juta.

Legassick, Martin. 1980. "The Frontier Tradition in South African Historiography." In *Economy and Society in Pre-Industrial South Africa*, ed. Shula Marks and Anthony Atmore, 44–79. London: Longman.

Levine, Lawrence W. 1977. *Black Culture and Black Consciousness: Afro-American Folk Thought from Slavery to Freedom*. New York: Oxford University Press.

Lloyd, T. C. 1935. "The Bantu Tread the Footlights." *South African Opinion* 8 (March): 3–5.

Magubane, Benjamin. 1979. *The Political Economy of Race and Class in South Africa*. New York-London: Monthly Review Press.

Mancoe, John X. 1934. *First Edition of the Bloemfontein Bantu and Coloured People's Directory*. Bloemfontein: A. C. White P. & P.

Manuel, Peter. 1988. *Popular Musics of the Non-Western World: An Introductory Survey*. Oxford: Oxford University Press.

Mariotti, Amelia, and Bernard Magubane. 1976. "Urban Ethnology in Africa: Some Theoretical Issues." In *A Century of Change in Eastern Africa*, ed. W. Arens, 249–73. The Hague–Paris: Mouton Publishers.

Marks, Shula. 1986. *The Ambiguities of Dependence in South Africa: Class Nationalism, and the State in Twentieth-Century Natal*. Johannesburg: Ravan Press.

_____. 1989. "Patriotism, Patriarchy and Purity: Natal and the Politics of Zulu Ethnic Consciousness." In *The Creation of Tribalism in Southern Africa*, ed. Leroy Vail, 215–40. London–Berkeley and Los Angeles: James Currey and the University of California Press.

Marks, Shula, and Richard Rathbone. 1982. "Introduction." In *Industrialisation and Social Change in South Africa: African Class Formation, Culture and Consciousness, 1870–1930*, ed. S. Marks and R. Rathbone, 1–43. London: Longman.

Marks, Shula, and Stanley Trapido. 1979. "Lord Milner and the South African State." *History Workshop* 8 (1979): 60–80.

Matthews, James W. 1887. *Incwadi Yami*. New York: Rogers and Sherwood.

McAllister, P. A. 1981. *Umsindleko: A Gcaleka Ritual of Incorporation*. Occasional Paper no. 26. Grahamstown: Institute of Social and Economic Research.

McNamara, J. K. 1980. "Brothers and Work Mates: Home Friend Networks in the Social Life of Black Migrant Workers in a Gold Mine Hostel." In *Black Vil-

lagers in an Industrial Society: Anthropological Perspectives on Labour Migration in South Africa, 305–40. Cape Town: Oxford University Press.

Meintjes, Louise. 1990. "Paul Simon's *Graceland,* South Africa, and the Mediation of Musical Meaning." *Ethnomusicology* 34 (1): 37–74.

Meintjes, Sheila. 1983. *Aspects of Ideological Formation Amongst the Kholwa of Edendale in Nineteenth Century Natal.* Centre for African Studies Seminar Paper. Cape Town: University of Cape Town.

———. 1984. *Law and Authority on a Nineteenth Century Mission Station in Natal.* History Workshop. Johannesburg: University of the Witwatersrand.

Mitchell, J. Clyde. 1956. *The Kalela Dance: Aspects of Social Relationships among Urban Africans in Northern Rhodesia.* The Rhodes-Livingstone Papers no. 27. Manchester: Manchester University Press.

Mokone, J. M. 1935. *The Early Life of Our Founder.* Johannesburg: A. S. Hunt.

Moloi, Godfrey, 1987. *My Life.* Johannesburg: Ravan Press.

Moodie, T. Dunbar. 1988. "Migrancy and Male Sexuality on the South African Gold Mines." *Journal of Southern African Studies* 14 (2): 228–56.

Mseleku, William J. 1936. *Zulu Solfa Music.* Durban: The Orient Music Saloon.

Mthethwa, Bongani. n.d. *Tradition and Change in the Music of an African Church: The Hymns of Isaiah Shembe.* Unpublished manuscript.

Muller, Carol, and Janet Topp. 1985. *A Preliminary Study of Gumboot Dance.* B. Mus. thesis, University of Natal, Durban.

Naledi/Medu. 1985. "Working Class Culture and Popular Struggle." *South African Labour Bulletin* 10 (5): 21–30.

Nathan, Hans. 1962. *Dan Emmett and the Rise of Early Negro Minstrelsy.* Norman: University of Oklahoma Press.

Nettl, Bruno. 1958. "Historical Aspects of Ethnomusicology." *American Anthropologist* 60:518–32.

———. 1978. *Eight Urban Musical Cultures: Tradition and Change.* Urbana: University of Illinois Press.

———. 1983. *The Study of Ethnomusicoogy: Twenty-nine Issues and Concepts.* Urbana: University of Illinois Press.

Nketia, J. H. K. 1982. "On the Historicity of Music in African Cultures." *Journal of African Studies* 9 (3): 91–100.

Nunley, John W. 1987. *Moving with the Face of the Devil: Art and Politics in Urban West Africa.* Urbana: University of Illinois Press.

Nxumalo, Henry. 1949. "How African Music-Makers Made the First Gramophone Record." *Umlindi* May: 7, 10.

Odendaal, Andre. 1984. *Vukani Bantu: The Beginnings of Black Protest Politics in South Africa to 1912.* Cape Town: David Philips.

Oliver, Paul. 1984. *Songsters & Saints: Vocal Traditions on Race Records.* Cambridge: Cambridge University Press.

Peregrino, F. Z. S. 1910. *Life Among the Native and Coloured Miners of the Transvaal.* Cape Town.

Perham, Margery. 1974. *African Apprenticeship: An Autobiographical Journey in Southern Africa, 1929.* London: Faber & Faber.

Phillips, Ray E. [1938]. *The Bantu in the City: A Study of Cultural Adjustment on the Witwatersrand.* Lovedale: Lovedale Press.

Phimister, Ian R., and C. van Onselen. 1979. "The Political Economy of Tribal Animosity: A Case Study of the 1929 Bulawayo Location 'Faction Fights.'" *Journal of Southern African Studies* 6 (1): 1–43.

Pinnock, Don. 1987. "Stone's Boys and the Making of a Cape Flats Mafia." In *Class, Community and Conflict: South African Perspectives,* ed. Belinda Bozzoli, 418–35. Johannesburg: Ravan Press.

Plaatje, Sol. T. 1982. *Native Life in South Africa.* Johannesburg: Ravan Press.

Ranger, Terence O. 1975. *Dance and Society in Eastern Africa 1890–1970: The Beni Ngoma.* London: Heinemann.

———. 1982. "Race and Tribe in Southern Africa: European Ideas and African Acceptance." In *Racism and Colonialism,* ed. Robert Ross, 121–42. Leiden: Martinus Nijhoff.

Ransom, Beverdey C. n.d. *The Pilgrimage of Harriet Ransom's Son.* Nashville: Sunday School Union.

Rich, Paul B. 1984. *White Power and the Liberal Conscience: Racial Segregation and South African Liberalism.* Johannesburg: Ravan Press.

Rycroft, David. 1957. "Zulu Male Traditional Singing." *African Music* 1 (4): 33–35.

———. 1971. "Stylistic Evidence in Zulu Song." In *Essays on Music and History in Africa,* ed. K. Wachsmann, 213–41. Evanston: Northwestern University Press.

———. 1975. "A Royal Account of Music in Zulu Life." *Bulletin of the School of Oriental and African Studies* 38:351–402.

———. 1975/76. "The Zulu Bow Songs of Princess Magogo." *African Music* 5 (4): 41–97.

———. 1977. "Evidence of Stylistic Continuity in Zulu 'Town' Music." In *Essays for a Humanist: An Offering to Klaus Wachsmann,* 216–60. New York: The Town House Press.

Saighoe, Francis A. Kobina. 1984. "Dagaba Xylophone Music of Tarkwa, Ghana: A Study of 'Situational Change.'" *Current Musicology* 37/38:167–75.

Samuelson, R. C. 1929. *Long, Long Ago.* Durban: Knox.

Sandilands, Alexander. 1951. *A Hundred and Twenty Negro Spirituals.* Morija.

Saunders, C. 1978. "F. Z. S. Peregrino and the South African Spectator." *Quarterly Bulletin of the South African Library* 32 (March): 81–90.

Schieffelin, E. L. 1985. "Performance and the Cultural Construction of Reality." *American Ethnologist* 12:707–24.

Schimlek, Francis. 1949. *Against the Stream: Life of Father Bernhard Huss.* Mariannhill.

Seroff, Doug. 1985. "On the Battlefield: Gospel Quartets in Jefferson County, Alabama." In *Repercussions: A Celebration of African-American Music,* ed. G. Haydon and D. Marks, 30–53. London: Century Publishing.

Simkins, Charles. 1981. *The Economic Implications of African Resettlement.* SALDRU Working Paper no. 43. Johannesburg.

Sitas, Ari. 1986a. "A Black Mamba Rising: An Introduction to Mi S. Dumo Hlatshwayo's Poetry." *Transformation* 2:50–61.

———. 1986b. "Culture and Production: The Contradictions of Working Class Theatre in South Africa." *Africa Perspective* 1 (1–2): 84–110.

————. 1987. *The Flight of the Gwala-Gwala Bird: Ethnicity, Populism, and Worker Culture in Natal's Labour Movement.* History Workshop. Johannesburg: University of the Witwatersrand.

Sithole, Elkin. 1979. "Ngoma Music Among the Zulu." In *The Performing Arts: Music and Dance,* ed. John Blacking and J. Keali'inohomoku, 277–85. The Hague-Paris-New York: Mouton.

Skikna, Shelley Z. 1984. *Son of the Sun and Son of the World: The Life and Works of R. R. R. Dhlomo.* M.A. thesis, University of the Witwatersrand, Johannesburg.

Skota, T. D. Mweli. 1931. *The African Yearly Register.* Johannesburg: R. L. Esson & Co.

————. n.d. *The African Who's Who.* Johannesburg: Central News Agency.

Slosberg, Bertha. 1939. *Pagan Tapestry.* London: Rich & Cowan.

Sole, Kelwyn. 1984. "Black Literature and Performance: Some Notes on Class and Populism." *South African Labour Bulletin* 9 (8): 54–76.

————. 1985. "Politics and Working Class Culture: A Response." *South African Labour Bulletin* 10 (7): 43–56.

Spiegel, Andrew, and Emile Boonzaier. 1988. "Promoting Tradition: Images of the South African Past." In *South African Keywords: The Uses and Abuses of Political Concepts,* ed. Emile Boonzaier and John Sharp, 40–57. Cape Town-Johannesburg: David Philip.

Statham, F. Reginald. 1881. *Blacks, Boers, & British: A Three-Cornered Problem.* London: Macmillan.

Tagg, Philip. 1989. "'Black Music,' 'Afro-American Music' and 'European Music.'" *Popular Music* 8 (3): 285–98.

Thomas, Harold J. 1988. *Ingoma Dancers and Their Response to Town: A Study of Ingoma Dance Troupes among Zulu Migrant Workers in Durban.* M.A. thesis, University of Natal, Durban.

Thompson, Leonhard, and Monica Wilson. 1971. *The Oxford History of South Africa.* Oxford: Oxford University Press.

Toll, Robert. 1974. *Blacking Up: The Minstrel Show in Nineteenth Century America.* Oxford: Oxford University Press.

Tracey, Hugh. 1948. *Lalela Zulu: 100 Zulu Lyrics.* Johannesburg: African Music Society.

————. 1952. *African Dances of the Witwatersrand Gold Mines.* Johannesburg: African Music Society.

————. 1954. "The State of Folk Music in Bantu Africa." *African Music* 1 (1): 8–11.

Turino, Thomas. 1988. "The Music of Andean Migrants in Lima, Peru: Demographics, Social Power, and Style." *Latin American Music Review* 9 (2): 127–50.

Uzzell, Douglas. 1979. "Conceptual Fallacies in the Rural-Urban Dichotomy." *Urban Anthropology* 8 (3–4): 333–50.

Vail, Leroy, ed 1989. *The Creation of Tribalism in Southern Africa.* London-Berkeley and Los Angeles: James Currey and the University of California Press.

Vail, Leroy, and Landeg White. 1978. "Plantation Protest: The History of a Moçambican Song." *Journal of Southern African Studies* 5 (1): 1–2.

————. 1986. "Forms of Resistance: Songs and Perceptions of Power in Colonial Mozambique." In *Banditry, Rebellion, and Social Protest in Africa*, ed. D. Crummey, 193–228. London-Portsmouth: Currey & Heinemann.

Van der Spuy, Hubert H. 1975. *The Musical Life of Pietermaritzburg, 1850–1902*. Ph.D. diss., University of Stellenbosch.

Van Onselen, Charles. 1982. *Studies in the Social and Economic History of the Witwatersrand, 1886–1914.* Vol. 1, New Babylon; Vol. 2, New Nineveh. Johannesburg: Ravan Press.

Vilakazi, Absolom. 1965. *Zulu Transformations: A Study of the Dynamics of Social Change*. Pietermaritzburg: University of Natal Press.

Vilakazi, Benedict W. 1942. "Some Aspects of Zulu Literature." *African Studies* 1:270–74.

Wachsmann, Klaus Peter. 1961. "Criteria for Acculturation." In *Report of the Eighth Congress of the International Musicological Society*, 139–49.

————. 1971. *Essays on Music and History in Africa*. Evanston: Northwestern University Press.

————. 1982. "The Changeability of Musical Experience." *Ethnomusicology* 26 (2): 197–216.

Walshe, Peter. 1971. *The Rise of African Nationalism in South Africa*. Berkeley and Los Angeles: University of California Press.

Waterman, Christopher. 1986. *Jùjú: The Historical Development, Socioeconomic Organization, and Communicative Functions of a West African Popular Music*. Ph.D. diss., University of Illinois.

————. 1990. *Jùjú: A Social History and Ethnography of an African Popular Music*. Chicago: University of Chicago Press.

Wesley, Charles S. 1931. "The Zulu Singers in London." *The Crisis* 38:24–26.

Wright, John. 1986. "Politics, Ideology and the Invention of 'Nguni.'" In *Southern African Studies*, ed. T. Lodge, vol. 4, 96–118. Johannesburg: Ravan Press.

Zindi, Fred. 1985. *Roots Rocking in Zimbabwe*. Gweru: Mambo Press.

Interviews

Caluza, Faith (interviewed by V. Erlmann)
    Edendale, February 10, 1983
    Edendale, November 4, 1984.

Cele, Jacob (interviewed by V. Erlmann)
    Inanda, October 5, 1984.

Kheswa, Job (interviewed by V. Erlmann and C. Ndlovu)
    Durban, February 24, 1986.

Khuzwayo, Selina (interviewed by V. Erlmann)
    Edendale, August 16, 1984.

Linda, Regina (interviewed by V. Erlmann and L. Mhlangeni)
    Soweto, February 8, 1987.

Madondo, Gilbert (interviewed by V. Erlmann and L. Mhlangeni)
    Soweto, February 8, 1987
    Soweto, February 21, 1988.

Mazibuko, Robert T. (interviewed by V. Erlmann)
    Edendale, November 11, 1984.

Mbambo, Eva Bathini (interviewed by V. Erlmann)
    Edendale, November 11, 1984.
Msane, Irene (interviewed by V. Erlmann and C. Ballantine)
    Soweto, February 13, 1987
    (interviewed by V. Erlmann)
    Soweto, March 3, 1987.
Mseleku, Elvira (interviewed by V. Erlmann and C. Ballantine)
    Lamontville, December 8, 1986.
Msimang, Walter (interviewed by V. Erlmann)
    Edendale, June 12, 1985.
Msimanga, Paulos (interviewed by V. Erlmann and C. Ndlovu)
    Durban, April 5, 1986.
Mzobe, Enoch (interviewed by V. Erlmann and C. Ngema)
    Durban, December 9, 1986.
Ngcobo, Thembani (interviewed by V. Erlmann and N. Jali)
    Inanda, March 6, 1984.
Ntombela, Samson (interviewed by V. Erlmann and C. Ndlovu)
    Durban, April 5, 1986.
Phewa, Thembinkosi (interviewed by V. Erlmann, I. Edwards, and C. Ndlovu)
    KwaMashu, November 11, 1985.
Shembe, Mbijana (interviewed by V. Erlmann and C. Ndlovu)
    Johannesburg, July 6, 1989.
Sithole, Isaac Mandoda (interviewed by V. Erlmann and C. Ndlovu)
    Durban, April 5, 1986.
Zondo, Ngweto Cornelius (interviewed by V. Erlmann and C. Ndlovu)
    Paulpietersburg, November 3, 1985.

Index

Abaqhafi, 103
Abdullah Ibrahim, xv
Accra, 54, 156
Adams College, 45, 61, 77, 147–53, 154, 163
African Jubilee Singers, 47–48. *See also* South African Choir
African Methodist Episcopal Church (AME), 46–47, 51, 117
African National Congress (ANC), 58, 93, 117, 119–20, 126, 171; music in, 119
African Own Entertainers, 142
African Quartette, 146
African-Americans: as missionaries in South Africa, 48; in South Africa, 38, 41; status as "honorary whites," 41–42
Afro-American culture: as defense against settler racism, 60–62; as model for South African blacks, 44
Afro-American music, 17–18; and Caluza, 145; influence on African music, 176. *See also* Spirituals
Aggrey, James E. Kwegyir, 52
Alabama, 53
Alcohol: and popular culture, 134–35
Allen, Mattie, 26, 35, 40
Alverson, Hoyt, 8
Amagosa, 105, 108
Amagxagxa, 101, 103
Amahubo, 9, 97, 106, 141
Amakholwa, 59–60, 70–71, 75, 118. *See also* Christianity
Amakhoti, 162
Amalaita, 75, 103
Amanzimtoti (isicathamiya choir), 163

Amanzimtoti Male Voice Choir, 163
Amanzimtoti Royal Entertainers, 72, 93, 150
AmaScotch, 70
Amathambo, 62
American Board of Missions, 66
American music: influence on African music, 177
Anderson, Benedict, 15, 120
Anderson, Susie, 36
Anglo-Zulu War, 97
Anikulapo-Kuti, Fela, 54, 181
Apartheid, 14
Australia, 35, 41

Ball, J. Stewart, 26
Ballantine, Christopher, 17
Balmer, J., 47
Bambatha rebellion, 117
Bantu Glee Singers, 66, 82, 164
Bantu Men Social Centre Quartette, 52
Bantu Social Centre, 77, 91
Barber, Karin, 16, 60
Basotho, xv, 56
Baumannville, 65
Beni, 97, 100, 176
Bhaca, 56, 100
Bhengu, John, 112
Black Consciousness, 18–19
Black music: as counter-world, 18; definition of, 17–18; ideological uses of the term, 16
Blacking, John, 9, 14, 17, 120, 121
Bland, James: *Dem Golden Slippers*, 29, 62
Bloemfontein, 34
Boer War, 21, 42